The Illustrated Encyclopedia of

MILITARY INSIGNIA

of the 20th Century

The Illustrated Encyclopedia of
MILITARY INSIGNIA
of the 20th Century

A comprehensive A-Z guide to the badges, patches and embelishments of the world's armed forces

Guido Rosignoli

Introduction by Will Fowler

CHARTWELL
BOOKS, INC.

A QUARTO BOOK

Published by Chartwell Books Inc
A Division of Book Sales Inc,
110 Enterprise Avenue
Secausus, New Jersey 07094

First published 1986
© Quarto Publishing Limited 1986

ISBN 1-55521-085-6

This book was designed and produced by
Quarto Publishing Ltd
The Old Brewery
6 Blundell Street
London N7 9BH

Senior Editor Lorraine Dickey
Editor Lydia Darbyshire
Art Editor Anne Sharples
Designer Phil Chidlow
Paste-up Elly King
Art Director Pete Laws
Editorial Director Jim Miles
Special thanks to Ursula Dawson

Typeset by Tradespools Ltd and
Ampersand Typesetting Ltd.

Manufactured in Hong Kong by
Regent Publishing Services Limited
Printed by Leefung-Asco Printers Limited
Hong Kong

Frontispiece
A selection of Austrian, Belgian, British and Danish
badges mounted or embroidered on a coloured backing.

CONTENTS

INTRODUCTION THE NEED TO distinguish between enemy and ally, leader and led, expert and novice has been a feature of war ever since men banded together to attack or defend their property.

The Romans, with their large armies composed of men from many nations, formalized rank and skills, although often the specialists could be recognized by the fact that they marched and fought beside their special instruments of war. The early Middle Ages and the rather unstructured wars that followed saw a new development in insignia. The knight or baron waged war accompanied by his retainers, who wore simple garments to show where they owed their loyalty. Heralds representing kings wore elaborate tabards, and so the French herald says 'You know me by my habit,' when he comes to parlay with the English in Shakespeare's *Henry V*. Earlier, the Crusades had seen the formalization of coloured crosses according to national grouping.

In the 17th century dress and the equipment of the soldiers were used to differentiate different ranks and groups. Musketeers, for instance, wore their distinctive bandoliers, while grenadiers had their slow matches and grenades. The cavalry wore riding clothes and carried a sabre, which allowed them to reach to attack other mounted men or to cut at foot soldiers. Many of these tools and weapons have re-appeared as the badges of modern soldiers and sailors.

By the 18th and 19th centuries the appearance of mass conscript armies made the wearing of uniforms essential, not only so that the armies themselves might be clearly differentiated, but also so that the status of the men within those armies might be identified. The armies of Europe and North America wore coloured tunics and headgear, carrying their food, ammunition and bedding in packs, canteens and haversacks.

Although Wellington wore a simple grey frock coat at Waterloo, many of his soldiers were more formally dressed, as were the men of the French and Prussian armies. Non-commissioned officers (NCOs) had stripes or chevrons similar to those worn today, and units could be recognized by the numbers and coloured facings on their shakos and tunics. Officers wore epaulettes and sashes, while senior NCOs carried a short pike. The tradition of the regimental colours kept soldiers together under the pressure of bombardment or cavalry attack. Sailors were the most resistant to uniform dress, and indeed services like the submarine crews still strive to retain some individuality even today.

An indication of how uniforms and insignia would develop was given in the Crimean War (1854-6) and American Civil War (1861-4). Mass-produced clothing began to be worn and there was a shift toward more practical designs. The Franco-Prussian War (1870-1) saw the British adopt the headgear of the winners. Previously British soldiers had worn kepis or shakos, but when the French were defeated, British troops adopted the Prussian spiked helmet. Experience in India, where tropical white uniforms were easy targets, led to the first adoption of camouflage when British troops dyed their uniforms khaki (the Urdu word for dust-coloured). Dressed in khaki they fought many of the colonial battles of the latter part of the century. The US Army retained blue uniforms, although they placed greater emphasis on comfort than the Europeans, up to the time of the Spanish American war. By the time they came to intervene in the rebellion in Mexico in 1911 they too had adopted khaki, but retained the smart and practical 'Montana peak', the wide-brimmed hat that is still worn by senior NCOs in the US Marine Corps.

The grim, grinding battles of World War I, the fast and accurate fire from machine guns and the improvement in aerial observation led to an increased awareness of the need for camouflage. The elaborate patterns of green, brown and tan that have become the common colour of soldiers in the field in the latter half of the 20th century, were the outcome of work by French artists, co-opted by the military to design patterns that would conceal guns and equipment.

Insignia grew smaller and more dis-

1. Prince Maurice of Orange-Nassau in an early 17th Century portrait, long before the introduction of badges, wearing an armour suit. Heraldic insignia already existed in order to distinguish friend from foe, in the form of painted or embroidered coat of arms, and coloured sashes were used for the same purpose (Bibl.3).

2. An 18th Century drummer boy of the British Army in a photograph taken in 1898. Regimental distinctions developed throughout Europe during this century in the form of facing colours and lace trimmings. Some old British regiments were authorized to wear special devices on grenadier caps, the 3rd Foot for instance displayed the Dragon in place of the Royal Cypher.

creet, although there was a need for a means of identifying a man at close range in what had become nations in arms. Corps, divisional, and even brigade patches were part of a man's uniform tunic. He wore his rank, stripes or bars to show his service. Other badges indicated his skills and aptitudes. Together with his medal ribbons, his badges and insignia revealed much of his life history. Predictably this became an art practised by intelligence officers on all sides.

Every nation contributed something to the evolution of insignia, and many countries still have reminders of early forms of insignia as part of their national army, navy or air force.

Before 1914 the air army had been a branch of the army or navy, its members wearing the same uniform. By 1918, however, the British had shown the way toward an independent force, and their lead was soon followed by every nation. As air warfare became more complex different skills were required. Mechanical and electrical equipment, radio and improved artillery to counter aircraft needed new technicians, and these too needed new badges and, in due course, new corps.

The inter-war years saw the development of airborne forces. Whether they were air-landed troops, who were transported in converted bombers and airliners, glider-borne troops or, in those days, paratroops, the high standards of fitness and aggressive initiative demanded of these men required a special type of soldier, and they received insignia to distinguish them from ordinary infantry.

World War II saw a vast increase in the number of men and women in uniform. Radar and jet aircraft entered service, and élite forces for attack above and below the water, by air and land, were trained and launched against vital targets. If much that is written about insignia in the 20th century appears to concentrate on World War II, it is because these years were an important formative time for the three services and their badges and insignia. Even insignia for modern equipment such as helicopters draw on the designs and motifs that

3. British cloth helmet model 1878/81, home pattern, as used by the Royal Artillery ie. with the ball instead of the spike, with appropriate helmet plate bearing the imperial Crown that was adopted in 1901.

(H.L. King collection)

4. Infantry helmet plate for other ranks, model 1881 with Victorian Crown, worn on the spiked helmet. The plate consisted of a base, the crown, star and laurel wreath, on which was placed the regimental helmet plate centre, which varied according to regiment.
(H.L. King Collection)

5. Blue cloth shako of the Highland Light Infantry displaying the green 'tuft', the black 'boss', the regimental 'badge' and the diced 'cap band' (Bibl. 50). Colonels and lieutenant colonels had two rows of thistle pattern lace round the top, majors had one.
(H.L. King Collection)

were made for airborne soldiers in World War II.

The role that insignia could play in boosting morale and providing political inspiration was clearly seen by both Nazi Germany and Soviet Russia, and both nations produced original designs. The trappings of the Third Reich may now be limited to collections, but their designs, suitably modified, may still be seen in the insignia of the armies of both East and West Germany. The Soviet Armed Forces wear uniforms that were introduced by Stalin in 1943 but that look back to the Tsarist days.

During World War I, women entered the services in numbers that had never been dreamed of in 1914. Members of the British First Aid Nursing Yeomanry put on an elegant khaki uniform and plunged themselves into the grime and blood of front-line nursing. The Soviet armed forces in World War II included women fighter, bomber and even stop-gap tank crews. These women wore the badges and rank of their male comrades. In the United States women served as nurses and specialists in all three services, while in Germany and Britain they crewed anti-aircraft guns and controlled the complexities of enemy intercept operations from fighter headquarters.

With the end of the war, many men and women put away their uniforms, but the armed forces remained. Independent air forces, no longer branches of the navy or army, were established, and for them new insignia and uniforms were designed. Missiles and helicopters, the technology associated with radio communications and interception, encouraged new units and badges to appear.

The Korean and Vietnam Wars and the many 'bush-fire' wars (such as the Mau Mau uprising in Kenya in the 1950s) produced new veterans. New developments such as night-vision equipment and infra-red detection have made camouflage and low visibility vital, and the soldier of the 1980s and his comrades in the navy and air force appear at first glance to have little in common with their predecessors of 1918. Yet ceremonial uniforms are still worn, even if they have been somewhat simplified, and service bands give us all a reminder of past glories. Royalty, politicians and dignitaries could hardly be met by a parade of men dressed in the overalls that they now wear to service equipment or in the pullovers or shirt sleeves worn in the office. Even these functional garments, however, retain some traces of the dashing uniforms of the turn of the century in the form of patches and cap badges.

9

6. An officer and two privates of the 7th Middlesex (London Scottish) Rifle Volunteers in a photograph of about 1900. They wear hodden grey regimental uniforms with dark blue glengarry, collar and cuffs and all the trappings of the 19th century uniforms, such as lace edgings and buttons on the cuffs and on the skirt of the doublet. They display the conventional badge on the head-dress and on the collar and being Scots they wear the 'hackle' and the sporran badge. The officer carries the claymore on the left and the dirk on the right of the waist belt which is fastened by the regimental-pattern locket, or 'belt-buckle' made of silver.

(The Regiment, April 1900)

FROM ITS ORIGINS military insignia has fulfilled one, two and sometimes three functions: it has denoted rank and station, a man's skills and trades, and finally his loyalty to service, arm or regiment.

Over the years insignia has changed from being essentially functional additions to tunics and jackets to the stylized loops, lanyards and badges that are worn today. The introduction of camouflage to land force uniforms has meant that many items of insignia have become parade accoutrements only, and stripes and stars are now reduced to inconspicuous additions to an anonymous pattern of green and brown. In smaller units, in fact, there is often no need to wear a badge of rank, since men recognize one another and know who is in command or who has a particular skill. When such a closely knit, specialized group encounters a more formal and conventional force, even when both are from the same national army, there can be confusion — sometimes funny, sometimes irritating — for both groups.

Rank and insignia also give men and women a visible authority and status. This system has been adopted in the civilian world, and companies dress their staff in different cuts and colours of overalls — the labour pool in blue, charge hands in brown and the foreman in a smart dark grey warehouse coat.

Some badges indicate membership of a special or privileged group. The paratrooper's wings, the submariner's dolphins, the diver's badge or the pilot's wings are outward indications of bravery and sustained application to training, as well as of successful completion of tests and courses designed to 'weed out' the unfit or unconfident.

It is in part this totemic element that makes badges so attractive to collectors

7. Lieutenant of the British Army in Egypt before World War I wearing the first officer's tropical uniform with open collar. Insignia are reduced to the minimum necessary to identify his rank, ie. stars on the shoulder straps and probably a 'puggaree insignia' on the left of the helmet.

and servicemen. To wear a ship's cap band or squadron or unit insignia is to show that you have been accepted as a member of a select group; being able to wear such a badge is as primitive in its own way as the initiation rites of a tribal group. There is, in the collecting of such badges, a sub-conscious element, in which the civilian owner possesses some of the magic that these badges exert in the military environment. If this were not so, why should there be such a fascination with airborne insignia?

Lest the collector be seen merely as a dealer in military voodoo, however, it should be added that many badges are both rare and beautiful. Some of the insignia designed for special forces are both rare and aesthetically pleasing. The insignia of the armed forces of Nazi Germany has become rare. It also included some striking and very attractive designs, many of which have reappeared in the insignia of the *Bundeswehr* of West Germany and the National *Volksarmee* of East Germany. The East German army has in fact retained more of the trappings of the *Wehrmacht*, than the *Bundeswehr*, and East German soldiers wear a dagger with their dress uniform and the *Waffenfarbe* (arm colours) piping on their epaulettes. Both East and West Germany have retained the grey colour worn by the Imperial Army before World War I and also the collar patches and metal breast badges for proficiency.

Soviet uniforms have a slightly theatrical quality, which makes them look good until they are closely examined. The badges, however, use enamel work, which has been a traditional skill for centuries, and they are therefore very attractive. It is worth noting that the insignia of the Imperial Russian Army was abolished after the Revolution, and a very simple uniform with collar patches was introduced. However, as part of a drive to sustain morale in the grimmer days of the 'Great Patriotic War' (World War II), Stalin authorized new rank insignia. The most notable change was the reintroduction of shoulder boards, which had been a classic Tsarist feature and which are, in effect, a 'hard' epaulette.

8. Italian 'alpino' in Libya during the Italo-Turkish War of 1911-1912. He wears the same uniform he did at his home station on the Alps, including the 'alpenstock', the only tropical provision being a dust cover for the rifle. He still wears the old cap badge with the crown, green collar patches and the company number on the shoulder pads.

Together with a high collar, the shoulder boards were the dress uniform of the Soviet Army in World War II.

Changes in uniform have also been introduced in the Chinese People's Liberation Army, and the soft cap and red-collared, green uniform bare of any insignia have been replaced by a hard cap and a tunic with epaulettes. These changes reflect the programme of modernization being undertaken in the Chinese armed forces. The absence of insignia in the Chinese Army had enhanced secrecy during operations in the Korean War for insignia can operate against its wearer. If he is captured a prisoner is required to give only his name, rank, number and date of birth. This information can then be passed through the International Red Cross to his home country, where he is listed as a prisoner of war and can then be contacted by his next-of-kin and the Red Cross.

To his captors, however, he is a potential source of information about the long- and short-term plans of the enemy. Cap badges, the coloured backing to rank badges and trade and skill insignia indicate the wearer's potential as a source of intelligence. An ordinary infantryman will have limited value, but a skilled technician or senior officer, who may know about equipment and future plans, will have a long-term intelligence value and will be worth retaining for a more detailed interrogation before he is is passed to a detention camp.

Soldiers on patrol 'sanitize' their equipment: they remove letters and personal possessions from pockets and wear a combat cap with no unit badge. Aircrew and men trained to infiltrate by canoe, sanitize their persons and equipment before missions.

9. British Army corporal wearing the khaki uniform adopted in 1902, with the cap badge of the General List, Infantry for Service Battalions, the 1914 predecessor of the General Service Corps instituted in 1942. He wears 'slip-ons' and the waist belt of the M. 1914 leather infantry equipment.
(Rosignoli Collection)

10. Warrant officer of the Australian 13th Light Horse Regiment wearing the standard British khaki drill uniform, officer's pattern, used during the Boer War and later in World War I. His uniform displays the regimental cap and collar badges, shoulder titles and rank insignia above the cuffs.
(Rosignoli Collection)

There are always exceptions, and a now respected British military historian, Michael Glover was captured on patrol in Italy, crossing the Rubicon 'the wrong way'. His German captors looked at his mixture of insignia, which included a cap badge from a British yeomanry regiment, a pistol lanyard from the Palestine Police and medal ribbons that showed that he had served in North Africa. Fascinated, his captors asked where he had served. When they learned that he had been in Tunisia, the questioning became more detailed, and, deciding that events over a year old did not constitute valuable intelligence Glover told the German officers about a small but violent action in which he had participated in Tunisia. His captors explained that they had been on the other side, and they began to exchange memories. Recalling the episode long after the war, Glover remarked, 'We had already had one bottle of Chianti and I managed to get them to open another on the strength of the conversation.'

11. Hungarian corporal of the pioneers of the Austro-Hungarian Army, in 1915, still wearing the field uniform adopted in peace time, with full length collar patches.
(Rosignoli Collection)

12. Private of a balloon observation unit in 1918, wearing the latest field service uniform with 'reduced' collar patches. Note that many soldiers kept on wearing the 'FJI' cockade to the end of the war.
(Rosignoli Collection)

13. Hungarian colonel in service dress during World War II.
The Hungarian uniforms retained many similarities with the pre-1918 imperial uniforms.
Namely the type of cap badge and rank insignia on the collar. The cap worn by this officer and the pocket flaps of his tunic are typically Austrian.

(Talas and Hingyi Collection)

BADGES ON BATTLEDRESS

Throughout history, convention and national custom have dictated that rank, skill and unit badges should be displayed on different parts of a serviceman's uniform and headgear.

The hat has been a common place for the name of the corps, regiment or ship to be displayed. Like major corps of the army, the air forces of the world wear badges that give no indication of their sub-group, be it squadron, regiment or battery. In the days before World War II, the air forces of many countries were under the control of the army or navy, and pilots and ground crew wore uniforms that were similar to soldiers' or sailors'. However air crew wore specialized insignia.

The corps or unit badge could be displayed on a peaked cap, reinforced with wire to make it an acceptable item of parade wear. Head-dresses include side hats or 'fore-and-aft' caps, which could be unbuttoned to protect the ears and neck, berets, which were common by World War II, and soft-brimmed hats, which were worn in the jungle fighting of the 1950s and 1960s. The US Army put insignia of rank on the helmets and hats worn in the field, and this practice was adopted by the Royal Marines, who currently display rank on the cold-weather headgear worn in Norway.

At the beginning of this century, pith helmets — known as 'Head-dresses. Foreign Service. Helmet Colonial Pattern' — were worn by British troops in the war in South Africa. The US Army had the 'smoky bear' hat, a broad-brimmed hat that was shaped into the 'Montana peak' by pinching the crown at four places. The smoky bear hat is still worn by the US Marine Corps Drill Instructors (DIs).

Officers' stars or pips were originally worn on the collar in the 18th century and then moved to the cuffs and/or shoulders. During World War I they were displayed on the cuffs of British officers' uniforms until it became evident that German snipers were looking for men with this obvious rank insignia; it was then made more discreet. The high casualty rate

among first lieutenants or subalterns in the British Army in World War I produced the bitter joke 'one star, one stunt': a first lieutenant would survive only one major attack (stunt). The actual statistics were that a soldier in one of the better divisions could count on a maximum of three months' service without being killed or wounded, while a junior officer at the front had a life expectancy of five months in an ordinary regiment and a chilling six weeks in a crack one. The antagonism felt by front-line soldiers for red-tabbed staff officers was powerful. Phillip Knightly recounts in *The First Casualty* that the sight of a staff officer was like a red flag, and all the battalion officers and men 'desired his death intensely'.

The convention that rank should be displayed on the shoulder is not exclusive to officers. Many armies find it both rational and tactical to display all rank on the epaulette. It is, however, customary among officers that the most junior wears one symbol — a star or bar being the most common — which is increased to three as he advances in rank. Sometimes the most junior officer is called a second lieutenant, sometimes a First. In his book *Winged Dagger* which described his service in the SAS in World War II, Roy Farran recalled the way that the one 'pip' of a second lieutenant could be mistaken for a major's one crown. When an Arab street vendor addressed him as 'Mister Major' he recalled, 'Of course it was really the touch of calling me Mister Major which did it. I prided myself on having such an air of authority that he had mistaken my single pip for a crown'.

Ethnic head-dresses not only identify the regiment but also the nationality of the wearer. Turbans, the Scottish glengarry, the Irish caubeen and even the

14. A British and Irish officer in a photograph taken in the 1920s. The former is a lieutenant colonel of the Leicestershire Regiment with two World War I overseas service insignia on the right forearm. The latter is a major general wearing the rank insignia adopted in 1923, ie. one gold bar between two red bars on the collar and on the shoulder straps.

Australian slouch hat served to identify the owner. Further, in the case of a glengarry, a coloured band might also display the tartan, thus giving a further indication of the loyalty of its wearer.

From the head, the observer would shift his gaze to the neck. The lapels of a shirt or tunic could show the rank or arm of a serviceman. The red gorgets with the small buttons at the top, which are worn by a British staff officer, are a throw-back to the two buttons that secured the metal gorget plate at the throat of an ensign of the British Army in the Napoleonic wars. Until the introduction of armour for snipers in World War I, this plate was the last remaining example of armour. In World War II the German Army gave its Military Police a gorget breast plate bearing the word *Feldgendarmerie* in luminous paint so that the police could be seen at night when they were on traffic duty. The plate hanging from its chain earned them the nickname *Ketten Hund* (chained dogs), since their duties, which included discipline, made them unpopular with ordinary soldiers.

Collars were often in a coloured material that indicated the arm of service. They indicated rank and also bore a motif such as crossed cannons, a lyre, crossed rifles, wheels, a tank or a flaming grenade.

Buttons could be a further indication of arm of service. In the British Army the minute detail of the regimental system provides black buttons for rifle regiments, while the cap badge was reproduced on each button of the khaki No. 2 dress uniform. Such detail is in sharp contrast with the Germans, who have a simple, stippled aluminium alloy button for all ranks.

Belts and belt buckles could be used to show rank, arm of service or nationality. The British Indian Army had exquisite belt buckles made in white and gold metal, while in World Wars I and II, the Germans produced a tough leather belt, which formed the basis of their load-carrying equipment. The Imperial Army had the Kaiser's crown in the middle of the buckle, and the *Wehrmacht* had the Nazi eagle and swastika in the centre of

the buckle. German officers had a brown, double-claw buckle belt.

With the exception of the Hungarians, the Warsaw Pact forces today have followed the Soviets in belt design, and they wear a brass or aluminium alloy plate buckle with a national motif in the centre. Thus, the Russians have a star with a hammer and sickle, the East Germans a hammer and dividers with a wreath of two hands of wheat, while the other national armies use motifs that have a national significance.

At the beginning of the century, officers wore complex gold and silver lace on leather parade dress belts, but, apart from supporting a sword, which was fast becoming a dress item rather than a weapon, the belt had little function. The Sam Browne belt, which was compulsory for officers and warrant officers of the British Army until 1939, had a functional use. It has now become a badge of rank for officers and senior non-commissioned officers of almost every military power in the world. Consisting of broad brown leather belt with a brass double-claw buckle, the Sam Browne belt was designed to take the pistol and ammunition pouches as well as the sword worn by an officer. The designer, General Sir Sam Browne VC, a veteran of the Indian Mutiny who gave his name to the equipment, had one arm, having lost the other in action. He was thus unable to handle his sword on the long sword frog designed for mounted officers. The Sam Browne belt carried both sword and pistol, and an ammunition pouch on a belt was supported by two leather cross-straps. The pistol holster is no longer used in the army, but is retained for police wear. The sword is still worn on parades, but only one cross-belt is retained.

Although not a badge, officers' and warrant officers' accoutrements like a Sam Browne belt and the 'swagger stick', cane or pace stick are a clear sign of rank in the eyes of the men they command. The cane that was carried by officers in the British Army up to the 1960s originated in the centurion's truncheon, which was used to administer punishment to the soldiers under his command. The threats offered on the parade ground by drill sergeants armed with a pace stick (a 3-foot long, brass-tipped pair of dividers, designed to check the correct pace of parade ground drill) would suggest that the centurion's spirit is still alive.

With a few odd exceptions, like the colour of footwear — black for soldiers, brown for officers — and a Scottish soldier's kilt and sporran, rank and unit identity are not displayed below the waistband. The major area of display is the tunic or jacket front, to the left and right of the buttons, the shoulders and the outer face of the sleeves.

The origins of shoulder epaulettes are obscure. Two versions have been suggested. The first is that the leather laces or 'points' securing a knight's armour to his leather doublet were retained when armour was no longer worn. On a doublet, the laces indicated that the owner had 'knightly status'. The second version dates from the comparatively recent introduction of the musket at the turn of the 17th and 18th centuries. The soldier loading a musket needed to secure to his shoulder the cross-belt carrying the cartridges. He therefore sewed a buttoned cloth loop on to his coat.

In Britain since World War II, the armed services have made changes. Because load-carrying equipment can cover conventionally displayed rank, rank has also been displayed on the chest and on

15. Lieutenant of the Norwegian Army wearing the service dress used in the 1930s. It is an austere uniform which displays the indispensable badges: the national insignia and rank stripes on the collar and green piping on the collar and cuffs and stripes on the trousers.

(Haermuseet, Oslo)

16. Two Danish officers photographed in 1939, wearing the M.1923 khaki service dress, with two different types of tunic's collar. The typical Danish officers' forage cap and the shoulder straps are ornated with silk lace. Different patterns of stars, according to class of rank, were worn on the shoulder straps by officers (rosettes by officiants) or administrative officers. All regular officers wore a four-pointed star on each side of the collar.

(Tojhusmuseet, Copenhagen)

the back on vertical epaulettes. The French during World War II moved rank insignia to the chest of combat clothing and their colonial armies followed this practice; thus in Vietnam, the US forces found that Vietnamese officers wore a loop of cloth on their chest, rather than on the shoulders or lapels, that showed rank.

Rank is also displayed on the sleeve near the cuff, although this is normally only done by senior non-commissioned officers. The Israeli Army has retained a simplified version of the British rank system, even to the extent of using a leather wrist-band to display the metal sergeant major's rank when the wearer is in shirt sleeve order.

It is difficult to establish exactly when non-commissioned officers began to wear insignia, but in the British Army, such insignia was being worn in the late 18th century. The most usual form goes from one to three stripes stripes taking the form of a V, either inverted or conventionally displayed. By the time the rank of sergeant is achieved, three stripes are worn, and above that they are embellished before disappearing completely in the insignia of warrant officers. The US Army, however, has a system by which stripes are added below the inverted V to produce a rather more complex pattern of NCO rank insignia. Moreover, the US Army has the rank of Specialist (or Spec), which was introduced in the 1950s and which has a parallel function to the line NCOs.

Above the rank of captain, a symbolic single motif can be used. A crown is convenient in an army that has a monarch as its titular head, and stars are used in armies of Warsaw pact countries. Eagles, flowers and sometimes simply more bars or bars of different thickness — a little like the navy — may be worn. The designs can be kept fairly simple by changing the colour of the epaulette or the stars. The Soviet Union combines stars with bars that run the length of the epaulette and uses different patterns and colours of gold lace as a backing. To indicate a more senior rank, the stars are increased in size. The epaulette may also

17. General Pietro Badoglio, later marshal, wearing the grey-green full dress used until 1934. His cap badge is gold embroidered on red backing and the aigrette was worn by officers in active command of regiments or higher formations — he was then chief of the general staff. He also wears the generals' silver aiguillettes and epaulettes, the latter with rank insignia, and on the forearm he displays seven badges of promotion for war merit, which account for his extraordinary career.

(Rosignoli Collection)

18. A Polish delegation in Italy, before World War II. In the foreground from left to right: Italian general commander of division wearing the greatcoat; Polish general of brigade in full dress uniform wearing the aiguillettes and decorations and medals; the city's mayor in Fascist party uniform with the tri-coloured sash, his badge of office, around his waist. Both generals display their traditional and somehow similar general's insignia, the Italian 'greca' and the Polish 'zig-zag', below the cap badge and on the cuffs and, the latter on the collar also. Note the staff badge and a regimental badge pinned on the pockets of the tunic of the Polish general. In the background on the right there is a general of the Polish mountain troops with his traditional brimmed hat with a cluster of feathers.

(Barbarski Collection)

19. A group of Italian fascists wearing the party uniform at a village fair, near Trieste. All wear the fasces on the head-dress and on the shoulder straps of the typical fascist jacket. The second man from the left displays his appointment — not rank — insignia on the breast, above the ribbons.

(Rosignoli Collection)

20. Black shirt of the 95th Legion of Italian Fascist Militia, with the fleur-de-lis of Florence on the breast above the ribbons, which include a medal for military valour, two crosses for war merit, four years participation in World War I and ten years service in the MVSN. It is unlikely, however, that an embroidered legion badge and embroidered fasces were worn on a summer shirt, which required daily washing.

(Rosignoli Collection)

21. 'Avanguardista' of the Italian Fascist Youth. He wears the cap badge used from 1938 to 1943, white collar patches with white metal badge and the GIL medallion on the lapel. The medallion depicted Mussolini's head surrounded by the motto of the youth organisation.

(Rosignoli Collection)

carry a miniature badge showing the arm of service that the officer belongs to: crossed cannon for an artillery regiment or a wreathed star for a motor rifle regiment.

Sometimes the epaulette was used to carry the regimental number of the soldier, and this could be amplified by adding a coloured piping to show his arm of service. Thus, in the German army during World War II an observer could, by looking at a man's epaulette, tell that the wearer was an NCO or officer in the 5th Infantry Regiment, colour and number providing the extra information.

It is easy to see why the War Office issued a little pamphlet in January 1942 called 'A Guide to the Identification of German Units'. With superb optimism it includes the most senior ranks of the German Army and Air Force but adds in the introduction: 'It should be remembered that for security reasons the enemy may do away with badges of rank, shoulder straps etc., in the case of troops selected for invasion.'

The British Army, however, has retained the practice of using a coloured backing to cloth pips to indicate the corps or divisional loyalty of the officer. First authorized in 1940, these colours were later amended.

The German Army both in the two World Wars and afterwards as two separate national armies had an impressive style of knotted gold and silver, or silver, epaulette. Superimposed on these cords were small metal pips. For ranks below major the epaulette was a simple pattern of parallel silver cords. NCOs had a border of silver lace with silver metal pips according to rank. Like the Russians, there were also small badges showing the arm or regimental number.

Metal shoulder badges are a feature of the Polish Army, and they are used to show that the wearer is attending a school or course. Cloth loops to show that the man or woman is an officer candidate are widely used. The white loops used in a number of British and Commonwealth armies are nicknamed 'candy stripes', a pun on candidate by South African soldiers.

In addition to the use of a V to show junior non-commissioned officer rank, single bars, either parallel or at an angle, have been used. The Army of the Irish Republic has a rank insignia that has both an upward and a downward V, producing something that looks a little like a wavy line. An NCO may sometimes display his speciality or skill above his stripes; crossed flags would be worn by the signals sergeant, for example, or axes by the pioneer sergeant.

Although the stripes may appear similar to an outsider, the names given to ranks by different armies can cause confusion. The rank of corporal can be referred to as brigadier in the French-speaking armies, while a brigadier in English-speaking armies is a one-star general. An adjutant in English-speaking armies can be a position held by a captain as an administrative officer in a battalion-strength organization; in Francophone armies a man with that title rank is a sergeant major. Even greater confusion can arise with English-speaking armies. An officer in the Royal Artillery discovered that one of the US Marines attached to his battery on a course held the rank of Gunnery Sergeant or Gunny. 'Actually we discovered that he knew nothing about artillery,' said the British gunner officer. British cavalry regiments and Guards regiments conjure up ranks with titles such as corporal of horse or lance sergeant, — which ordinary line infantry or corps can find confusing.

Rifle regiments in the British army wear black rank insignia on their sleeves; in dress uniforms these are black with a gold or silver border, while in the field they can be black and green. These colours reflect the tradition of camouflaged rifle-green clothing that was worn in the 19th century.

The US Army has a variety of slang and nicknames for officers. The single gold bar of a first lieutenant can be a 'butter bar' or 'brown bar', while the full colonel, with his eagle insignia, is a 'bird colonel' (the British refer to lieutenant colonels rather unkindly as 'half colonels'). Young platoon commanders, who were made up from conscripted

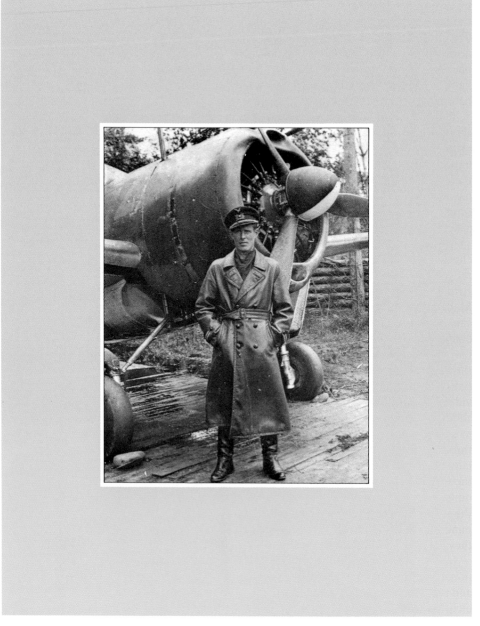

men, were nicknamed 'shake 'n' bake' officers after the quick-bake cake mixes.

Epaulettes are also used in the British Army to carry regimental initials. The tradition is an old one, dating back further than the introduction of battledress in the late 1930s. Some regiments have a facsimile of the cap badge with initials, like the Welsh Guards with their leek and WG; others, like the Duke of Wellington's Regiment, spell out their title almost in full. The original titles were in brass or bronze, but they are now produced in an alloy that requires no clean-

22. Finnish Air force officer, World War II period. He wears a dark blue uniform with the cap badge shown on page 97, army pattern collar patches with black frames and fir twigs on blue background, which displays the usual rank insignia.

(Sotamuseo, Helsinki)

ing. A split-pin backing used to secure the brass titles to the epaulette, but now, like most badges in the west, they are normally held in place with a clutch-pin backing. In the armies of Warsaw Pact nations, badges are still of the brooch-backed or screw-pin type.

Rank was not displayed only on the shoulders, however. Non-commissioned officers wore their rank insignia on the upper arms, while naval officers wore theirs as bands on their sleeves. This naval practice was adopted by many air forces when separate air arms were established.

The French Army and Marines have citation lanyards or *fourragères*, which are more elaborate in design than the British corps or regimental lanyard. Made in two or three colours, *fourragères* can be worn in one of three different configurations. They are attached to the battalion or regimental standard and in this respect are similar to a US Presidential Citation, being both a unit and individual decoration. Worn on the left shoulder, the *fourragère* can be attached to a button under the epaulette or passed through the epaulette like a conventional lanyard. After the protests and mutiny in the French army in Algeria in 1962, some units who were only at the periphery of the protests were deprived as a unit punishment of some of the *fourragères* they had been awarded for past heroism.

Insignia that at one time had a functional role but that has become symbolic and that is also based on knots and cords, includes sword knots. Originally these were the cords that allowed the owner to hang the sword from his wrist, so that it would not be dropped in battle and, if its owner was mounted, lost forever. Later, sword knots became a trimming to the guard on the sword, indicating, by their colour and the way in which they were twisted through the guard, the corps or regiment of the owner. The Germans had an elaborate system of side arm knots in a variety of colours, which were attached to the bayonet frog. Since German officers also carried a dagger, this too had a knot, normally in aluminium thread. The East German Army has retained this tradition

in its parade dress.

Aiguillettes have also been retained in both the *Bundeswehr* and the National *Volksarmee*, and the German use of this insignia can be traced back to the Prussian army of 1730, although a 'modern' version was introduced in 1808. Soldiers other than a general's ADC are qualified to wear them, including unit adjutants and music directors, as well as men on headquarters staff.

Another form of identification that is

used for NCOs in some armies is the lanyard. This knotted cord hangs from the left or the right shoulder, where it is held in position by the epaulette, and it is tucked into the top pocket of the tunic or combat jacket. Traditional colours include blue for engineers and signallers, white for gunners and black and green for riflemen. The lanyard is meant to have a whistle at the end, although some officers' lanyards have a 'dog clip'. One national service soldier of the 1950s recal-

23. German officer holder of the Iron Cross of I and II Class, with the 'Wounded badge' and SA Sports badge. Although he wears the SS eagle on the left sleeve it is not clear to which of the multifarious Third Reich organisations he belonged.

24. Polish rifleman of a mountain battalion in Britain during World War II. He wears the cape instead of the greatcoat. The eagle and the small strips on his beret identify his nationality and rank — lance corporal — respectively. Collar patches identify the branch of service.

(Polish Institute and Sikorski Museum)

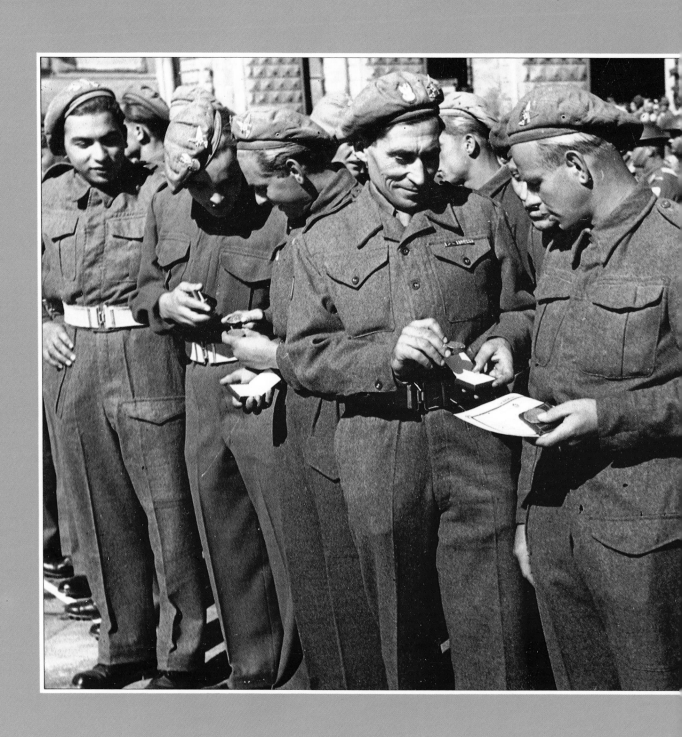

25. Fusiliers of the 9th Battalion of the 3rd Carpathian Division in 1945 have just been awarded the medallion and certificate for the liberation of the city of Bologna, Italy in 1945.

On the beret they already wear their special battalion badge (see page 110) on the side of the Polish spreadeagle.
All wear shoulder titles which identify their

nationality and the divisional 'formation sign'.
(Polish Institute and Sikorski Museum)

led that it was a measure of how serious an officer was whether he had a whistle or a bottle opener at the end of his lanyard; very smart officers had a corkscrew. In some regiments in which the rank chevrons were displayed on the right arm only, NCOs wore lanyards on the left so that soldiers would have no excuse for thinking that they were addressing a member of the other ranks.

Lanyards can come in the rather grander form of aiguillettes, which are worn by the aides-de-camp to senior officers. ADCs to a monarch, Admirals of the Fleet and generals wear them on the right side, while attachés to foreign governments wear them on the left. These striking and rather elaborate cords originated in the days when an ADC to a general carried the rope and tent pegs to tether his chief's and his own horse. The easiest way to carry them was slung over his shoulder, and so this cluster of cords became the insignia of an ADC.

The colour and design of badges reflected the fact that uniforms were generally dark 'navy' blue and white. The choice of this colour dates back to 1748 when, according to a popular story, King George II noticed the Duchess of Bedford, the wife of the First Sea Lord, riding in Rotten Row dressed in a striking blue and white habit. It may also be true that she was so dressed to help the king make up his mind because the Admiralty had itself already chosen this colour combination.

Epaulettes, which are now a common way of denoting commissioned rank in working dress, were introduced in 1795, when it was said that officers of the Royal Navy suffered a loss of prestige among foreigners who all wore them. However, until 1812 captains of under three years' seniority and commanders wore only one. The epaulettes worn today are, moreover, a simple loop of gold ribbon on blue, or for the air force, of pale blue on darker blue; those worn in 1812 were more complex creations in gold lace.

During the 20th century the navies of the world have faced many technological changes, and the air forces, even though they had a rudimentry existence at the beginning of World War I, only properly came into their own some 60 years ago. Many of the sleeve badges of these arms are, therefore, less traditional than those of the army. Non-substantive badges worn by the Royal Navy in World War II included those for trades like air mechanic ordnance, torpedo gunner's mate and higher submarine detector. In contrast, there were badges for officer's cook, chief sailmaker and stoker fire fighter, although by the 1980s many of these had gone. The army, on the other hand, sometimes retains old badges, but gives them new meanings: semaphore flags are still used to indicate skill as a signaller, but now a signaller may be using satellite ground station, or encryption and burst transmission on radio messages. Post-war navies working with this type of equipment have adopted a simple working dress of shirt and trousers, or sometimes overalls, but it is still used to display rank and trade. On more formal and traditional dress, the pullover with square collars and black scarf also displayed rank. Colours for badges were commonly red or blue. In tropical water, uniforms were either white or khaki.

The Japanese, who were widely influenced by western, particularly British, teaching, adopted a uniform and rank that had much in common with those worn by their American and British enemies. Although rank could be displayed on the cuffs, epaulettes were used on white uniforms. The Imperial chrysanthemum served as 'pips', taking the place of the crown used in other 'royal' navies. The wreath and anchor dominate naval insignia, just as eagles and wings are a traditional theme in air force badges.

As masters of iconography, the Japanese adopted a series of simple, understandable badges. Thus an engineer third class had a spanner in a wreath; an engineer second class two spanners, and an engineer first class had two spanners with the silhouette of an aircraft.

The arms have, however, been used to display a variety of insignia since the turn of the century. Insignia designating skills and trades, long service, or membership of regiments and corps are the most

26. Technical Sergeant of the USAAF displaying the unofficial chevrons with winged propeller used during World War II. He has blue and yellow piping on the top of the curtain of the garrison cap, the winged propeller on the disc of the left lapel, the air force patch on the left upper sleeve and the specialist badge (Photographer) on the right forearm. On the right upper sleeve he wears the official photographer's 'tab' and four overseas service bars on the other sleeve.

obvious, but brigade and divisional insignia have also been sewn on to shirts, combat jackets and battledress.

Some of these badges are also worn on the chest. Paratroopers in the US Army, for instance, wear their wings on the chest, while the British carry them on their shoulders. The Soviet Union has a series of arm badges: motor rifle regiments have a red backing and airborne regiments a pale blue backing, while other arms, including armour, artillery and engineers, have a black backing. All these badges include the Soviet star and hammer and sickle motif above the arm insignia.

The air forces and navies of the world use the arm of their jackets to display skills and trades. The British Royal Navy had a great influence on training and uniforms before World War I, and many badges worn by navies today look very similar.

During World War II, the British Royal Navy adopted the practice of reducing a cap tally to HMS for 'His Majesty's Ship' so that the ship would not be identifiable from the cap. Commonwealth nations followed suit, changing their tallies to HMCS (Canada), HMAS (Australia), HMNZS (New Zealand) and HMIS (India). South Africans placed an anchor between the letters SA on their tally. the Royal Navy made a distinction in rank between the Women's Royal Naval Service (WRNS), which had pale blue rank on their cuffs, and the Royal Naval Volunteer Reserve (RNVR) and Royal Naval Reserve (RNVR), whose distinctive 'wavy' rank bands gave them the nickname 'the wavy navy'. The unusual British tradition of volunteer reserves, which produced the Territorial Army, RAFVR for the Royal Air Force and the Royal Corps of Observers, provided a vital element in the defence of the United Kingdom in 1939–45. They still exist and have a parallel in the National Guard and Air National Guard in the United States.

The United States, with its Atlantic and Pacific coasts, has always needed an effective Coast Guard. The insignia worn

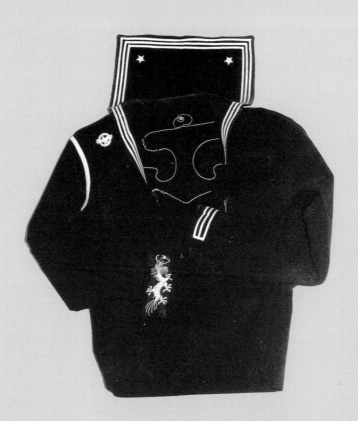

27. Blue jumper of a seaman 1st class (white braid around the right shoulder and three white stripes on the cuffs) of the US Navy, with discharge insignia on the right breast. Note the yellow anchor design embroidered inside on the inner lining. There is a pocket on the left breast and another one in the inner lining at the back within the anchor. On the back of each cuff is sewn a patch which depicts a silk woven Chinese dragon.
(Rosignoli Collection)

28. OD field jacket, pattern dated 1944, used by a technical sergeant of infantry, attached to the 5th US Army in Italy. Its wearer had two years of overseas service and displayed the combat infantryman insignia above his ribbons. His ribbons refer to a Bronze star, the medal for the American Defence Service and for the European-African-Middle Eastern Service. The latter carries a bronze arrow-head, a silver star and a bronze star.
(Rosignoli Collection)

29. OD service jacket used by a US Army sergeant on demobilisation, after World War II. The insignia on this jacket identifies its wearer as a sergeant of the medical corps, who had served overseas for three years in the US Army Forces Pacific Area and was later attached to the 6th Army. The meritorious service insignia is displayed on the right forearm and the discharge insignia above the right breast pocket.
(Rosignoli Collection)

by the Coast Guard is similar to that of the US Navy, but efforts are made to distinguish the two forces. For example, the officer's cap badge is different: the navy has two anchors held in the claws of the US eagle, the Coast Guard only one. An interesting rationalization of naval, air force and army insignia involved the wearing of miniature metal badges on naval garrison caps and the khaki shirts used in the tropics. Army-style rank bars and stars were used, although naval rank applied; thus the two silver bars of an army captain were worn by a naval lieutenant. The army's 'butter bar', the single gold bar of a 2nd lieutenant, is worn by a naval ensign.

A commonly used and widely respected badge is the dolphin to indicate that the sailor is in a submarine fleet. Both the US Navy and the Royal Navy use it — as a breast badge, which is uncommon in many navies — and indeed, the Royal Navy shore establishment for training submariners is named HMS *Dolphin*. The German navy adopted the *Luftwaffe* and army practice of awarding metal breast badges, which looked very similar to those of the Army. Included were breast badges for submarines, destroyers, the high seas fleet, coastal artillery and E-boats. One of the more unusual ones was awarded to blockade runners, Axis ships that had evaded the Allied blockade of occupied Europe conducted by the Royal Navy and Royal Air Force and, with the entry of the United States into the war, by USAAF aircraft and ships.

One Allied navy that saw little action in World War II was the Soviet Navy. Russian sailors have always enjoyed a

30. Staff sergeant, US Army, in about 1946. He displays his chevrons on both upper sleeves, the divisional shoulder sleeve insignia on the left upper and the distinctive insignia of the 350th Infantry Regiment on the left side of the garrison cap, the piping of which denotes branch of service — light blue for infantry. After World War II the senior sergeants started to wear the officer's dark brown garrison cap but with enlisted men piping.

(Tessier Collection)

special place in the history of the Soviet Union since they spearheaded the Bolshevik uprising

After the war, the new Soviet Airborne Force were given a uniform that included a striped, T-shirt vest, similar to a navy vest, as an indication of the special role assigned to the airborne forces.

Russian sailors did, however, fight on land and were present at the battle for Stalingrad and in raids and operations on the Baltic coast and in the Crimea. Soviet naval rank is displayed on the shoulder boards that had been instituted in 1943 as part of the new uniforms and insignia. Previously, rank was displayed on the cuff only. The cuff insignia remained, but as short bars rather than as the full ring of gold lace. Shoulder boards were used to show the fleet in which the officer or rating served: the Pacific Fleet, Arctic Fleet or Lake Onega Flotilla, for example, was indicated on the shoulder

boards. Cap bands or tallies were retained, and they must be one of the most widely used forms of insignia in the world, although they are not worn in the US Navy.

Army-style chevrons on uniforms displayed rank and special skills. Any serviceman who has tried unsuccessfully to draw stores or equipment from an unhelpful storeman, will find the crossed keys of a storekeeper peculiarly appropriate. The predictable lightning bolts indicate a signaller. Cooks have several grades, from cook third class or officer's steward up to a chief officer's steward, and including cook and a baker cook.

The use of diamond-shaped badges with one or two letters marked a move from symbolic insignia. Symbols had the advantage of being easily understood by men who might have a low level of literacy; letter badges were used to represent trades like photographer, teacher,

shore patrol and gunnery instructor. While some badges indicated the trade, others could show the standards attained by the rating; an unenclosed E in blue stood for excellence in gunnery, and the same letter in red represented excellence in engineering.

One badge that was worn by US servicemen and is still found in the British

31. A group of Americans of the 350th Infantry regiment photographed in a US servicemen's club in Italy, in 1945. Most are war veterans judging by the number of their ribbons and by the overseas service insignia visible on the left forearm of two men. All wear on the shoulder straps the combat leader identification insignia, although distinctive insignia at this time were still worn on the lapels. The shoulder sleeve insignia of the 88th Infantry Division could be seen on the left upper sleeve of the fifth man from the left.

(Tessier Collection)

armed forces, is the Combined Operations badge. An elegant combination of anchor, Thompson sub-machine gun and either an RAF eagle or an Americanized version of the eagle, the badge was worn by men who were among the forces landed by small boat or parachute into Occupied Europe during World War II. As the war progressed, it was more widely worn, and RAF ground crews operating in temporary air strips on the Normandy beach-head wore it on their battledress. The British version was red on blue; the American yellow on red.

The US Marine Corps and the Royal Marines have always been closely involved with their respective navies. They have also always enjoyed a friendly rivalry. One of the most notable distinctions between a Royal Marine and his US counterpart is that, although the cap badges of both show the globe, that of the US Marines has the two continents of America, while that of the Royal Marines has the other side of the world, and depicts Africa and India. The US Marine Corps cap badge has the American eagle with an anchor; the Royal Marines badge has a wreath with the royal lion and crown insignia. On badges worn by officers, the 'dog and basket' are detached, while for NCOs and marines the crown is joined to the wreath.

A much larger force than the Royal Marines, the US Marine Corps has aircrew, as well as their own artillery arm. The Royal Marines draw on the Royal Navy and British Army for these resources, although gunners, sappers and other supporting arms complete the 'all arms commando course' and are 'green hatted'–that is, qualified to wear the green beret. When these soldiers return to their parent units they are permitted to retain the World War II army commando

32. Four pages taken from *Know Your Allies*, **an identification booklet published by the Supreme Headquarters Allied Powers Europe in the early 1950s. This publication shows that most Western European Nations wore at that time British-style uniforms although retaining, when applicable, their own traditional insignia.**

(SHAPE)

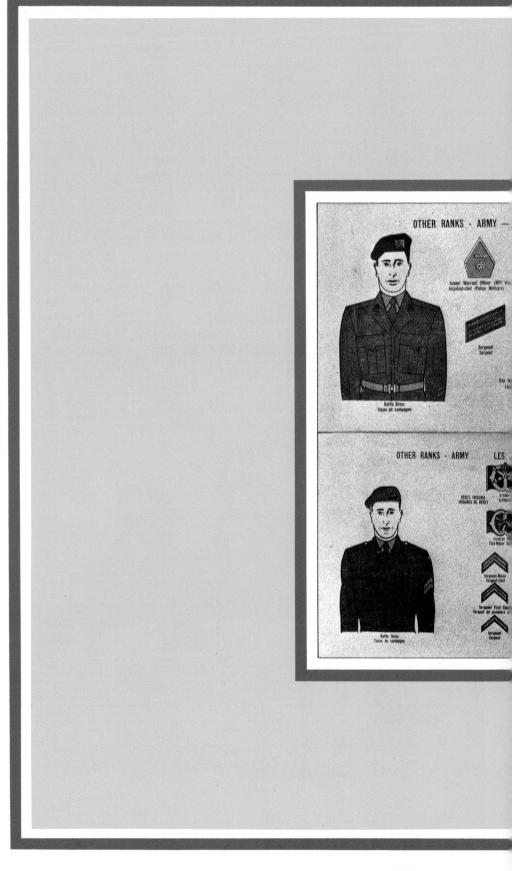

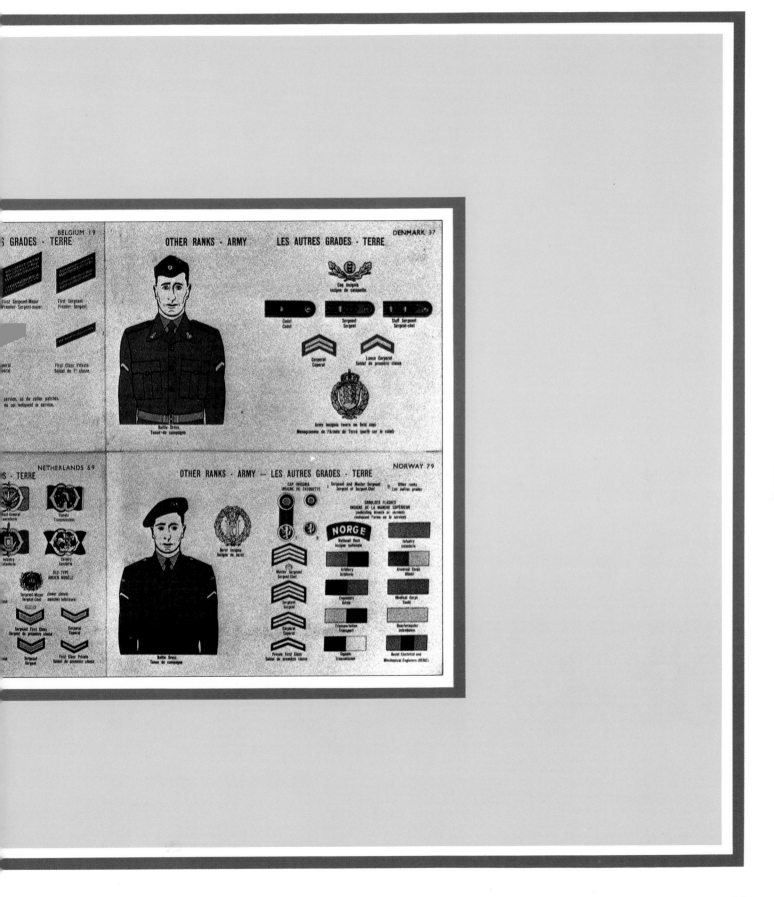

33. The flag of the '1er Regiment Etranger' on parade at Sidi-bel-Abbes, Algeria, in 1955. The 'sergent-chef' in the foreground wears the additional gold edged chinstrap which identifies his rank and the senior NCOs' dress epaulettes.

(Rosignoli Collection)

35. NCOs of the Foreign Legion relaxing before a meal, 1956. Note the re-enlistment chevrons worn below the main sleeve insignia.

(Rosignoli Collection)

34. The platoon of IA of the 1st REI on parade at Sidi-bel-Abbes in 1955. The officers and the NCRs in the foreground wear the dark blue kepi while all other ranks wear the kepi 'blanc' typical of the 'legionnaire'.
(Rosignoli Collection)

36. As above, but the 'Compagnie des Elèves Grades'. Two officers, one NCO and other ranks, all displaying the distinctive insignia on the right pocket.
(Rosignoli Collection)

insignia of the red commando dagger on a blue background.

Although the Soviet Naval Infantry has a long tradition, it is, in fact, a post-war force. The men are well trained and highly motivated. Insignia includes army-style rank worn on shoulder boards and metal badges for skills and qualifications like paratrooper. Naval infantry wear an anchor badge on the left sleeve, while on their stiffened, dark blue berets they have either an other rank's or officer's badge. The other rank's badge is a star in a pierced gold circle, while the officer's badge resembles a naval one. On the left

side of the beret is a red, pennant-shaped cloth patch with a metal anchor badge. The belt buckle, which is similar to the navy buckle, has an anchor and star. The naval infantry have the blue and white striped jersey T-shirt similar to the one worn by the navy and paratroops.

37. The Earl of Derby inspects the East Lancashire Regiment on Somme Day, 1950. The officer on the left wears the war-pattern battledress while the other ranks wear the post-war (M. 1949) battledress. On the blue beret the 'cap badge' is worn on a primrose yellow backing and no collar badges are worn on the battledress. In 1948 the officers replaced the bronze badges of the service dress with silver badges and brass buttons. The formation sign of the Lancashire Brigade and the regimental cloth shoulder title are clearly visible on the sleeve of the sergeant.
(The Chester Chronicle)

CUFF TITLES

Cuff titles are a peculiarly German institution. Adopted by the army before World War I, they became more significant during World War II, reappearing after the war with the West German armed forces. In his authoritative book, *German Army Uniforms and Insignia 1933–1945*, Brian L. Davis identifies three types of cuff title: battle honour or campaign medal, élite army unit insignia and training school, and command staff or special formation. The cuff titles of the *Waffen* SS are part of the second category, and some army units have been confused with *Waffen* SS units because of this, for names like *Grossdeutschland* and *Feldherrnhalle* sound like SS titles.

Waffen SS cuff titles range from the famous through the notorious to the obscure. The LAH, Hitler's Body Guard, which had grown to divisional strength by the end of the war, had a cuff title that was based on Hitler's signature. During the heavy fighting in Hungary at the close of the war, Josef 'Sepp' Dietrich, who had commanded the division until July 1943, heard that Hitler had questioned the courage of the *Waffen* SS. Enraged, he and some of the officers dispatched their cuff titles to Hitler in a chamberpot. *Waffen* SS units were sometimes given names of figures from German history — Hohenstaufen, Götz von Berlichingen — Florian Geyer or Prinz Eugen, for instance and the title was normally in white lettering on a black band with white borders. The lettering could be in gothic script or a simple script like that for *Totenkopf*.

Totenkopf, Death's Head, was the 3rd SS Panzer Division, and its insignia raises an interesting point about the use of this motif in military badges. The death's head has become popularly associated with the SS, but it has, in fact, a longer and more respectable history. It was a tradtional badge for German units as far back as the mid-18th century, and it was worn by the Black Hussars who fought with the Prussians at Waterloo. In World War II the insignia, in two forms, was still worn as a cap badge beneath the national emblem by Wehrmacht units. German

armoured units adopted the death's head as collar dogs worn with a black uniform.

The death's head was the cap badge of the British 17th Lancers, who wore it in memory of General Wolfe who died on the battlefield at Quebec in 1759. It is now the cap badge of the 17/21st Lan-

38. Two British Army sergeants in Japan, in the 1950s. Both wear the UN Korean ribbon. The Scot on the left wears the regimental tartan flash above the formation sign of the Commonwealth Division and hackle above his cap badge. The RASC sergeant on the right wears conventional cloth shoulder titles and a lanyard.

(Fisher Collection)

cers. Elsewhere, the skull appears as the cap badge of the 17/21st — the badge of the Spanish Foreign Legion — the Brides of Death — a force formed by Franco during the Spanish Civil War. Syrian commandos have a death's head badge, and young PLO fighters were photographed in early 1982 with the badge on their camouflaged uniforms.

Cuff titles, like the death's head, should not be seen as a uniquely SS insignia. A number were worn by the German Army and Air Force, including *Afrikakorps*, *Kreta*, *Met*, and *Spanien* 1939, and *Kerland*, and were, in effect, battle honours. Titles like *Grossdeutschland*, *Brandenburg*, *Feldherrnhalle* and *Infanterie* were granted to élite army units. At the other end of the scale were titles like *Propagandakompanie*, *Feldpost* or *Feldgendarmerie*. Female assistants working in army offices were given the title *Stabshelferinnen des Herres*. In the post-war *Bundeswehr* cuff titles have reappeared for the NCO school, *Unteroffizierschule*, and for the *Wachbataillon*, the Guards Battalion, which is based at Siegburg near Bonn. The West German *Luftwaffe* has followed a cuff title tradition that was developed in the war. *Geschwader* names like *Mölders*, *Udet* and *Immelmann* perpetuate the names of fighter aces of World War I, and officer air reporters were called *Kriegsberichter der Luftwaffe*. There were also commemorative cuff titles for men who had served with famous formations in World War I.

Arm bands tend to be associated with the political swastika insignia worn before the war in Germany, but, like the death's head, they have a longer and more re-

39. Staff of the NATO headquarters at Heidelberg in 1965, which includes Belgian, British, Canadian, German, Italian and US Army officers and NCOs.

The date of this photograph is important because in that year the Royal Army Service Corps of Transport and all ranks were re-badged. However, as the new badges were not yet available at Heidelberg the RCT personnel stationed there wore RAOC cap and collar badges temporarily — third row, first man on the left.

(Fisher Collection)

spectable history. They are perhaps most widely known for their use by stretcher parties, recovering wounded or dead on the battlefield. During the Falklands campaign in 1982, there were complaints that British stretcher parties had come under fire: Argentine soldiers observed the letter of the law and said that they would not have fired at the men if they had been properly and clearly identified. In addition to arm bands, members of stretcher parties can also wear a simple pullover waistcoat with large red crosses on the back and front.

Arm bands were worn to identify staff officers in World War I, different colours being used according to arm of service and staff position. The arm band has also been retained by shore patrols, military or regimental police, and by men who assume a temporary status, such as a movements officer at a port, airfield or railway station.

White arm bands have been widely used as a means of identifying umpires on training exercises, and they may also wear the umpire's cap or helmet and use a vehicle marked with a white cross. On exercises, 'enemy' troops are often distinguished by their coloured helmet bands, since all the uniforms are similar in appearance.

In more recent times the arm band has been replaced by the brassard, an arm band with a loop extending up to the epaulette to secure the band and prevent it sliding down the arm. A brassard also has a larger area, which allows more information to be displayed. Men with the United Nations or other peace-keeping forces can show their nationality, organization and rank on a brassard, which can be quickly moved from shirt to combat jacket, or simply removed altogether. Brassards can also be used as a supplementary pocket on the sleeve, which may be invaluable if the man is wearing a fragmentation vest.

Another form of battle honour adopted by the Germans in World War I was the arm shield, which was a pressed metal plate, worn on the upper left

40. An international gathering at the Heidelberg NATO headquarters in the mid-1960s. From left to right: a British staff sergeant, a German officer, a Canadian corporal, a Belgian private, another Canadian and another British staff sergeant. Collar badges on collar patches identify the branch of service of all except the Canadians who wear cloth shoulder titles.

(Fisher Collection)

sleeve. If a man was awarded three, one was displayed above two. Most shields were made of white metal, but the one awarded to troops who had fought in the Crimea and the Kuban in Russia was of bronze. The first shield awarded was for the Narvik campaign in 1940, but others followed, particularly during the desperate actions at the close of the war. A shield was to have been produced for the 6th Army that fought at Stalingrad, but it never materialized. Other shields were struck for the defence of Lorient and the fighting in Warsaw in 1944, but it is likely that, in the pressure of war, the shields never reached the men who had earned them.

PATCHES AND BADGES

The US armed forces, notably the Army, have the distinction of being the originators of the unit patch. As far back as the Civil War, General P. Keary gave the officers and later the men in his corps a red patch to wear on the front of their caps to identify them. From this beginning in 1862, patches and metal badges proliferated in the Union army, and some designs may still be found in today's US Army.

The corps dictated the shape of the emblem, the division within the corps the colour; in World War II the 24th Corps still had its heart-shaped patch and the 1st Corps its round patch. World War I witnessed the arrival of shoulder patches for the US forces when the 81st Infantry Division wore a 'wild cat' badge on the left shoulder. This and the other patches that were subsequently adopted in France were unofficial, and it was not until October 1918 that they were officially permitted.

The patches worn in France in World War I were often locally made. In World War II, the embroidery techniques and skills of the Far East allowed original and attractive designs to be made with metal thread and silks.

In World War II machines were used to make a vast range of embroidered patches. At first they were embroidered on khaki cloth but after the war, when the US Army changed to army green, the patches were produced on an army green backing. Later, in Vietnam many badges were made in 'subdued' black and green. The 1st Infantry Division, which had fought with distinction in North Africa, Sicily, Normandy and Europe had been universally known as 'The Big Red One', after the red number on its shield shaped patch. And although red was hardly a tactical colour, tradition won.

41. A group of Italian paratroopers wearing camouflage combat dress, escorted by two 'carabinieri' in full dress. They wear the old pattern pre-1964 parachute insignia on the upper left sleeve and rank insignia on the beret and on the left breast. At the front, from left to right, a 2nd lieutenant and a captain, followed by two warrant officers.

As other divisions had 'Airborne', the 10th Mountain Division, which trained for mountain warfare, had a tab reading 'Mountain'; it fought in Italy at the Gothic Line and the Po Valley. The 25th Infantry Division, made famous by the American writer James Jones in his accounts of the pre-World War II Army in Hawaii, has the famous 'tropic lightning' patch, which features a red taro leaf with a bolt of yellow lightning. Memories of World War I are recalled by the 26th Infantry Division, which has the initials YD (for Yankee Division). A pun is hidden in the patch of the 27th; it shows the constellation Orion, and in World War I its commanding officer was Major General J.F. O'Ryan. The 29th has the Oriental symbol of yin and yang, but whereas the interlocked shapes are often in blue and red or yellow and red in the Far East, the divisional patch is in the blue and grey of the North and the South in the American Civil War. The 34th and the 35th look to the Mid-West with the 34th's tab featuring a red steer's skull on a black olla (Mexican flask), while the 35th's has the cross in a circle that was used to mark the Santa Fé trail. The 39th, which did not serve overseas, has a triangle surrounding the letter D. The triangle symbolizes the three states of the Mississippi delta, Mississippi, Louisiana and Arkansas. The 41st has a patch symbolizing a Pacific sunset, and it looks a little like the insignia adopted by the short-lived state of Biafra, which fought a civil war in Nigeria in the 1960s. The 41st lived up to the image in the patch during fighting in Salamaua, the Marshall islands, Mindanao and Palawan. The 45th Division's thunderbird with its yellow bird against a red background draws on Red Indian art. The 79th had the cross of Lorraine long before it was adopted by the Free French in World War II; the divisional patch dated back to World War I. The 90th has a patch that could be mistaken for a brand: an O on its side bisected by a T. The orthodox version is that this stands for Texas and Oklahoma, but the wearers of the patch asserted that it stood for 'tough ombres' (tough men). The buffalo on the 92rd patch was a

42. Captain of the Royal Engineers wearing No. 1 dress in a photograph taken in 1969. The gilt and silver cap badge is worn together with bronze collar badges and anodised rank insignia and buttons. A bronze badge was used on the khaki service dress cap.

(M. Gaffney Collection)

reminder that Red Indians called black soldiers 'buffaloes', and the division was a traditionally black unit in the then-segregated US Army. The 93rd has a French *Casque Adrien*, the French helmet of World War I, to show its participation in that war. The screaming eagle of the 101st is based on a bird called 'Old Abe', which was the mascot of a regiment in the Iron Brigade in the Civil War. The black shield commemorates the Iron Brigade, and the Airborne tab was added in World War II. The division served with great distinction in World War II, seeing action at the defence of Bastogne, and earlier it was in part of operation Market Garden. The 1st Cavalry Division, with its large shield patch with a horse's head and diagonal bar, saw action in the Philippines in World War II. It returned to the Far East in 1965 during the Vietnam war as the 1st Air Cavalry.

Among the other shoulder patches

43. Recruits of the 'Volksarmee' being sworn in at the Sachsenhousen National Memorial, built on the grounds of a former Nazi concentration camp. They wear the parade dress uniform with cuff patches on the tunic, steel helmet and the officer on the right wears the dress belt and sword. The emblem in the centre of the flag is worn on all head-dresses except the steel helmet.

(Press Office of the Ministry of National Defence of the GDR — 1971)

44. Captain, USAF, in flying overalls. The squadron insignia of the 61st Tactical Air Squadron 'Green Hornets' is visible on his right upper sleeve. On the other sleeve he displays the Select Lead Crew badge and on the breast he has the Tactical Air Command patch on the right, and a composite tag which shows the pilot wing and his name on the left side.

(Hayes Collection)

worn in World War II were insignia designating theatre. They included China-Burma-India, and this shield-shaped patch had the Chinese Nationalist Sun, and a US star and bar. It was most memorably worn by the pilots of USAAF fighters, bombers and air transport units operating with the British and Chinese.

Other patches included those of the base commands set up to defend areas that had been established abroad as bases for operations. The only foreign base that did not need protection was Britain, so although a patch showing Big Ben against a red and blue background was worn by men in the UK, they were not required to defend the island. Threats to the US mainland seemed very real in 1941, and in 1942, after the bombing of Pearl Harbor, several Frontier Defence Sectors were established. They wore patches for the Pacific Coast, Chesapeake Bay, New England, New York-Philadelphia and Southern Coastal, and AA Artillery Command Control D.C. and AA Artillery Command Southern D.C.

The Allies trained a large number of men from occupied territory, and the US Army provided badges for men from France and China, even issuing a patch for the US Mission to Moscow. The French Forces training with the US wore a patch that looks rather like the French *Wehrmacht* volunteer badge worn by Frenchmen who were serving with German forces during World War II. Each has the French national colours in vertical bars with the national name above it.

With its total commitment to war, the US put actors and entertainers into uniform as part of the USO Camp Shows, which toured the different theatres to entertain the troops. The patch they wore was a red and white curved design with a winged motif.

At the bottom of the cuff, men had overseas service stripes or chevrons. The chevrons indicated time served in World War I, each one standing for six months. Stripes worn on the right sleeve indicated wounds received in action.

The US Army Air Force and the US Marine Corps aviation wings had a series

of patches during World War II. The Marine corps had a red shield with wings and stars and Roman numerals; the headquarters for the USMC Air Force in the Pacific had a crown in place of the numeral. There were four wings, and although the shield patch had been adopted in March 1943, it was changed to a diamond-shaped patch with the Marine Corps badge, wings and the number of the wing.

45. Chief Petty Officer, Fire Controlman, US Navy. The 'cap badge' and the rating insignia on the upper sleeve identify his rate and the emblem within the 'arc' and 'chevrons' identifies his speciality mark. The bars on his forearm denote 12 years service. Twelve years service with good-conduct (top row, central medal) made him eligible to wear gold arc, chevrons and service stripes. The eagle and the speciality mark are of silver.

(Hayes Collection)

The US Army Air Force was rather less formal. It chose as its dominant colours blue and yellow, with red at the centre of the white star.

Triangles were, however, used for specialist cuff insignia for trades like engineer, armourer, photography specialist, communications and weather specialist. These patches were yellow on blue, and they bore a symbolic representation of the trade — a bomb, a camera and, for the weather specialist, a weather vane.

US personnel attending the War Crimes trials at Nuremberg and Tokyo wore special patches, which, predictably, featured the scales of justice. Commands set up in former Axis-occupied or owned territory also had their own patches. Troops in Guam in the Philippines had two different patches: one showed a palm tree, sandy shore and fishing boat; the other, less like a holiday poster, had a palm tree. Commands in Berlin District had the Brandenburg Gate, while US Forces Far East had the snow-covered peak of Mount Fuji. The Ryukus Command based in Okinawa had a traditional Japanese torii gate.

As new nations, which had been colonies or had been under Axis occupation, began to adjust to freedom, the US government sent military assistance missions to help with the training of their armies. The Military Assistance Advisory Groups (MAAG) in Laos, Taiwan and Vietnam had their own patches.

The Korean war produced its quota of insignia. The Imjim River Scouts pocket patch of the Advanced Combat Training Academy of the 2nd Division featured a Red Indian chief's head on an arrow pointing northward through the Demilitarized Zone into North Korea, the patch itself being a map of Korea.

Out of the US Army presence in

Europe, the concept of special forces that could train insurgent groups inside the Eastern Bloc grew into the Special Forces or Green Berets. Some of the insignia for this force looked back to earlier specialized units in the US Army, but the shoulder patch with its dagger crossed by three lightning bolts came to be known as the 'Saigon Electrical Works' badge. Since most of its members were qualified with other skills, the patch was topped off with the Airborne tab or, sometimes, the Ranger tab. The raid in November 1970 made by Special Forces men on a suspected North Vietnamese prisoner-of-war compound at Son Tay, 23 miles from Hanoi, yielded no prisoners, which was a tragic ending to a well-planned operation, but so thorough had been the secrecy surrounding the raid that the participants had created an unofficial shoulder patch. It showed a pair of worried eyes looking out from under a toadstool – otherwise the patch was black. Beneath it the tab read 'KITD/FOHS' which stood for 'Kept in the Dark/Fed Only on Horse Shit'.

Other Special Forces insignia worn in Vietnam included those adopted by the Mobile Strike Forces, and they tended to mix South Vietnamese and US motifs. The Mobile Strike Forces had a very simple patch, the death's head with MF below it on a black shield. The tiger featured in some patches, and when the 1st and 2nd Mobile Strike Forces became more formalized, the Death's Head was replaced by patches showing a knife with SF-style lightning bolts. Between 1968 and 1970, the 2nd Mobile Strike Force Command (USSF only) wore a patch depicting a dragon against the yellow and red bars of the South Vietnamese flag with the tab 'Airborne Mike Force' above it. ('Mike Force' was the universal corruption of Mobile Strike Force.)

The Military Assistance Command Vietnam Studies and Observation Group (MACV SOG) advised and assisted the South Vietnamese Special Exploitation Service, which was later called the Strategic Technical Directorate. Behind these rather vague titles were the operations that penetrated Viet Cong and North Vietnamese Communications on the Ho Chi Minh trail. The patch, which one can hardly believe was worn, was a death's head on a Special Forces green beret; it had a cheerful Oriental flamboyance.

A major characteristic of the war in Vietnam was the use of helicopters to lift both men and supplies. The assault helicopter changed tactics, but before these could become standard practice they had to be tested. The 11th Air Assault Division, formed in the United States, worked through the drills and techniques, and wore a new patch: a blue shield with the figure 11 in a red circle with wings below the tab 'Air Assault'. The 11th became the 1st Cavalry Division (Airmobile) in July 1965. Other units became air mobile as the war progressed, and new patches appeared, but perhaps the most interesting was the 163rd ACR (Air Cavalry Regiment), whose patch featured a steer's head on a yellow shield with a diagonal black bar. The 163rd ACR had been the 163rd RCT (Regimental Combat Team) and could look back to 1884–7, when it was the 1st Infantry Regiment of the Montana National Guard. Redesignated the 163rd Infantry Regiment in 1922, it became part of the Federal armed forces in 1940 as part of the 41st Infantry Division. In 1945 it became the infantry regiment of the 163rd RCT and in 1953 an armoured cavalry regiment.

The wearing of foreign decorations and insignia is carefully controlled out-

47. A group of Warsaw Pact soldiers wearing combat uniforms, with the exception of the two Soviets with peaked caps who wear service dress. In the foreground from left to right: Hungarian, Czechoslovak, Russian, German, and Polish other ranks, and others of the same nationalities in the background. The cap badge seems to be the only item of national identification for the rankless private, therefore when the steel helmet is worn, any means of national allegience disappear. Nevertheless the men wear a different uniform according to their nationality and speak a different language. Rank badges are the only important insignia in modern warfare.

(Militärverlag der DDR (VER))

side an operational area. US Army Special Forces advisors in Vietnam sported a number of the patches and badges awarded to the élite forces with whom they were serving. The Vietnamese, Cambodian and Civilian Irregular Defence Groups produced patches that reflected their national and local tastes as well as the earlier French influence on the area. Thus the Cambodian Army Airborne Reconnaissance had French-style parachute wings, but in place of the parachute there was a skull with a red beret. Above the skull was the word 'Recon'. The South Vietnamese Jump Status patch drew on the French airborne beret badge with its winged Roman sword; the French badge is enclosed in a circle. The Vietnamese adopted the US practice of classing parachutists by the number and type of jump made, but they retained a badge similar to that worn by the French, and they also had a gold thread on a red background badge for non-airborne honorary parachutists.

Unauthorized patches for air mobile units included the vertical winged sword on a black shield below an airborne tab, the component of the 1st Aviation Brigade with parachute competence. The 11th Aviation Group Medical Evacuation had a helicopter bearing a Red Cross, with open hands and wings and the motto 'Dust off', the slang name for an airborne evacuation of casualties. The 95th Evacuation Hospital had the motto 'We care for all'. The Reconnaissance Team Asp CCN, the Recon Team Kansas CCN MACV-SOG, and the Recon Team Alaska CCN, however, wore patches that had various unauthorized motifs like winged skulls, snakes and daggers. All shared the same motto — 'We kill for peace'.

Although shoulder tabs have not been a traditional part of US military insignia, they grew as accepted or unauthorized additions to uniform. Colours varied, but common were white letters on blue with a red border, or yellow on black with a yellow border.

During the early days of US involvement, a 'Viet-nam' tab, printed as white lettering on a red background, appeared on items of uniform. It was even sewn on to non-standard camouflaged hats made from parachute silk. Following the US invasion of Grenada and the peace-keeping mission in the Lebanon, other non-standard tabs were produced. Patches and tabs have been produced for men who served in World War II, Korea and more recently Vietnam. They can be worn on non-military clothing, although they have also appeared on old combat fatigues at reunions and pilgrimages.

The chest has been a common place to display rank and skills: medal ribbons, pilots wings and numerous unit and qualification insignia are positioned to the left and right of the buttons of a jacket or tunic.

The French have traditionally worn some very fine metal regimental badges on leather fobs from the right pocket of their shirt or tunic. This insignia came into use informally between the wars as a metal badge pinned to the tunic. In their colonial postings, units would have commissioned local metal workers to make unit insignia, but after World War II the badge became more formalized.

The French Foreign Legion adopted and modified these unit and regimental badges in a way that allows an observer to trace the origins and history of each unit. The 1er Régiment Étranger has a badge featuring the Mexican eagle with a snake in its beak. This recalls the heroic battle to the death by men of the Legion at Camerone in Mexico on 30 April 1863. Some badges are private jokes. The 1er Escadron du 1er Régiment Étranger Cavalerie has a crab motif: during their operations in the swamps of Indo-China in the 1950s they had been mounted in ex-US Marine Crab and Alligator tracked amphibious vehicles. The 13ème Demi Brigade de la Légion Étranger (DBLE) became part of the Free French forces fighting in North Africa and later in Europe in World War II, and it has the

48. Although well camouflaged in his combat dress, wearing the red beret with winged badge as the only colourful item of his uniform, this 'para' still seems to be very conspicuous in civvy street.

(Hayes Collection)

cross of Lorraine in its badge. Beneath the cross and the seven-flamed grenade of the Legion, a serpent lies crushed. The Legion's service in Indo-China and North Africa appears in the shape of outlines of Vietnam, dragons or Moorish symbols.

A less well known élite of the French armed forces are the Commando-Marines. Like their British opposite numbers, they wear green berets, but they draw their traditions from World War II. Their bronze, shield-shaped cap badge has a motif that includes a commando dagger, a small fishing boat and the cross of Lorraine. The unit badge fobs worn on the breast include the Commando Jaubert, which alludes to Indo-China with its dragon motif, and the Commando de Montfort, which uses heraldry from pre-revolutionary France. They were among the French forces sent to Beirut as part of the multi-national peace-keeping force in 1983–4 — a curious twist of history, since to the south, on the Israeli border, the PLO had held Montfort castle, a crusader fortification, which fell to Israeli commandos. The French Groupement Aéroporté (GAP), of which the commandos were part, has an eagle motif, and there is now a version backed by the cedar of Lebanon to commemorate this deployment.

The unit fob badge has been adopted

by other armies and has even been worn by British soldiers attached to allied forces. The practice of wearing other national badges is a carefully guarded privilege. Normally the wearer has undertaken training or a course, and parachute wings are, therefore, most common. Normally soldiers are allowed two foreign badges, more can make them look like Boy Scouts collecting qualification badges. One British soldier, who completed a course with the US Army when it was in the Panama Canal Zone, returned to his unit with a very colourful 'jungle expert' badge. It proved to be too colourful for his commanding officer, who would not allow the soldier to wear it on his combat jacket.

An exception was made for a British sergeant who passed the US Army Ranger course. He still wears his Ranger tab with great pride, having a black on green 'subdued' version for his combat jacket and a gold on black version for his dress uniform. The Ranger course, spread over several months and through a variety of terrains including mountains and swamps, is probably one of the hardest courses in the US Army. As one three-tour Vietnam veteran said, 'After the Ranger course nothing seemed hard in Vietnam.' This veteran had Cambodian parachute wings, which looked very

like the French wings.

Like a number of armies, the French wear their parachute wings on their chest. Known as the plaque à vélo (bicycle badge) because the wings resemble a bicycle registration disc, the badge received a good deal of attention from its wearers in the 1950s and 1960s. Pierre Leulliette, in his autobiography *St Michael and the Dragon* (a title chosen from his parachute regiment insignia), recalls: 'There were a thousand ways, all in defiance of orders, of wearing this distinguished symbol. The artists chromed it over: so that it shone like silver, even at night. The careful ones backed it with red leather so as to set it off. As for the born scrappers, obeying some deeper dictate, they twisted it, wore it down, and tarnished it until it became yellow, the way that kids in St Tropez used to sandpaper their jeans at the knees...'

The Israeli Defence Force has a number of distinctions for the insignia of its experienced forces, and men who made the parachute assault at the Mitla Pass in 1956 have a red backing to their parachute wings, and there are campaign ribbons for 1948, 1956, 1967 and 1973.

US Army parachute wings have always been a source of interest to other airborne soldiers. Some protest that they

49. Miscellaneous Western European Insignia:
1. Pocket badge of the 4th Allied Tactical Air Force 2. Cockade for officers and NCOs of the Danish Army and Navy 3. Forage cap badge of the 'Bundeswehr' 4. Beret badge of French parachutists 5. Beret badge of the Royal Artillery, British Army 6. Shoulder strap badge of the Belgian 'Chasseurs Ardennais' 7. Collar insignia of the Turkish tank units 8. Breast badge of the Italian 'San Marco' marines 9. Breast badge of the Italian 77th/78th Infantry Regiments 10. Norwegian cockade.

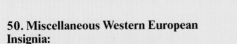

50. Miscellaneous Western European Insignia:
1. Formation sign of the Headquarters Allied Forces Northern Europe 2. Distinctive insignia of the French 3rd Parachute Regiment of Marine Infantry 3. Distinctive insignia of the 1st Company, 'Aosta' Battalion, 4th Alpine Regiment of the Italian Army 4. Collar badge of the Netherlands Army engineers 5. Nationality insignia of the Netherlands Army.

receive only one set of wings while the US forces have three and, if Para Ranger or Rigger are included, four. There are three classes of wings. Master Parachutist has made 65 jumps, including 25 with combat equipment, four at night and five mass tactical jumps. The wearer must also be a qualified jumpmaster or have served as a jumpmaster on at least one combat jump or 33 training jumps.

A Senior Prachutist receives his wings after 30 jumps, including 15 with combat equipment, two at night and two mass tactical jumps. He too must be a qualified jumpmaster or have taken part in one or more combat jumps or 15 non-combat jumps as a jumpmaster. Master and Senior Parachutists must also have served on jump status for 36 and 24 months respectively. Army-qualified parachutists wear a winged parachute insignia, and Ranger qualified men wear the badge topped with the ranger tab.

The development of helicopter air mobility has produced the Air Assault badge, which is seen as an equivalent of parachute wings. To duplicate the challenge of a parachute jump, abseiling (or rapelling) from a hovering helicopter has been introduced. Men are also required to rig helicopters for underslung loads and to be able to lay out a landing zone. Pathfinders in Vietnam, who fulfilled a similar role with air mobile forces, wore the winged torch insignia on the front of their uniform.

The rivalry between the 82nd and 101st Airborne dates back to their inception in World War II. The 101st maintains that the AA for 'All American' of the 82nd Airborne shoulder patch (insignia that predates its airborne role) in fact stands for 'Almost Airborne'. However the 82nd has had the last laugh, because it is now the only truly airborne unit in the US Army since the 101st became a helicopter air assault division.

The combination of chest and arm insignia for airborne forces is not confined to the US Army. War-time and post-war practice has repeated the combination with German, Italian and Soviet airborne forces. The *Bundeswehr* has a badge that is similar in design

to the war-time *Fallschirmjäger* badge; the eagle on the post-war badge is in white metal, and there is no swastika on the wreath. In World War II the *Luftwaffe* had a variety of qualification badges, all of which used an oval wreath of oak leaves. With the exception of air crews, whose wreath was horizontal, the wreaths were vertical. The eagle had been adopted by the Nazi party as an Aryan symbol, but this did not preclude its being used by many other national air forces. The RAF, for example, had a blue eagle shoulder title, while the RAF Regiment had a red eagle shoulder title.

Luftwaffe badges included aircrew, pilot, observer, wireless operator air gunner, pilot observer, air gunner flight engineer, glider pilot, parachutist, AA artillery, ex-flyer (the eagle had folded wings) and un-qualified air gunner. Badges were also introduced for *Luftwaffe* units pressed into ground combat. These included a ground combat award, a similar award for 100 engagements, a sea battle award, a tank battle award and a 75 tank engagements award.

In the strange empire-building world of Nazi Germany, the *Luftwaffe* fielded well-equipped ground units before it lost control of the skies, and its men wore a curious mix of army uniform and air force insignia. In World War II the Germans included a good deal of information in the collar patches of their air force uniforms. *Waffenfarbe* were yellow for airborne and flying personnel, red for gunners and blue for medical personnel. Collars also showed rank and status. However, the *Luftwaffe* also had trade badges, although these were combined with metal breast badges. Unencumbered by tradition, they produced some pleasing and clear designs: an armourer for light bombs had a grenade with a cluster of five flames emitted from one port; heavy bomb armourers had flames coming out of three ports; AA artillery crews had a recognizable outline of an 8.8 cm Flak gun barrel.

For its chest badges, the US Army Air Force adopted a winged motif, and the badges had a pleasing consistency of design. They were standardized on a

design by Herbert Williams, which had been adopted in 1919, and they were made in sterling silver. The design has been continued, with some alterations, to the present day. In 1941, three classes of wings were authorized to distinguish more experienced pilots; the initial badge was pilot, advancing to senior pilot and to command pilot. Other qualification badges included balloon observer, balloon pilot and senior balloon pilot, navigator, aircraft observer and technical observer. The rank of senior balloon pilot was for men who had piloted airships or motorized balloons for 100 hours and had 10 years' service. Though this may seem rather antiquated in a war that saw missiles and jet aircraft in action, powered balloons or blimps, with their low speed and high endurance, had an important role in anti-submarine operations.

Glider pilot badges were adopted by all the major combatants. They were perhaps among the most demanding of pilots' wings to be awarded, for the man at the controls of a glider had to put his unpowered aircraft down in a safe landing zone to deliver the cargo and passengers intact. (Many gliders 'nosed over' if they hit rough ground, killing the pilot and many of the passengers.) After this hazardous landing, the pilot joined his passengers to fight as a conventional soldier. In the British Army glider pilots' wings were worn on the left breast above medal ribbons, a patch showing a white glider on a pale blue background was also worn on the forearm of the left sleeve.

Glider pilots in the US Army Air Force had wings with the letter G on a shield flanked by wings. Other badges using the same design were for bombar-

52. Miscellaneous World War II Insignia: 1. Canadian General Service cap badge 2. Red Army cap badge 3. Formation sign of the British 9th Armoured division 4. Cap badge of the Australian Commonwealth Military Forces 5. Branch of service badge of the Yugoslav Motor Transport 6. Collar badge of the 12th 'Wolynski' Rifle Battalion of the Polish 5th 'Kresowa' Infantry Division 7. Formation sign of the India Eastern Command 8. Branch of service badge of the Red Army tank unit.

51

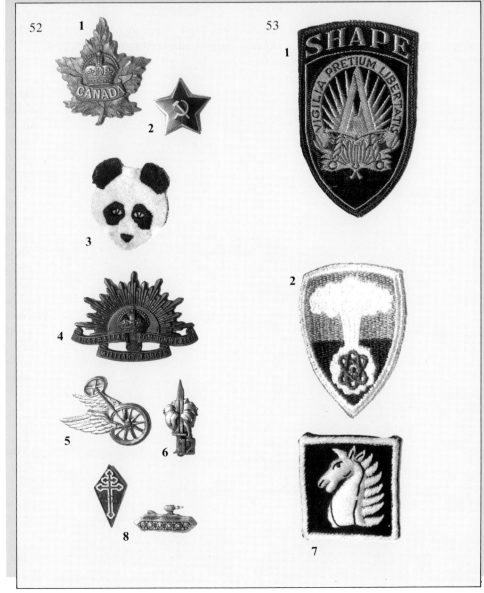

52

53

51. Miscellaneous Eastern European Insignia:
1. Collar insignia of the Hungarian Border Guards 2. Other ranks' forage cap badge of the Yugoslav proletarian divisions 3. Collar badge of the Yugoslav tank units 4. Polish Navy proficiency badge 5. Soviet Army officer's cap badge 6. Rank star of Hungarian 2nd lieutenant 7. Other ranks cap badge of the 'Volksarmee' 8. Breast badge of Yugoslav Border Guards.

53. 1. Formation sign of the Supreme Headquarters Allied Powers Europe 2. Shoulder sleeve insignia of the Defence Atomic Support Agency.

dier, aerial gunner and air crew member, and there were also similar designs for the women's services including Women's Army service pilot, Women's Air Force service pilot and flight nurse. It is interesting to note that today women have assumed a greater responsibility for flying duties in the US Air Force, including piloting tanker aircraft, and, as army pilots, they crew troop-carrying helicopters. The Soviet Air Force, however, has the distinction of having the first women pilots to fight in air combat. They had a similar uniform and rank badges to their male comrades, but they introduced some individual touches when they embroidered the collars of their flying overalls with traditional motifs. Like the army uniforms, Soviet air force uniforms and insignia changed in 1943 to a high collar and shoulder board design. The British Women's Auxilliary Air Force (WAAF), which became the WRAF after the war, did front-line work in the Battle of Britain in 1940. The women wore similar insignia to the RAF, but with the addition of the letter A to officers' lapels and beneath the non-commissioned ranks' 'vulture' (the nickname for the RAF eagle) on the shoulder. A separate, dark blue uniformed force, the Air Transport Auxiliaries, included many women, who ferried aircraft to RAF bases from factories. The blue grey uniform of the Royal Air Force was adopted by most of the Commonwealth air forces that fought in World War II, however, in addition to the shoulder title, the Australian, New Zealand, South African and Canadian air force cap badges included letters to indicate the nationality of the wearer. The wings worn on the tunic breast were also different in colour or design. Interestingly, the Canadians had the crown above their aircrew badges, while the RAF and RAAF had a simple letter or motif surrounded by a wreath and with one wing. Badges included observer, navigator, air gunner, wireless operator, flight engineer, bomb aimer, parachute training instructor and signaller.

The air forces or men from the occupied countries of Europe and volunteers from the United States who joined before December 1941 who served with the RAF in World War II displayed ranks and trades in a variety of ways. US volunteers had the Eagle Squadron badge: a US eagle with the letters US. In his autobiography *Tumult in the Clouds*, James Goodson, a former Eagle Squadron pilot, recalls one man who improved on King's Regulations: 'Vic had gone one better for Texas. On the shoulder of his jacket where foreign volunteers in the RAF had their "USA", "Canada", "New Zealand" "Rhodesia", etc Vic had a neat "Texas".' Vic France also wore a tailored RAF uniform and a pair of highly polished, black, pointed-toe, high-heeled Texas boots.

The Dutch and Poles adopted parts of the Royal Air Force insignia when they served with the RAF, normally retaining parts of their own national insignia to keep a sense of identity. However, in war time, British rank insignia assisted identification and reduced the danger of their being mistaken for enemy air crew if a pilot landed by parachute.

The Polish Air Force, which had seen action against the early Soviet Air Force during the Russo-Polish war of 1919, had some striking breast badges. All depicted an eagle in flight, but some had an ingenious chain that, when attached to the tunic, gave the impression that the badge was hanging although in reality it was secured by a screw-backed pin. Badges were worn high on the tunic under the left lapel. The 1919 pattern badge, which was still in evidence at the beginning of World War II, was either an eagle with a green enamel wreath in its beak, or a silver eagle with wreath. The wreath could be used to enclose letters or motifs to indicate specialities like radio operator (R) air gunner (S), flight meteorologist (M) or bombardier (B). The eagle's claws were used also to grasp lightning bolts, which, by their number

54. Wearing their characteristic pale blue berets, troops of the United Nations Peace Keeping forces check in by radio during a patrol. The UN forces wear blue berets or helmets, arm band brassards with the UN badge and their own national insignia, and sometimes blue cravat chokers.

and direction, indicated other qualifications; for example, three gold lightning bolts and no wreath was the 1933 Observer Second Class badge, and the 1928 Pilot Observer wore a similar badge, which included a wreath, but in gold.

In the early 1930s the Italian Air Force had some badges that looked a little like the US Army Air Force insignia. Earlier in World War I an eagle and crown, which looked rather similar to the RAF other ranks' 'vulture', had been used. With the advent of the Fascist state, two types of breast badge were added: a stylized winged air crew badge, which was echoed in white metal for trades like photographer, armourer or driver, and a wreathed badge for rescue, transport, dive bombers, interceptors, bombers, torpedo aircraft, assault-combat, reconnaissance at sea and strategic reconnaissance and aerial observation. These badges were rather similar to those adopted by the *Luftwaffe*. Although this may merely be an indication of the way Nazi Germany and Fascist Italy copied some aspects of their respective regalia, it also shows the fairly limited choice of wings, eagle, wreaths and symbolic bombs, flashes of lightning, or parachutes that can be used for air force badges and insignia.

One original badge was designed in Britain as a result of attacks by the *Luftwaffe*. The Royal Engineers Bomb Disposal teams wear a yellow bomb on a red field as a patch on their pullover or tunic. It was designed during World War II by Queen Elizabeth the Queen Mother as a tribute to the teams who were engaged in this hazardous work.

Although air forces throughout the world have displayed their aircrew status on the tunic fronts, a wide variety of metal and cloth badges has been used by armies past and present. A significant development in the production of embroidered badges was mechanized multi-coloured embroidery, which allowed unit badges to be produced in a more attractive way, as well as being more durable than printed cloth. Hand-sewn badges have not completely disappeared, for in Vietnam men could have all their rank

55. A US Army Captain in combat kit talks with a Soviet observer during the US Reforger Exercises in 1983. The Soviet presence was part of the Helsinki agreement between President Carter and Brezhnev — the West sent observers to Warsaw Pact exercises in return.

56. A US Air Force pilot with national insignia on his shoulder and his pilot's wings and name tag on the front of his flying overalls.

and qualification badges sewn directly on to the shirt fabric by local tailors, who replaced the cloth patches produced in the United States.

One notable addition to US Army and Air Force uniforms came in the 1950s, when name and arm badges were introduced. Name tabs have been adopted by a number of countries, but some would argue that, while it is useful to know the name of the man or woman to whom one is speaking, an officer should make it his business to know his soldiers' names.

Arm-of-service insignia worn on the front of shirts or jackets has even reached the Israeli defence Forces. The Nahal badge, which is worn on the left shirt front is a source of wry amusement to some observers in the Middle East. Until Israel became involved in the Lebanon she had no need to identify her forces – she had no allies in the area. Contact with Christian forces, and later the peace-keeping forces in Beirut, however, obliged her to identify her troops.

During the protracted guerrilla war in Rhodesia in the 1960s and 1970s the universal camouflaged uniforms adopted by the police and army led to the intro-

duction of force name tags. Unit 'slides', which were cloth loops over the epaulettes, also displayed the rank and arm of the member of the security force.

The French, as we have seen, display rank on the front of their uniforms. Name tags too are attached to combat jackets with a 'velcro' fastening, which allows the wearer to 'sanitize' his clothing, by removing the name and rank.

In the US Army breast badges that are worn as metal insignia on service dress tunics, are reproduced in cloth for wear on combat clothing. During the Vietnam war there was a move from the full-coloured badge to a 'subdued' pattern in black and green. Though this led to a slight loss of detail, the shape and pattern of the badge were unchanged. One member of the Special Forces recalled that the A and B team members could be distinguished when they met at the unit club house. An outsider would assume that the 'front-line' A team men were those men in camouflage clothing with subdued badges, while the B team men were those sporting flamboyant badges on shoulder and shirt pockets, with colourful Vietnamese special forces

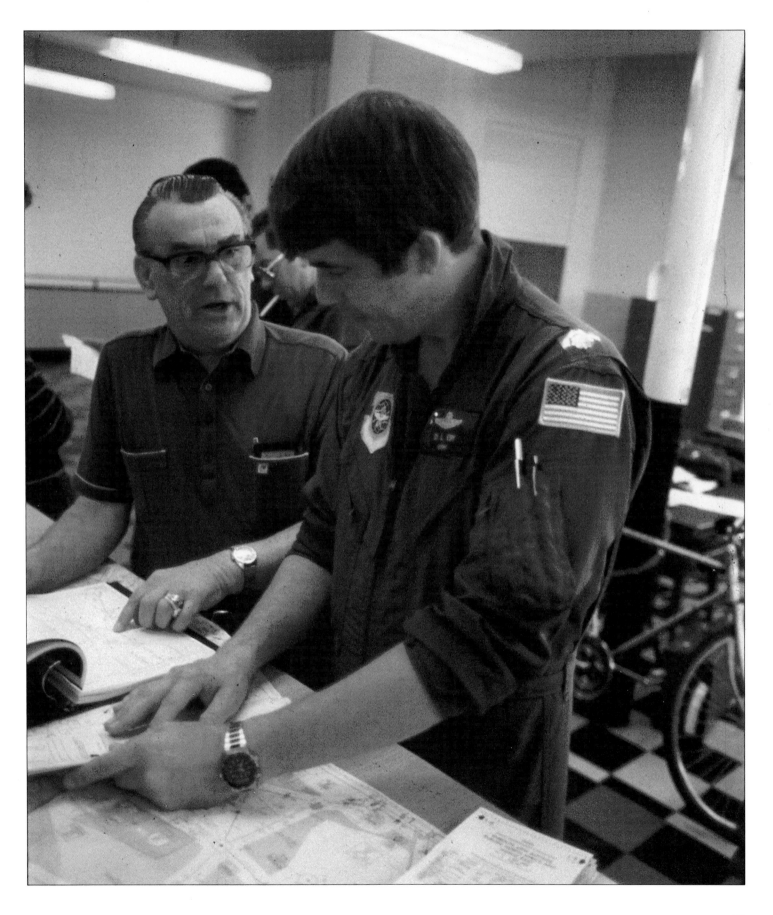

scarves knotted at the neck. The reality was the opposite: the A team men who worked with the Vietnamese adopted their allies' mode of dress, and the B team men wore the subdued insignia. Another soldier in Special Forces said that they kept their badged shirts on a hanger and wore them only when there was a 'threat' of a high-ranking visitor; otherwise the uniform could be a T-shirt, 'tiger stripes' and boots.

Among the breast badges available for the US Army are the combat infantryman, expert infantryman and, since World War II, a second and third award for combat infantryman as well as a combat armored cavalry and combat field artillery. On dress greens, breast badges are worn for work in the Department of Defense, the White House, Joint Chiefs of Staff, General Staff and for being a member of the Guard at the Tomb of the Unknown Soldier, Washington.

The use of badges to indicate the experience and training of a soldier is not exclusive to the US Army. In World War I the Imperial German Army instituted wound badges, a concept not dissimilar to the US Purple Heart. This practice was continued with the operations of the Condor Legion during the Spanish Civil War. In World War II a standard badge, a helmet in a wreath with crossed swords and a swastika, was issued, but, following the July Bomb Plot of 1944, a wound badge was produced for the survivors that bore Hitler's signature and '20 Juli 1944'.

A tank battle badge came in three classes. It consisted of an oval wreath with a stylized tank and eagle and swastika. There was an ordinary badge, one for 25 to 50 engagements and one for 75 to 100 engagements. Other combat badges included the infantry assault, army parachutist, army balloon observer and army anti-aircraft. Anti-aircraft guns and parachute forces had been appropriated by the *Luftwaffe*, and so army-qualified men were unusual.

57. Riggers from the 82nd Airborne prepare a heavy drop pallet — they are wearing the red beret that has become the trademark of airborne soldiers in the west.

58. Soviet Observers with US Army officers during Reforger 83. The Soviet officers in summer working dress have the characteristic shoulder board insignia for their rank.

Up to four tank destruction badges could be awarded, and, with the destruction of a fifth tank, the badge was awarded in gold. It consisted of a tank motif on a silver aluminium cord backing with black borders.

A more sinister award dating from World War II was the SS-instituted anti-partisan war badge, which was awarded from the end of 1944 to members of the armed forces who had engaged in anti-partisan operations. Many of the awards produced during the war can now be worn in West Germany — provided the swastika is not included — but the anti-partisan war badge is proscribed.

As observed earlier, the two Germanys have incorporated some of this insignia in their post-war uniforms. The West Germans have cloth and metal parachute wings, and the earliest post-war version looks rather like the close combat badge of World War II. Sports qualification badges are also worn, and to achieve promotion a man must pass the fitness tests. The National *Volksarmee* of East Germany has, like other Socialist countries, political as well as sporting badges made of enamelled metal. These include insignia for the GS Academy of the Soviet Army, the Military Academy of the Soviet Army, the Military Academy F. Engels and the Military Medical Section of E-M Arndt University, as well as a graduate officer's badge. Other badges worn by ordinary soldiers include those for parachutist, exemplary soldier, army proficiency, border troop proficiency and military sports. Drivers of tanks, trucks and trades, such as signaller and diver, have a white and gold metal breast badge, some of which include a number indicating first, second or third class. The most notable adoption from Nazi Germany is the aluminium thread marksman's lanyard. It is awarded in three classes for infantry, artillery and armour marksmanship, and, but for a lack of an eagle and swastika, it looks very similar to the version awarded from 1936 to 1945.

A general assault badge was produced in three classes: general assault, 25 to 50 assaults and 75 to 100 assaults. It was awarded to men who were not eligible for the infantry or tank assault badges, and the initial qualification was to have participated in three assault actions on three different days.

Although the tank destruction badge, which was awarded for the single-handed destruction of a tank, was a sleeve decoration, it was, together with its aircraft equivalent, produced in the same spirit as some of the breast awards. The tank badges were instituted in 1942, but back-dated to 1941, but the aircraft destruction badge came out near the end of the war, and it is not certain if any were awarded.

CAP BADGES

The cap badges of the 20th-century armed forces owe their origin to the helmet plates of the 18th and 19th centuries. These normally had a number indicating the regiment in which the soldier was serving.

By World War I, the Imperial German Army had produced some superb examples of *pickelholben* (spiked helmets), which had the imperial eagle and regimental number on the front. The British had moved away from using number designation to regional or corps badges, and in this practice they were not alone. During World War II there was a certain wry amusement when Italian units, with splendid names like the 'Wolves of Tuscany', were captured by men with self-effacing regimental name like The Buffs. However, many armies wore their distinctive unit insignia on their lapels, shoulders or as a badge on the chest. The cap badge was thus a simple national or arm insignia, indicating membership of the cavalry, infantry, artillery or support arms. Officers often had a different badge from ordinary men.

The Soviet Union has an oval surround in gold, flanked by oak leaves, with a red star in the centre for officers' caps, while other ranks have a simple red star with a hammer and sickle in the centre. The US Army distinguishes between officers, warrant officers and enlisted ranks, although in some armies warrant officers have the same cap badge as officers. The cap badge of US Army officers has the American eagle with olive branch and arrows in its claws; warrant officers' badges are simpler, with the eagle surrounded by a wreath, and enlisted men have the eagle on a circular gold backing.

In East and West Germany the national colours of black, red and yellow are used. The addition of badges to the side of a ski cap for alpine troops in the West German Army follows a tradition dating

59. A crude and simple piece of insignia — the name on helmets or uniforms, sometimes with the wearer's rank. Here a US armoured vehicle commander has his name stencilled on his helmet.

back to World War II. The edelweiss mountain flower, which is worn on the side of caps, was also worn as sleeve insignia in World War II.

Breast badges had been awarded in the Soviet Army during World War II, the most famous and prestigious being the Guards insignia, a status that was conferred in September 1941 on units that had performed particularly well in battle. Fighter and bomber squadrons were also awarded Guards status, and the insignia was painted on the fuselage of aircraft or the turrets of tanks. The badge was instituted in March 1942, and, like later introductions in the war, was an attempt to sustain morale and give units identity. In the post-war Soviet Army, Guards units retain this status by their consistently high standard of readiness. The badge is a simple red star with a banner bearing the word 'Guards', and a wreath and the cyrilic 'CCCP' (USSR). Soviet badges are either pin- or screw-backed. Pin-backed badges are the less substantial.

Although the badges are worn on the right side, either below medals and orders or, in their absence, in their place, there are exceptions. The Komsomol (Communist Youth League) badge is worn on the left. A shield and wreath design is widely used for infantry and proficiency badges, although armour and rocket troops have stylized wing backing to their badges, which are awarded in three classes. The most common colours are gold metal with red, blue and sometimes white, enamel. Badges include athletics awards, one of which, 'Ready for Labour and Defence', depicts a sprinter crossing the line. The extended service badge shows how long a man has remained with the army after completing his military service. Conscription is not popular with the Soviet public, and this badge is one of the inducements for trained men to stay on after their two years. Parachute insignia includes instructor parachutist, proficient parachutist and parachutist, and they are based on the figure of a parachutist, with numerals and other details added according to class. A common badge worn by marines,

60. Sometimes headgear and badges are created for a specific role — here the beret and badge of the Combat Control Team on Reforger 83 — the red beret, like the umpires white arm band is designed to be readily recognisable at a distance.

61. A mass colour party of the NATO participants in Reforger 83; though a regiment's colours were once the rallying point in battle the role of flags has diminished except as a means of identifying national groups in a multi-national exercise or peace keeping force.

paratroops and ordinary soldiers is the proficiency award. In three classes, it has the numeral in white on a blue enamel background.

Operations in Afghanistan may have led to the reintroduction of wound stripes. Instituted in July 1942, they were sewn above the left-hand side of the right breast pocket. Two classes were produced: a gold stripe for a serious wound, a red one for a minor wound.

Historically, badges, medals and retired rank have played an important part in Soviet life. The 'Great Patriotic War' has been portrayed as a time of inspired sacrifice, unity and loyalty, something like the 'Dunkirk Spirit' but on a larger scale. Old soldiers wearing their medals and uniforms are, therefore, a reminder and an inspiration. Badges and qualifications are things to aspire to while the young man is doing his two years' service. Conscripts to the navy who do three years, may need even more inspiration.

Naval and air force uniforms have often used simple cap badges to differentiate between officer, warrant officer and other ranks. In the navy, the cap band might show the ship in which the rating serves. Sometimes a distinction within a basic design might be used to show that the officer is an engineer, line or aviation specialist, as happens in the Royal Netherlands Navy. The cap badge of chaplains in the Italian Air Force in World War II took the form of a cross, and an elaborate range of badges in the *Regia Aeronautica* showed the role and status of the wearer. Thus administration, medical, flying and technical badges were grasped in the claws of an eagle flanked by oak leaves and topped by the royal crown. The Commonwealth Air Forces have retained the basic RAF badge but, like their wings, it has included their national identity: RCAF for the Royal Canadian Air Force, for example. When Rhodesia (now Zimbabwe) unilaterally declared independence, the Rhodesian Air Force adopted the initials RAF, but altered its insignia.

It is however on land that individuality in cap badge becomes most notable. The Italians, Belgians and British are among those nations that retain or have developed this tradition. The amalgamation of British regiments in the 1960s posed the problem of blending two or more badges, an exercise that rarely satisfies all concerned. But, in the 20 years that have passed since these changes, most soldiers are happy to serve in such anonymous regiments as the Royal Regiment of Wales or the Duke of Edinburgh's Own Regiment. The Light Infantry and Rifle Regiments have been amalgamated, but their cap badges seem to have worked well.

In World War II cap badges included some logical and simple designs as well as baffling and historic ones. The Royal Scots Greys sported the French eagle that they captured at the Battle of Waterloo; the 9th, 12th, 16/5th and 24th Lancers had crossed lances in their badge. The Royal Tank Regiment bore the outline of a World War I tank with a wreath, royal cypher and the motto 'Fear Naught'. The Royal Armoured Corps had a simple, but rather brutal, design of a mailed fist with arrows moving round the flanks as it punches the centre of the objective. The Royal Artillery, with its motto *Ubique Quo Fas et Gloria Ducunt*, has a Napoleonic cannon, and some versions of this badge were made with a moving wheel on the gun. Of the Guards Regiments, the Grenadier and Welsh Guards had the most attractive designs: the Grenadier Guards have a flaming grenade and the Welsh Guards a Welsh leek — few military formations can have a vegetable as their cap badge.

Fusilier regiments retain a flaming grenade design, while the light infantry have the bugle horn, a motif that dates back to the days when, as élite troops in the Napoleonic wars, they used the light bugle horn instead of the conventional drum to signal manoeuvres on the battlefield. It is a motif that has been used by the Belgians as well as the Italians. The Somerset Light Infantry, now part of the Light Infantry, having previously been amalgamated as the Somerset and Cornwall Light Infantry, had the battle honour Jalalabab, which dates back to the British Afghan wars. One of the more unusual badges is one of the two worn by the Glosters. The smaller badge on the back of their caps reminds them of the 'thin red line' that fought French troops attacking from both front and rear in Egypt in 1802. The sphinx on the back is a smaller version of that on the front and is surrounded by a wreath. Like the Argyle and Sutherland Highlanders and the Royal Welch Fusiliers, the Glosters have avoided disbandment or amalgamation, even though there were plans in the 1970s to merge them with the Hampshire Regiment and a badge was designed.

The Duke of Edinburgh's Royal Regiment, which incorporates the former Royal Berkshire Regiment, has retained the red triangular backing worn by that regiment to commemorate the battle of Brandywine in the American War of Independence, when the regiment fought as the 49th Foot. The cap badge is a combination of the badge of the Wiltshire Regiment and that of the Royal Berkshire Regiment.

The sphinx as a cap badge is not unique to the Glosters, for it was also worn by men of the East Lancashire Regiment, the South Wales Borderers, the Lancashire Fusiliers, the Dorset Regiment and the Essex. However, some of these cap badges incorporated the sphinx as part of larger design. The Rifle Brigade and King's Royal Rifle Corps (the 60th) passed on a tradition to the Royal Green Jackets of displaying battle honours on their cap badge. The tradition is that these regiments, operating as small independent skirmishing and scouting groups in advance of the squares of soldiers in the Napoleonic battlefield, could not have a regimental colour within the security of a square; their battle honours were, therefore, displayed on their badge. The Royal Marines have one battle honour only: that awarded for the capture of Gibraltar in July 1704 and its subsequent defence against the French and Spanish during a nine-month siege.

The Italian Army currently has a range of cap badges, many of which include a flaming grenade as part of the design. These badges cover the different types of artillery from missiles through heavy, medium and horse artillery to light and heavy AA artillery. They include variations on crossed cannon barrels and a flaming grenade, while the infantry have crossed rifles, and support arms, such as railway engineers, miners, bridging en-

62. A trooper of the 1st Cavalry Division gets a helping hand with his pack as he boards a US Air Force Transport. The female US Air Force ground crew is wearing a jacket with the squadron badge on the shoulder.

63. Sporting both US and West German paratroopers wings a US NCO in his bright red Combat Control Team cap talks to a US Airborne officer. The wearing of foreign wings is a popular, but carefully controlled, practice — some men like to 'collect' wings by jumping with different armies.

gineers and combat engineers, have crossed axes or anchors topped by a flaming grenade.

Belgian badges have a pleasing logic, although there is more variety than those of the Italians. Corps are identified by fairly obvious motifs like lightning bolts for electrical and mechanical engineers, or crossed cannon and flaming grenade for the artillery. Lancer regiments have variations on crossed lances while *Chasseurs à Cheval* have crossed sabres, with the numeral superimposed with a bugle horn, a means of communication for men spread out and moving fast on horseback. It is, however, the Belgian infantry who have some of the most original badges. For example the 4e *Linie* has a rather aggressive bear, and the *Chasseurs Ardennais* a wild boar, similar to those that still inhabit those mountainous areas. Some of the old fortress units have retained a symbolic connection with castellated motifs. Many Belgians served with the British forces in World War II, and they have their own SAS unit, which retains the winged dagger and motto 'Who Dares Wins', and with this they retain the characteristic SAS parachute wings.

INSIGNIA IN THE TWENTY-FIRST CENTURY

Camouflage has removed much of the colour and glamour that silver, gold and coloured uniforms gave to the appearance of sailors and soldiers. Practical uniforms for work in ships and on airfields have led to simplified insignia — colours have become more subdued. The armed forces, however, are a conservative organisation with a strong sense of tradition and the badges and rank of an earlier generation represent continuity in a changing and sometimes very dangerous and short-lived world.

As security against terrorist or special saboteurs becomes an important consideration for men manning missile sights, airfields or even stores and offices, so insignia must move towards an individual form of identification. At present flying overalls have a clear pocket on the chest to take the air crew members name and rank badge. This principal of visual identification is being extended. The era of the intelligent microchip credit card will soon be with us and will vastly increase the amount of information that insignia will be capable of carrying. The 'smart card' will know next of kin, religion, medical history, any other relevant information of a non-tactical variety, and will soon replace credit cards, passports and national identity cards.

The current range of night vision devices give the viewer a very good image of a human moving in the dark — but do not show great detail except at very close range. The new rank could be used to give a pre-programmed response to laser interrogation. The sentry on duty would send an eye-safe laser pulse at an incoming patrol and the rank reflectors would give a return signal that identified the men. Systems like this could be used to trigger remotely controlled signals, or even an ambush. If this all seems rather fanciful it is worth remembering that sensors have been in use since the Vietnam war, and laser interrogation of vehicles is now a common training technique in anti-tank gunnery exercises. Insignia that can answer for itself is not such an unbelievable idea — it is after

all the logical extension of the visual information that was given and received by the sergeant's stripes, or the officer's epaulet.

If the reader fears that a presidential honour guard will one day appear in overalls with multi-function name tags on the chest, nuclear biological and chemical warfare kit, light-weight 5.56mm rifles and carbon fibre helmets, he or she can be assured that the day will be a long time coming. Ceremonial uniforms will always be needed to give due weight and dignity to public functions, and with them will go all the gold braid, embroidery, gold, silver and bronze metal work, and the

64. The brassard in action — a Military Policeman assigned to Customs duties watches as US troops disembark in Germany. The brassard can also be used as a sleeve pocket for pencils or a note book.

rainbow of colours that have been used for centuries for military insignia.

A–Z
OF
MILITARY
INSIGNIA

A

Note: Words in **bold** in the description indicate that the word in question forms an entry elsewhere, and reference should be made to it.

AIDE-DE-CAMP A term of French origin, whose usual abbreviation is ADC. An aide-de-camp is an officer whose duty is to assist and generally attend on an officer of high rank. Distinguished officers are appointed aide-de-camp to a monarch or to the president of a republic.

The appointment is identified by uniform trimmings, **aiguillettes** or badges, which vary according to custom.

In a monarchy, the ADC to the sovereign usually wears the sovereign's **cypher**. In Britain the personal aide-de-camp to King George VI wore a special cypher in block letters, 17.5mm (⅔in) high, but the other high-ranking officers and equerries who held the appointment wore the official royal cypher in dull silver. The cyphers are worn on the plaited cords of the aiguillette, on the **epaulettes**, on the **shoulder straps** or on the **slip-on** of the shirt's shoulder straps.

Officers who held the appointment under more than one sovereign could wear the cypher of each of the sovereigns under whom they had served.

In the former Kingdom of Italy the ADC to the king or to the households of the royal princes wore special stars on their collars, with the king's or princes' cypher upon the star and the crown or a coronet above it. The ADC also wore a crowned cypher on the epaulettes of his dress uniform (*see* Epaulette).

In the Republic of Italy the ADC to the President wears special stars on the collar: a mural crown above the star on which the initials RI are embossed. Aides to high-ranking officers wear a silver star on both sleeves of their uniforms.

In the United States of America the aides' badges depict the eagle perched on the national shield; the number of stars in the blue chief indicates the grade of the general served by the aide. The insignia of aides to generals, which were adopted in 1902, are worn on both lapels of the jacket or, if no jacket is worn, on the left of the shirt collar (Bibl. 164).

The badge with five stars shown on the cover of this book belonged to an ADC to General Eisenhower; it was made in London by Gaunt Ltd.

After World War II the badges of the aides to General of the Army were changed to a blue shield with five white stars arranged in a circle. The highest aide's appointment is that to the President of the United States, and the insignia consists of 13 white stars arranged in a circle on a blue shield ensigned by the eagle (Bibl. 167).

AIGRETTE A word of French origin, an aigrette is an ornament made of straight feathers and worn on the head-dress. Italian generals and colonels in active command wore an aigrette of heron feathers in dress uniform until 1940. The word plume is synonymous.

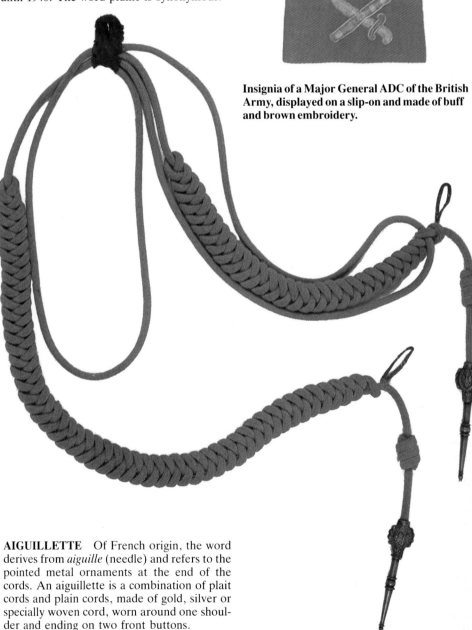

Insignia of a Major General ADC of the British Army, displayed on a slip-on and made of buff and brown embroidery.

AIGUILLETTE Of French origin, the word derives from *aiguille* (needle) and refers to the pointed metal ornaments at the end of the cords. An aiguillette is a combination of plait cords and plain cords, made of gold, silver or specially woven cord, worn around one shoulder and ending on two front buttons.

The aiguillette is a mark of special appointments, and it is worn in specific orders of dress according to regulations.

Aiguillette of a Polish Army general, worn from the right shoulder strap to the front buttons of the tunic.

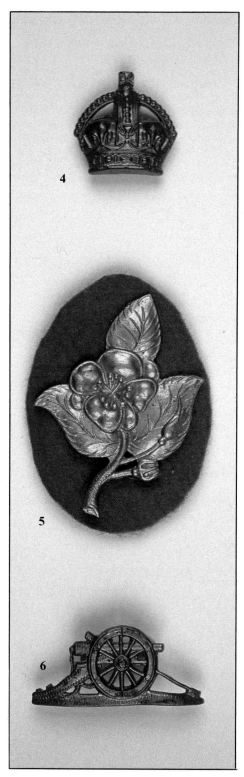

Embroidered arm badge of the 4th Queen's Own Hussars (1) and, in metal, the Prince of Wales's Plume (2) and the Irish Harp (3).

ARC A word of US origin. The non-commissioned officers of the US Marine Corps wear inverted V-shaped **chevrons**, which, from the 3rd grade upward, are joined below by one or more stripes. Non-commissioned officers of the Line have the two bars of the lowest chevron joined by arcs — ie, curved stripes — while those of the Staff have the bars joined by ties, as they are straight.

In the US Navy, the rating insignia (*see* Rating) of the chiefs are surmounted by an arc, and the senior non-commissioned officers of the army also wear chevrons combined with arcs, which are sometimes called rockers (Bibl. 164).

ARM BADGE Any insignia worn on the sleeve could legitimately be described as an arm badge. In British military terminology, however, this designation is reserved for the crowns, regimental badges or similar devices that are worn by warrant officers and non-commissioned officers of certain regiments and corps in association with their **rank insignia** or at the top of the sleeve of the jacket (*see* Shoulder flash). The wearing of arm badges is particularly common among cavalry regiments (Bibl. 52).

Although arm badges are associated with rank insignia, they are also regimental or

The small metal crown (4) and the gun (6) were worn in combination with chevrons to identify some specific NCOs' ranks. Both are still used but in anodised metal versions – the pattern of the crown was changed in 1953. The pear blossom (5) was worn by NCOs of the Queen's Own Worcestershire Hussars.

appointment badges, and they therefore belong in a category of their own.

Embroidered arm badges were worn with full dress; otherwise metal ones were worn. It is often difficult to distinguish between the embroidered badges used by officers on forage caps and on collars, and those worn by non-commissioned officers. In the case of the badges illustrated there can be no doubt, however, as they were completely different.

The Prince of Wales's Plume was worn by the 3rd Dragoon Guards, the 10th Royal Hussars, the 12th Royal Lancers and the Royal Wiltshire Yeomanry. There are also examples on which the coronet is in gilding metal and some on which it is embroidered; and there are some smaller, metal badges. The Irish Harp was used by the Irish cavalry regiments, and the pear blossom belonged to the Queen's Own Worcestershire Hussars.

The sergeants' crown and the gun of the gunners are also seen in embroidered versions. (*See also* Chevrons.)

ARM FLASH See Shoulder flash.

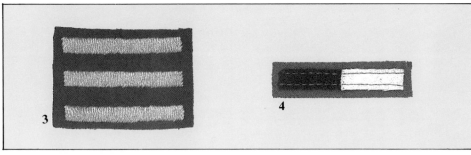

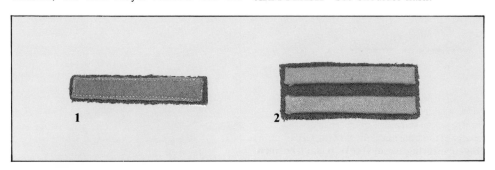

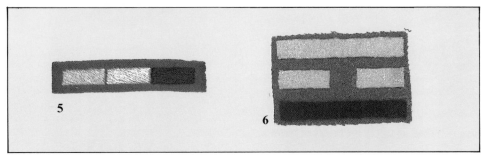

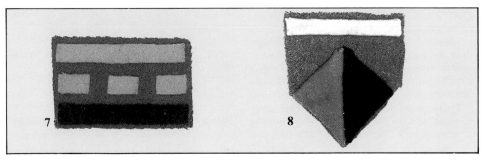

The first three are the conventional arm-of-service strips of divisional brigades, followed by those of the R. Signals (4) and REME (5), followed by strips modified in order to identify individual battalions and with additional flash.

ARM-OF-SERVICE STRIP The Army Council Instructions dated 18 September 1940 introduced a new system of branch-of-service identification because collar badges were not worn on battledress and, when a helmet was worn instead of a cloth head-dress, no alternative branch-of-service identification was displayed.

These Instructions provided for the adoption of coloured cloth backing to the officers' rank insignia (*see* Rank insignia), and for the introduction of worsted **shoulder titles** and arm-of-service strips.

The strips, which measured 50×6mm ($2 \times \frac{1}{4}$in), were of coloured material and were placed on each sleeve of the battledress blouse immediately below any corps or divisional sign, and on the sleeves of the greatcoat. The number of strips worn by the personnel of infantry battalions in divisions identified the brigade's seniority — eg, the personnel of the first divisional brigade had one strip, the second brigade, two and the third, three. The guards were exempted from wearing these new markings.

Arm of service	Colour
Staff	red
Royal Armoured Corps	yellow—red
Royal Artillery	red—blue
Royal Engineers	blue—red
Royal Signals	blue—white
Infantry (except Rifle Regts)	scarlet
Rifle Regts	rifle-green
Royal Army Chaplains' Dept	black (later purple)
Royal Army Service Corps	yellow—blue
Royal Army Medical Corps	dull cherry
Royal Army Ordnance Corps	dark blue (later red—blue—red)
Royal Electrical and Mechanical Engineers	red—yellow—blue (adopted later)
Corps of Military Police	red (with MP armlet)
Royal Army Pay Corps	yellow
Army Educational Corps	Cambridge blue
Army Dental Corps	green—white
Auxiliary Military Pioneer Corps	red—green
Intelligence Corps	green
Army Physical Training Corps	black—red—black (adopted later)
Army Catering Corps	grey—yellow (adopted later)
General List	scarlet

Where more than one colour is mentioned, the first colour was worn to the fore.

Most strips were cut out from felt, but some were embroidered and others were printed directly below the **formation sign**. The illustration shows some different types of strips: on the left are the one, two and three scarlet strips that would officially be worn by the 1st, 2nd and 3rd infantry brigades of an average infantry division.

However, during the course of World War II, many battalions added regimental devices to their strips, others modified them, and many battalions were changed from one brigade to another but did not change the number of strips accordingly. As a result, a great deal of confusion ensued.

The 183rd was the 2nd brigade of the 61st Division, and it was composed of the 7th Battalion, the Gloucestershire Regiment (which correctly wore two scarlet strips), the 10th Battalion, the Worcestershire Regiment (which had two scarlet strips, the second one broken, and a green strip below), and the 4th, Northamptonshire Regiment (which had the second strip in three segments and a black strip, its regimental colour, below). The 1st Battalion of the Sherwood Foresters became part of the 183rd Brigade in August 1944, but it wore only one scarlet strip above its regimental flash.

Arm-of-service strips were also used by men of other nationalities who wore battledress, and the Norwegian Army, for example, still used the strips in the 1950s.

ARMLET Sometimes known as armband, the word derives from the word 'arm'; it is synonymous with the term brassard, which derives from the French *bras* and which is used in the United States. In modern terminology the word armlet refers to a cloth device worn around the upper arm. A typical armlet is that used by the Military Police, but thousands have been used for different reasons and at different times.

An armlet may be worn in lieu of a uniform. During World War I, for instance, many recruits of the British Army were issued with special armlets when stocks of uniforms were not yet available. The armlet was lined with holland material and buttoned up at the back. Other examples used for the same purpose displayed the crown only.

White armlets bearing the title of the military districts were issued to recruits in Italy for the same reason, and armlets with green, white and red horizontal stripes were worn by workers engaged in reserved occupations. On the armlet was pinned a white metal star bearing the name of the establishment, usually ammunition factories.

Paramilitary forces and partisans often wore armlets in lieu of uniforms (Bibl. 156), as the armlet, although serving its purpose of identification, could be easily hidden or destroyed if its wearer was captured by the

Two British armlets: the first was worn by recruits during World War I in lieu of a uniform, the second one was worn on the left sleeve of the blue battledress of the Civil Defence during World War II. It could be worn on civilian clothes.

enemy.

In Britain during World War II the armlet was adopted as a badge of office by many civilian organizations, including the Home Guard, before it was given a uniform, and the Civil Defence. After the publication of the Fire Prevention Order of January 1941, the Fire Guards also wore armlets, which were dark blue and had the words FIRE GUARD in yellow or white block letters in two lines.

Armlets were and are used on uniforms so that their wearers may be seen at a distance or distinguished among others at a glance. The most important of these is that worn by representatives of the International Red Cross, which is always white; Muslim nations, Turkey for instance, have adopted the Red Crescent. Armlets could also be worn by personnel engaged in manoeuvres, with different colours being used to distinguish one faction from another.

Belgian staff officers used to wear a crimson armlet, and by the late 1930s the French Army used about forty armlets to identify different appointments.

In June 1943 the US armed forces used only a dozen brassards (Bibl. 164), four of which identified the type of formation to which general staff officers were attached; however, several others were adopted later. The US forces that landed in Morocco wore the Stars and Stripes on a white background as a national identification device, and the personnel of the Transportation Corps later obtained a brassard in branch-of-service colours. The personnel of the Headquarters Allied Forces in the Mediterranean sector wore a special armlet with hand-embroidered initials

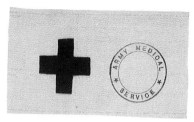

3

4

5

6

Top: Armlet of the Army Medical Service (3), with the red cross, and of the Transportation Corps, US Army (4). Above. The armlet of the Headquarters Allied Forces (5) was later replaced by the 'AF' shoulder sleeve insignia. The last armlet was worn by civilians in 'Wehrmacht' service, one of many used by the multifarious organisations of the Third Reich.

on a grey cloth background, edged by gold lace.

In the early 1950s, the US Military Police on duty at Checkpoint Charlie in Berlin adopted a new type of brassard, which was attached to the shoulder strap and incorporated the Berlin **shoulder sleeve insignia**.

The German Third Reich made extensive use of armlets for the armed forces and its auxiliary services, and for various political organizations.

Armlets were and are used by international

contingents assigned to the United Nations forces. The normal type displays the UN emblem only; others incorporate nationality insignia as well.

Belgium
Coloured backings are worn under the badge of the khaki beret; corps that have coloured berets wear the badge only. Most backings are in the shape of shields — except that of the 4th Lancers, which is square — and are made of thin plastic — except that of the Guides, which is made out of cloth and sewn directly

on to the beret. The colours of the backings are as follows:

scarlet	Line Infantry Regiments
	Artillery
	Military Police
	School of Infantry
	School of Artillery
	School of AA Artillery
deep green	*Carabiniers*
	Cyclistes, Carabiniers Cyclistes
	Chasseurs à Pied
	Security Sections
dark blue	Administration
	Signals
royal blue	Logistical units
black	Engineers
	School of Engineers
amaranth	Medical Service
crimson	Guides
white	Lancers
	HQ 16th Armoured Division
yellow	*Chasseurs à Cheval*
	Reconnaissance units

The *Chasseurs Ardennais*, Commandos, the personnel of the Army Air Corps, airborne units, Armoured Engineers and recruits in training do not wear any backing under the cap badge.

Armlet of the Hitler Youth and the common type used by United Nations Forces. Several variations of the UN badge are in existence.

Britain
The use of backing on cap badges is common practice in the British Army, but there were no strict rules governing its use until 1940. Before then, the backing was often worn on a particular type of head-dress only or it was worn unofficially and then abolished. The Durham Light Infantry wore a round, light infantry-green patch behind the beret badge during World War II, but it is not known if all the DLI battalions wore it. The distinction of wearing a patch of brown holland material was granted to the South Staffordshire Regiment in 1935 by King George V, but it appears that the 2nd South Staffords favoured a smaller patch than the one used by the 1st battalion.

Most Scottish regiments had tartan patches under the head-dress badge, and in some cases the **hackle**, with or without the cap badge, was worn.

The Army Council Instructions of 18 September 1940 introduced worsted rank insignia on coloured backing for officers to wear on the shoulder straps of battledress. The colour of the felt backing depended on branch of service and was the first colour shown on the **arm-of-service strip**. The first embroidered rank insignia were flat, but padded stars and crowns in different sizes were also made and worn for many years after the war.

Warrant officers' **rank insignia** may also be found embroidered on coloured backing, and the **chevrons** of the non-commissioned officers' dress uniform are of gold lace sewn on coloured backing. Regimental and corps arm badges are usually displayed on a coloured patch or directly embroidered on to it (*see* Arm badge).

B

BACKING A badge's backing is any coloured background that is added under the badge or on which the badge is embroidered and that has a special significance. It usually serves to identify a branch of service or organization, but it can also identify an individual qualification.

Austria-Hungary
The edelweiss was the emblem of the Austrian mountain troops. The officers' badge was embroidered on grass green, the colour of the *Schützen*, while the other ranks had aluminium badges.

Left and opposite. A selection of Austrian, Belgian, British and Danish badges mounted or embroidered on coloured backing are shown in these two pages.

The light infantry green backing worn under the cap badge of the DLI (2) reappeared after World War II in the form of background colour on the shoulder titles (see page 203) of the light infantry regiments. The brown holland patch (4) was also worn by the South Staffords behind the collar badges and it is still in use today (see page 124).

Three Danish badges are shown here (5, 14, 15) and several others complete with backing are shown on page 127.

Two representative Belgian beret badges, of the Engineers (8) and of the 1st Regiment 'Chasseurs à Cheval' (9) are illustrated, others are shown on page 80.

The green backing of the chevron (9) identifies the Royal Army Dental Corps or the Intelligence Corps and the black on red warrant officer 1st class insignia (13) was the type used by the King's Royal Rifle Corps. The embroidered Prince of Wales's Plume is an arm badge.

8

10

9

13

14

15

16

Denmark

Before World War II the other ranks of the Danish Army wore as branch-of-service identification button-shaped badges on coloured backing above the right breast pocket of the tunic. The colours of the backing were:

scarlet	Infantry
light blue	Cavalry
crimson	Artillery
black	Engineer
blue	Train
violet	Army Technical Corps
red/white	Medical Service
	Sanitary Troops
green	Veterinaries

Branch-of-service and regimental badges were adopted in 1948 and are worn on coloured felt backing, the colour changing according to battalion, numerical order of the unit or service:

crimson	Regimental commander and staff
scarlet	1st battalion
white	2nd battalion
light blue	3rd battalion
yellow	4th battalion
green	5th battalion
violet	6th battalion

The badges illustrated belonged to the 6th battery of the 3rd Field Artillery Regiment, now the North Jutland Artillery Regiment, and to the Staff of the Royal Life Guards.

Holland

During World War II, and until about 1948, the personnel of the Royal Netherlands Army wore on the beret the Netherlands lion on an orange oval backing. Later, however, a series of about fifty large beret badges was adopted, each with a coloured cloth backing:

Backing	Piping	
crimson		General Staff
		Technical Staff
		Quartermaster Staff
crimson	gold	Special Duty Officers
black (velvet)		Protestant Chaplain
		Jewish Chaplain
black		Security Corps
		Technical Service (Ord/EME)
black	white	Judge Advocate Corps
black	Nassau blue	Mobile Defence Corps
black	green	Commandos
black	orange	Infantry Regt van Heutsz
black	red	Field Artillery
		Anti-tank
		Artillery
		Anti-aircraft Artillery
Nassau blue		Military Police
		Transport Corps
		Medical Corps
Nassau blue	white	Signal Corps
light blue		Army Women's Corps
light blue	dark blue	Hussars van Boreel
light blue	poppy red	Hussars Prins Alexander
light blue	white	Hussars van Sytzama
light blue	orange	Hussars Prins van Oranje
dark blue (velvet)		Catholic Chaplain
green (velvet)		Doctors (gold badge)
		Dentists (silver badge)
		Pharmacists
green		Military Medical Corps
light green		Neth. Indies Instruction Bn
green	yellow	Jager Guards
green	crimson	Limburgse Jagers Regt
poppy red		Royal Military School (NCO)
		Stoottroepen
		Infantry Regt Johan Willem Friso
		Infantry Regt Oranje Gelderland
		Infantry Regt Menno van Coehoorn
		Infantry Regt Chassé
poppy red	with yellow vertical stripe	Royal Military Academy
poppy red	Nassau blue	Grenadier Guards
wine red		Supply Corps
pink-red		Army Pay Corps
orange	Nassau blue	Fusiliers Guards Prinses Irene
dark brown		Engineers
		Officers and Supervisors of Fortifications
		Pioneers
		Pontoneers
yellow ochre		Reserve Officers General Service
turquoise		Humanistic Adviser

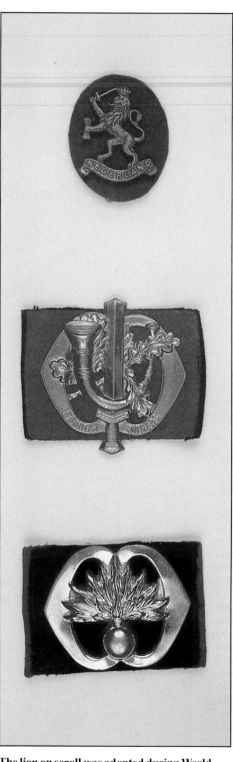

The lion on scroll was adopted during World War II by the Netherlands Army in Britain and as a beret badge it was worn on an oval orange backing.

Shown above are the badges of the 'Limburgse Jagers' Regiment and the Grenadier Guards, others are shown on page 102.

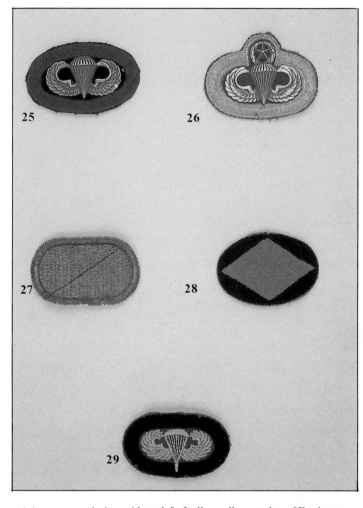

Italy

The divisional collar patch was adopted by an Army Order of July 1940 in order to establish an alternative way of identifying the personnel of the divisions that, by the same order, were forbidden to wear the formation sign.

Previously, all army personnel had the collar of the jacket faced in branch-of-service colour, and, since 1936, the personnel of corps attached to infantry divisions had added the collar patches of the divisional infantry to their coloured collars. As coloured collars were also abolished in 1940, composite collar patches, identifying the branch of service and the type of division, were adopted instead.

The engineers of an infantry division, for instance, who used to have black collars piped in crimson, wore the engineers patch, which was black piped in crimson, sewn on to the collar patch of the divisional infantry. The personnel of supporting corps and services of the mountain divisions wore their patch on a rectangular deep green backing, and those attached to motorized divisions wore a patch on a blue rectangular backing.

A special uniform was adopted in September 1938 for the personnel of the Civil Service. All wore a special pattern of the Roman eagle on the peaked cap (*see* Cap badge), the eagle being embroidered in gold, silver or oxidized silver, according to the Civil Service group — A, B or C — represented. In addition, the badges were embroidered on different colours of felt, the colour indicating the Civil Service branch of the wearer as follows:

Colour	Administration
white	Council of Ministers
dark carmine	Foreign Affairs
crimson	Interior
pink	Justice
light yellow	Customs and Excise
scarlet	War
blue	Navy
light blue	Air Force
lilac	Education
violet	Public Works
green	Forestry and Agriculture
grey	Communications
yellow	Corporations (Trade Unions)
bluish-green	Propaganda
golden yellow	Treasury

Above left: Italian collar patches of Engineers, 'Brescia' Infantry Division (20) and of the Mountain Artillery (21) adopted in 1940. Cap badges of Italian Civil Service officials, of the Customs and Excise Group B (22) and of the War Ministry Group C (23), used from 1938 to 1945.
Above right: Wings of Italian Parachute Instructor (24), with red backing. US Army Parachutist badge on the oval backing of the 501st Airborne Regiment (25) and examples of different types of backings, including the domed backing used by Senior and Master Parachutist (26).

In some cases, the backing indicates that its wearer possesses a special qualification. Italian Parachute Instructors wear red backing under their **wings**, just as, in the US Army, Combat Leaders have a green tab or slip-on, on the shoulder straps.

United States of America

American paratroopers usually wear the wings on an oval cloth backing, the colours of which identify the unit. The backing was initially conceived mainly as a branch-of-service identification, but, as many small units adopted it, there are now hundreds, with the colours set in every possible way. In addition, some have a domed extension on the top to accommodate the star and wreath of the upper parachutists' grades. Some parachute ovals have the wings embroidered in the centre, and technically, the backing is an integral part of the badge.

BADGE   A badge is a sign or device worn to show the relation of the wearer to an organization or occupation. A military, naval or air force badge, on the other hand, is a specific item made of a specific material, metal, cloth or embroidery, worn to show the function of the wearer within an organization.

The word badge does not have the same meaning as 'insignia': the phrase cap insignia, for example, refers to all the devices worn on the cap — including the chinstrap and the cap band if they have any special significance — while a **cap badge** is a single item worn on the cap.

BAR   In general terms the word bar refers to any stripe, usually short, worn on its own or in combination with other devices. However, as a **chevron** is composed of two diagonal bars, only a single diagonal stripe should technically be called a bar. Belgian sergeants and corporals use bars, and the corporals of the *Bundeswehr* have worn two patterns of bars since 1955, the first in gold woven silk, the second in silver silk. Two French bars as worn on the combat dress are illustrated, as are the small bars that in the 1960s used to be sewn on a tab below the second button of the blouse. The last illustration is a Spanish set of bars of a *Cabo* of the air force.

Small rectangular devices, such as the rank insignia of American lieutenants, are also called bars, as are the devices worn by field officers of the Belgian Army on the collar patches.

Bed badge of Private Bayton F. of the North Staffordshire Regiment.

BED BADGE   Bed badges are a peculiarity of the British Army and were adopted about 1900. They were hung on a hook at the end of the soldiers' beds and bore the regiment's title and details of the bed's occupier. The type and shape vary according to regiment.

Both the South and North Staffordshire regiments used the Stafford Knot as a bed badge because both shared the knot as their main regimental device.

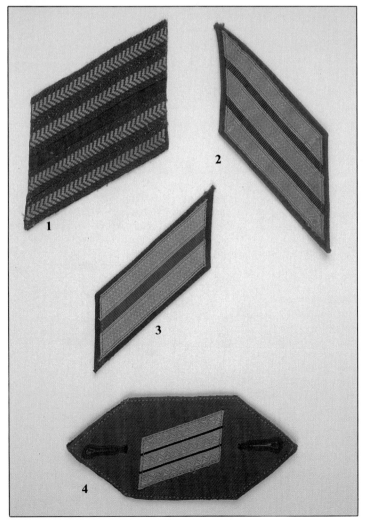

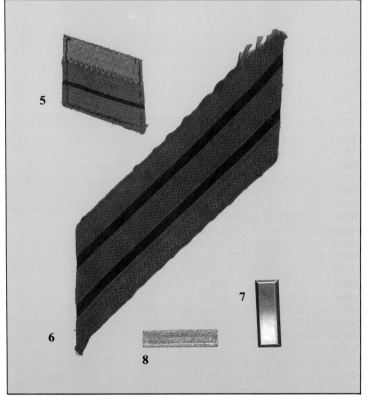

The bars of Belgian First Sergeant (1) are of British-pattern braid, for battledress. Those of the 'Bundeswehr' identify the ranks of 'Hauptgefreiter' (2) and 'Obergefreiter' (3) and the French Army bars identify the ranks of 'Sergent Chef' or 'Maréchal de Logis' (4) and of 'Brigadier Chef' of the Hussars (5), respectively.

The rank insignia of 'Cabo' of the Spanish Air Force is followed by the metal bar of American Lieutenants (7) and by the narrow bar used on the collar patches by Belgian field officers (8).

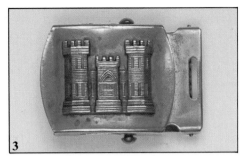

This selection of belt buckles includes the Austrian (1), German ((4) Württemberg) and Turkish (5) patterns used during World War I, a British Victorian buckle of the Royal Engineers (2) and the other ranks' universal pattern 1881/1902 (6) of the British Army. It shows also the locket-type clasp of Turkish officers (5), a Spanish Infantry buckle (8), the US Army buckle ((3) Engineers) and the latest Italian Army model (9).

BELT BUCKLE After the decline in miltary fashion of the shoulder-belt plate, the armed forces of many nations displayed a national or regimental emblem on the plate of the waist belt. The belt buckle is also known as a waist-belt clasp.

During World War I, the Austro-Hungarians wore the double-headed imperial eagle on the plate of their buckles. The Italian officers had a similar buckle made of brass or white metal, but on the plate was the Savoy eagle, which had only one head and a cross in a shield on its chest.

The officers of each regiment, corps and department of the British Army had a different waist-belt clasp. The infantry favoured the round locket-type clasp, while, in Queen Victoria's reign, the Royal Engineers preferred a rectangular pattern, in the centre of which was the Royal Arms and, within a wreath of thistles, the *Ubique* scroll that also appeared on the helmet plate.

A rather large locket-type clasp was adopted in 1881 for the other ranks of the regular army. Described as a 'universal pat-tern', this clasp was re-issued after 1901 with the Imperial Crown.

During World War I German troops wore belt buckles made of brass, with the different state emblems in white metal in the centre. During the course of the war, Prussian buckles were issued to recruits regardless of their state of origin, and white metal buckles later replaced the two-metal pattern.

Turkish buckles for both officers and other ranks display the Crescent and Star, Turkey's national emblem. The rectangular buckle is similar to the German pattern, for Turkey and Germany were allies during World War I.

The Spanish infantry buckle illustrated was worn during the Civil War (1936-9). It has the maker's name on the back — *Castells—Barcelona.*

For over forty years the US armed forces have used a remarkable buckle on the trouser belt, which, because of its unobtrusive efficiency, has been copied by other nations. Corps badges were often unofficially soldered on the plate. The Italians adopted a similar belt buckle in the 1960s, but unfortunately it is too large for its purpose.

BOSS A boss is a protruding round or oval badge made of coloured silk or braided cord wound on to a padded centre (*see* Cap badge).

The boss could have round or oval shape, the British type shown is usually worn with a regimental badge fixed in the centre (see page 90).

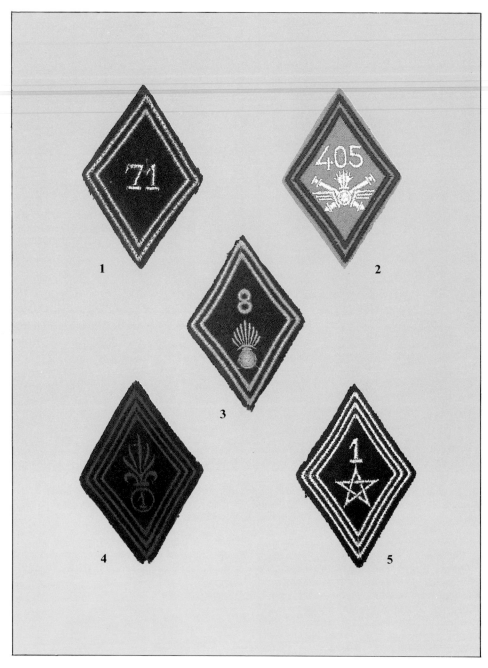

Uniforms have developed on a national basis and according to national traditions, and branch-of-service insignia are therefore displayed in a variety of ways. They often take the form of coloured collar patches or of badges worn on the collar, the shoulder straps or the head-dress. In addition, some organizations display branch insignia according to rank or order of dress.

The officers and warrant officers of the modern French Army, for instance, wear branch insignia in the form of patches on the collar of the jacket; the other ranks, however, wear branch insignia on the left upper sleeve of the jacket in the form of diamond-shaped patches.

When in shirt sleeves and working orders, the officers and warrant officers wear the sleeve badge instead of collar patches. Their badges have the central device and/or the regimental or battalion numbers embroidered in gold or silver thread; the sergeants have devices and numbers embroidered in yellow or white cotton; while the devices and numbers for the rank and file are embroidered in the same colour as the frames. This rule, however, is not strictly observed, and sergeants usually wear officers' type badges.

Overseas troops, formerly known as North African troops, are distinguished by three frames, while metropolitan troops have two only or none.

BREAST INSIGNIA Many different types of badges have been and are worn on the breast by the armed forces of most nations to identify the wearer's nationality, branch of service, rank, unit, qualification or proficiency, and other specific insignia are worn according to national custom and type of uniform.

Most of these are described under their appropriate entries. US breast pocket insignia are listed under **pocket insignia**; French pocket insignia, however, are discussed under **distinctive insignia** because they are unit insignia made of metal or metal and enamel, and they are not necessarily worn on the pockets. Italian Alpine troops used to wear their unit insignia on the head-dress, but these badges are now worn on the pocket.

BRANCH-OF-SERVICE INSIGNIA The devices that identify the branches or arms of service of the armed forces are known as branch-of-service insignia. As the infantry, the cavalry and often also other arms or corps are divided into regiments, regimental badges are an integral part of this category.

From the 1960s the massive regiment of three or four battalions, which had been the backbone of the army since the early 18th century, has been replaced by small mobile units of battalion strength, which inherited the regiments' traditions and badges.

The type and colour of the uniform, combined with the colour of the facings, were the

Some examples of post-World War II French branch insignia: 1 – Engineers, 2 – Anti-Aircraft Artillery, 3 – Infantry of the Line, 4 – Foreign Legion, 5 – Moroccan 'Spahis'.

first means of branch-of-service identification; they were later replaced by badges. Nevertheless, the branches-of-service colours have never disappeared, and coloured collars, cuffs, trouser stripes and piping are still displayed on dress uniforms. In fact, several armies wore them on service dress until the 1940s.

BUTTON Regimental buttons have been used for at least two hundred years and possibly longer, for their dual purpose, both practical and ornamental, must have been discovered centuries ago, although information on this subject is scarce and often ambiguous.

All the regiments of the British infantry and some of the cavalry regiments were numbered in 1751, and buttons bearing the regimental number were adopted by the Royal Warrant of December 1768. Instead of numbers, the three regiments of dragoon guards displayed the initials of the regiment on the

The pictures show a selection of British Army buttons, of large size, which display regimental devices, except the first one, used by generals.

buttons.

Officers' buttons were made of gilt or silver; the other ranks had pewter buttons. Some unassuming ornaments were later added to the regimental numbers, and eventually regimental devices or emblems replaced the regimental numbers (Bibl. 52, 67).

The buttons of other European nations went through similar stages, although some nations adopted a single type of national button. Other nations went through the cycle, from numbered to regimental buttons, but ended with a single button for all ranks and regiments. The choice of buttons used in Europe during the 20th century has, of course, been influenced by both economic and political factors, as well as changing fashions.

In the past officers' buttons were superior in quality to those of the other ranks and were often of a different size. Moreover, as many firms were involved in the manufacture of buttons, their quality and the design of the devices embossed on them varied considerably. In recent years new economic priorities, the modernization of the armed forces and social changes have led to the gradual simplification of miltary uniforms and their accessories.

Buttons made of anodized aluminium or of similar materials are now used worldwide by all ranks, and zips and press-studs have replaced them on field and fatigue uniforms.

Britain
Of the three services the army has been the most prolific in the use of buttons, and each regiment and branch of service had and still has its own type (Bibl. 50). They came in different sizes, the smallest being the buttons supporting the chinstrap of the peaked cap. The Royal Horse Artillery has worn a ball-shaped button since the 1790s, with the crown above the field gun since 1873.

Some regiments and corps had their **cap badge** modified, often more than once, and these changes were also recorded on their buttons or, alternatively, the design of the emblem on the button was changed. The type of crown changed according to the sovereign: the Victorian Crown was used until 1901; it was followed by the Imperial Crown, which was replaced in 1952 by the St Edward's Crown, which was adopted for the reign of Queen Elizabeth II. Buttons displaying the Royal Cypher also changed according to the reigning sovereign.

Between 1871 and 1924 only the officers and the non-commissioned officers of the infantry of the line wore regimental buttons; the rank and file wore general service buttons. Later, however, all ranks had regimental buttons, until buttonless battledress was adopted in 1937.

Gilded or brass buttons were used by army personnel apart from the Militia and the Volunteer Force, which were distinguished by silvered or white metal buttons until 1908, when both organizations were embodied in the newly formed Territorial Force. In addition,' rifle regiments and some light infantry regiments had black buttons, and bronze

25 **26** **27** **28**

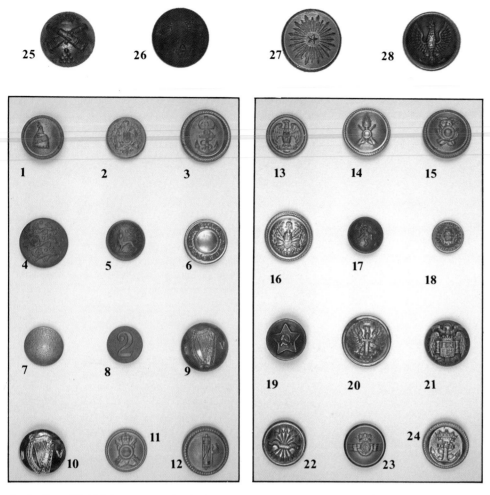

1 **2** **3**

4 **5** **6**

7 **8** **9**

11
10 **12**

13 **14** **15**

16 **17** **18**

19 **20** **21**

22 **23** **24**

29 **30**

31 **32**

1 — Albania
2, 3 — Imperial Austria
4 — Denmark
5 — Ethiopia (pre-1935)
6 — France
7, 8 — Germany (pre-1945)
9, 10 — Republic of Ireland
11–16 — Italy. The last button, officers'
pattern, was adopted in 1975 to replace all the
regimental and branch-of-service buttons
previously worn.
17 — Holland
18 — Vatican
19 — USSR
20–25 — Spain, including a button of the
Falange Española and an old button of the
'royal' artillery.
26, 27 — Sweden
28–30 — Poland, showing the two different
types of eagle.
31, 32 — USA for greatcoat.

A selection of British buttons varying in size and type, made of different metals, or plastic, with devices embossed, engraved, or soldered on the button, and with different crowns.

buttons were used by the officers on the khaki service dress.

Some of the smallest buttons, worn on the front of the officers' forage cap, had the regimental or corps emblem as a separate piece, riveted on to the button. Some regimental blazer buttons had the regimental insignia or regimental initials engraved on their surface.

Five naval buttons are illustrated, including that of flag officers and of the officers of the Merchant Navy. The Royal Marines have brass and bronze buttons, while the Royal Air Force has brass buttons, with the eagle and crown as separate pieces for the full dress. (The initials CD stand for Civil Defence.)

Other buttons
Most collectors of buttons tend to collect examples from their own country only, as the numbers of buttons involved combined with the lack of information on the subject deter the enthusiast from extending his interest to other countries.

Illustrated are a few examples of buttons from well known countries; all were used during this century.

C

CAP BADGE The phrase cap badge is popularly used to describe a badge that is worn on a cap, a peaked cap, a brimmed hat or any other type of soft head-dress. Technically, however, the badge worn on the beret is known as a beret badge, but in several armies beret and forage cap badges are also worn on the collar or on the shoulder straps. The expression head-dress badge refers to badges worn on all types of head-dress, including helmets.

The main types of cap badges are discussed below: those that identify the nationality of the wearer by displaying the national emblem or colours, and those that identify his, or her, branch of service or regiment. The cap badge usually also indicates rank, especially in the case of general officers, or class of rank, since the same badge often exists in two patterns — or in three — for officers, non-commissioned officers and the rank and file.

Albania
Little is known about Albanian badges except that extensive use was made of the Skanderbeg helmet and of the black Albanian eagle (*see* Formation sign) until the end of World War II.

In the 1930s, according to regulations, the *Gjeneral Armate*, who was King Zog, wore the Skanderbeg helmet above a sceptre superimposed upon crossed sprigs of laurel and oak; the generals had the same, helmet above the king's cypher, and above one or two chevrons below the oak sprigs.

The black and white illustration, which is taken from the regulations, shows the other officers' cap badge, complete with measurements.

The badges were changed after Italians invaded Albania in 1939. The white metal star worn by the Italians was combined with the Skanderbeg helmet and worn on the collar by the new Albanian Army. Some Albanian units also wore this badge on the fur hat.

The pre- and post-1939 Skanderberg badge.

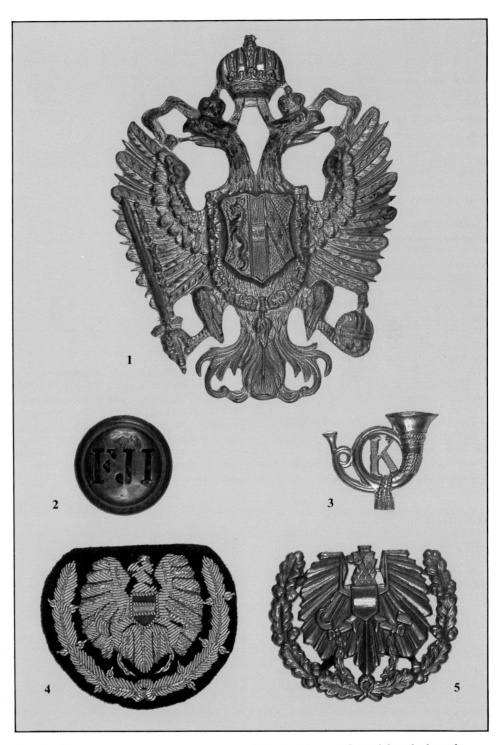

Austria–Hungary
Before World War I two badges were worn on the shako: a **boss** at the top, with the Emperor's cypher on a black background in the centre, and below that, but above the **chin-strap,** the double-headed Austrian eagle. The boss was made of gold metallic wire for officers and of brass for other ranks; the eagle was made of gilt and brass respectively.

The gold boss and its black centre echoed

The first three are Imperial cap badges: the eagle (1) of the officers' dress shako, the metal boss (2) worn on the field cap during World War I and the bugle (3) with the initial of Emperor Karl I.

Two versions of the post-1955 Austrian eagle for the peaked cap. It holds in its claws the hammer and sickle.

the national colours of Imperial Austria, yellow and black.

The officers' field service shako carried only a boss, smaller than on the dress shako and with a diameter of only 30mm (1¼in), with a double gold cord at the bottom looped around a small button. The other ranks' field cap had at the front a brass version of the officers' boss, with the Emperor's cypher cut out in the centre. Austrian units had the cypher 'FJI' while the Hungarians had 'IFJ'.

The *Jäger* and *Schützen* regiments wore a bugle on their head-dress. A large bugle was worn on the dress hat above the holder of the cockerel feathers, and smaller versions of the bugle were worn on the field cap. The emblem or number displayed in the centre of the bugle identified the type of unit (Bibl. 38).

After the death of Emperor Francis Joseph in 1916, the cypher of the field cap badge was changed to 'K' for the Emperor Karl for Austrian and Hungarian regiments alike, and, since metal buttons were not worn on field uniforms, there was no way of distinguishing the number of a specific regiment (*see* Collar insignia).

To solve this problem a new system of unit identification was introduced in 1917. Patches were worn on the left side of the field cap and on the shoulder straps of both the tunic and the greatcoat. The number of the regiment or battalion, together with letters of the alphabet, was stencilled on the patches in different colours according to the branch of service (Bibl. 17,38).

Austria
1933-8   After World War I the Austro-Hungarian Empire broke up, Hungary regained its independence and territories that had been part of the empire were integrated into new nations.

Austria became a republic, and the imperial emblems were abolished. The new Austrian cap badge displayed a small red, white and red cockade in the centre of a boss.

1955-86   The cockade within the boss that had been used before World War II was re-adopted in 1955 as the main head-dress badge.

The boss is all in gold for officers down to the rank of *Fähnrich*, gold with an inner silver circle from the rank of *Vizeleutnant* to that of *Wachtmeister*, and of yellow metal for the rank and file.

The cockade is worn on the crown of the peaked cap and on the field cap. The modern version of the Austrian eagle is worn on the cap band, in silver embroidery for officers, silver metal for sergeants and in bronze for the rank and file.

Belgium
The red, yellow and black **cockade** is the

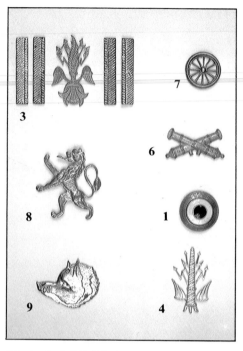

The 'cockade' (1, 2) is the main Belgian cap badge. Generals wear a pair of vertical double bars on the cap band (3, General 'des Armes'), GS officers are identified by the 'demi-foudre' (4) and the other officers have the branch – of – service badge (5, 6, 7) on the cap band.

The lion (8) was used by the Belgian troops in Britain and the other badges without (9) or with backing are worn on the beret.

Belgian national emblem, and it is worn on army and navy peaked caps. The red comes from the red cock of Wallonia, the black from the black lion of Flanders, and, as both these regional emblems are on a yellow ground, the central ring of the cockade is yellow.

The modern version derives from the larger cockades of conventional pattern that were worn on the model shakos of 1831, 1845 and 1895. Large, oval, embroidered cockades have also been used since the middle of the 19th century, and a large, round cockade, embroidered in whipcord pattern, was worn on the round, brimless model 'pillbox' hat of 1868 (Bibl. 46).

All these head-dresses became obsolete during World War I, and they were replaced by the peaked cap and by the *bonnet de police*. A khaki beret was adopted in the early 1920s for tankmen, and in the 1930s the *Chasseurs Ardennais* were issued with dark green berets, while the *Unités Cyclistes Frontière* obtained royal blue berets.

Since its adoption, the modern army's peaked cap displays the national cockade on the crown at the front, while insignia of branch, combined with class of rank insignia, are worn on the cap band.

Large, medium and small cockades are available either embroidered or enamelled. The small pattern, which is 20mm (¾in) in diameter, is made of enamel, and it is usually worn by all ranks except generals, who have a medium size cockade embroidered in whipcord. The larger enamelled badge is preferred by naval ratings, who wear it on the sailor hat. However, no strict rule governs the wearing of one or another type of cockade, particularly as far as the officers are concerned.

A cockade used before World War II had the cypher of King Leopold III (LIII reversed) in its centre. It was larger than usual and had narrow red and yellow rings.

Class of rank is displayed on the cap band in a variety of ways. The generals have two sets of vertical bars with the category badge within; the generals *des armes* wear the *foudre*, while the generals of the services wear the insignia of their service or corps. The field officers have one vertical bar on either side of the arm- or branch-of-service insignia, and the other officers wear the insignia only, without bars.

All ranks of the cavalry (Lancers) and also the warrant officers and non-commissioned officers of all corps wear silver badges.

Metal or embroidered badges and bars may be worn on the cap, but metal is more usual, its surface being finished to imitate embroidery. General Staff officers wear the *demi-foudre*, while all other officers and the other ranks entitled to wear the peaked cap have their branch-of-service badge on the cap band.

The crown of the Infantry of the Line and

of the *Chasseurs à Pied* comes in different sizes and finish, and although the pattern that is 25mm (1in) wide should be worn on the peaked cap, the smaller crown for the **shoulder strap** is often used on the cap as well. The Guides wear the crown above crossed sabres, and the personnel of the pre-war Fortress Artillery also wore a crown, but it was above crossed cannons. The gunners wear crossed cannons, and the Engineers have the Roman helmet (*see* Shoulder strap).

The *bonnet de police*, the typical Belgian forage cap with the tassel, was in use until 1940. It displayed the branch-of-service insignia and the unit's number on its right side. The *Chasseurs Ardennais* wore the boar's head above the regimental number on their green berets, and the regiments and battalions of the Frontier Cyclists were identified by a bicycle wheel on their blue berets.

In 1940 the Belgian Army was re-formed in Britain, with British uniforms and equipment, and, although the officers endeavoured to use Belgian-type badges on their peaked caps, the Belgian lion was the only insignia worn by all ranks on forage caps and berets.

In 1948-9 regimental and branch-of-service badges were adopted for use on new coloured berets, and they are still in use today, although in the meantime many of the original badges have been abolished, modified or changed. These badges are in yellow or white metal with a polished or dull finish according to class of rank and branch of service.

Most badges are worn on coloured, shield-shaped backings (*see* Backing). The exceptions are the *Chasseurs Ardennais* who wear the boar's head on green berets, Parachutists, who wear maroon berets, Commandos, with dark green berets, Army Air Corps, with light blue berets and Armoured Engineers who have black berets.

The badge of the Reserve Infantry Battalions is a smaller version of the Infantry's pre-World War I shako plate, which had the regimental number in the centre instead of the lion. The beret badge of the 1st *Chasseurs* on Horse — *1 Jagers de Paard*, a Flemish regiment — is a warrant/non-commissioned officer's silvered badge, which is privately purchased and therefore different from the general issue badge (*see* Backing). The badges of the Artillery, which have a polished gilt finish, and of the Engineers, which have a dull gilt finish, are also non-issue items.

Britain

Britain's comparatively early achievement of unity, together with the benefits arising from being geographically separated from mainland Europe, spared the United Kingdom the upheavals and revolutions that shook the rest of the continent. The steady continuity of power is reflected in the vast numbers of British insignia, which differed according to class of rank and were, therefore, constantly changed to meet the requirements of the time.

Naval cap badges are discussed first, because the Royal Navy is the first in order of priority of the three services. The cap badges of the Dominions, now the Commonwealth, follow in type and style those of Britain, and only a few examples are shown therefore.

Royal Navy : The first dress regulations were issued in 1748 by Lord Anson's Board of Admiralty, which sought to distinguish naval officers from other officers.

The officers' cap badge consists of a wreath of gold laurel leaves surrounding a silver **foul anchor** with the Royal Crown above. This pattern of badge was adopted in 1856, and such was the great power and prestige enjoyed by the Royal Navy during the 19th century that it was copied by other nations throughout the world.

Between *c*1870 and 1891, the badge was usually embellished by a gold ring set around the anchor, and earlier badges were considerably smaller than those prescribed in the 1937 Uniform Regulations, which were and still are 65mm (2½in) high and 85mm (3¼in) wide.

Cap badges may be hand embroidered in gold and silver, usually with the anchor partly of metal, or they may be made of gold or silver metal. They are also sometimes made of bronze, which was used with khaki uniform 'when exposed to enemy fire'.

The officers' cap badge of the Women's Royal Naval Service is smaller than the men's cap badge, and its laurel wreath is embroidered in blue silk. The chaplains obtained a special badge in 1940: it has the wreath embroidered in black silk and veins in gold wire.

Cap badges for chief petty officers were introduced in 1879. A gold and silver crown above a silver anchor in a gold ring was worn by seamen, and non-seamen ratings wore a similar badge but all in gold. Gold and silver badges were adopted for all chief petty officers in 1918. 'Senior' petty officers were allowed to wear the peaked cap in 1920 with the badge described above, and a gold wreath was added to the cap badge of the chief petty officers. The ring around the anchor was purely ornamental and often consisted of two cords; in 1970, however, a new order specified that only the Fleet Chief Petty Officer would wear two gold rings and that the others should wear one ring only.

The red cap badges for junior ratings originated in 1890, when non-seamen branches obtained cap badges similar to those of the chief petty officers but embroidered in red thread.

Ratings' badges were also made in metal, and those for non-seamen branches were painted in red.

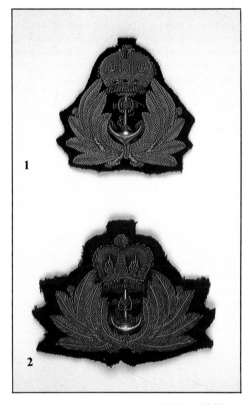

Above: Comparison between old ((1) c.1910) and modern (2) naval officer's cap badges.

Below: two metal badges, for officer (3) and chief petty officer (4), and embroidered cap badges for chief petty officer (5) and petty officer (6, 7) with different crowns.

During World War I six battalions of sailors formed the Royal Naval Division, which was deployed as an infantry formation. Each battalion had a different cap badge bearing its title on a scroll — Anson, Drake, Hawke, Hood, Howe and Nelson.

Army : Most British Army cap badges identify a regiment or a branch of service. However, as they are also found in different versions for officers and other ranks, they also identify a specific class of rank. A few cap badges denote rank or class of rank, although some of these should still be classified as regimental badges.

Field marshals, general officers, brigadiers and substantive colonels wear special badges indentifying a specific rank in the first instance. In addition, they indicate class of rank for the generals and a rank with special appointment for the others. Two examples of embroidered general officers' badges are shown, the small badge is worn on a forage cap or beret and the full size badge on a peaked cap. The field marshal's badge has two crossed batons in its centre, embroidered in red and gold. The brigadiers, substantive colonels and staff officers not on the cadre of a unit wear the Royal Crest.

Some regimental badges vary according to rank, a practice common within the guards regiments. For instance, there are three cap badges for other ranks of the Grenadier Guards: warrant officers, orderly room sergeants and band sergeants wear a bronze grenade with the Royal Cypher reversed and interlaced, in silver, pinned on to the ball of the grenade; sergeants and musicians have the cypher embossed on the grenade in gilding metal; the others have a plain grenade, without the cypher.

The warrant officers and sergeants of the Gordon Highlanders wear the stag's head in relief, a badge known as the 'staff badge'.

The cap badge is the main form of regimental and branch-of-service identification of the British Army, although collar badges, arm-of-service strips and other means are, or have been, used for the same purpose.

The Royal Warrants of 1751 and 1768 abolished the practice of naming regiments after their colonel and ordered that regiments should be numbered, thereby initiating an order of precedence among them that exists to this day. First in order of precedence is the cavalry, followed by artillery and engineers, the infantry of the line and branches of service.

Above right: Cap badge for the peaked cap of junior ratings, embroidered in red thread.

Right: Embroidered cap badges of British Army generals, in two sizes, for forage cap (1) and peaked cap (2) and the Royal Crest worn by brigadiers and substantive colonels (3).

4

5

Above and left: Cap badge for warrant officers, orderly room sergeants and band sergeants of the Grenadier Guards (4) and for warrant officers and sergeants of the Gordon Highlanders (5).

1

2

3

4

5

In modern terms, the number of cavalry and infantry regiments that existed in 1900 (Bibl. 50) was disproportionately large in relation to the few support arms and branches of service. There were 104 regiments of regular cavalry and infantry, plus yeomanry, volunteers and militia battalions, all of which wore different cap badges.

Many special volunteer battalions, all with different badges, raised during World War I (Bibl. 56), were disbanded after 1918. The Machine Gun Corps and the Tank Corps were formed during World War I and the 'armour' was reorganized in the 1920s, in the 1930s and again during World War II. The airborne forces, parachutists and glider-borne troops, were constituted during World War II, and the Parachute Regiment is still in existence.

During the 1920s the number of cavalry regiments was reduced through the amalgamation of regiments, and some Irish regiments were disbanded after the creation of the Republic of Ireland. The process of merging regiments continued after World War II, particularly affecting the infantry of the line.

The modern regimental cap badges of the British Army are the product of a long process of development that started in the middle of the 18th century.

The Royal Warrant of 1 July 1751 authorized some regiments to display 'devices and badges' on the colours or on grenadiers' caps, drums and bells of arms. The 3rd Regiment of Foot, The Buffs, obtained the mythological dragon, which later became the regiment's head-dress badge. The 5th Regiment obtained St George killing the dragon, which was later displayed on the grenade of the Royal Northumberland Fusiliers (*see* Collar insignia). The 6th Regiment obtained the antelope, and the 7th, which was already a fusiliers regiment, was granted the rose within the garter with the crown over it. The 8th, the King's Regiment, obtained the white horse of Hanover, the 23rd, The Royal Welch Fusiliers, had the Prince of Wales's feathers, and the 27th obtained Inniskilling Castle.

Two other important devices were granted by the same warrant but only for display on the three corners of the second colour: the lamb to the 2nd Foot and the lion of England to the 4th.

The Royal Warrant of 1768 adopted the flaming grenade as the badge of the grenadiers, and initially it was worn at the back of the hat. In 1814 the bugle horn was granted to the regiments of light infantry.

Left: Examples of embroidered British officers' cap badges: 1. 1st King's Dragoon Guards 2. The Queen's Own Worcestershire Hussars 3. The Yorkshire Hussars (Alexandra Princess of Wales's Own) 4. The North Somerset Yeomanry 5. The City of London Yeomanry (Rough Riders).

Until 1881 it was usual for only officers to wear a regimental device on the helmet plate, while the other ranks displayed the regimental number only in the centre of their helmet plate. After 1881, however, following the amalgamation of regiments and their redesignation on a county basis, the other ranks' helmet plate centre displayed the regimental device. In the late 1890s, when cap badges were adopted following the introduction of the blue field service cap, the regiment's device — the dragon, lamb, sphinx, or English rose and so forth — became the centrepiece of the badge, while a scroll, inscribed with the regimental title and often surrounded by wreaths, was added.

The Scots retained the glengarry and therefore wore, and still wear, larger badges. The badge of the Royal Scots (The Royal Regt) is based upon the star of the Order of the Thistle; the officers' pattern has the thistle in its centre and the other ranks' badge has St Andrew and the cross. Most Scottish cap badges are decorated with a wreath of thistle.

The badge of the South Wales Borderers is decorated by a wreath of immortelles, an honour granted to the 24th Foot after its participation in the Zulu War (1879).

Some cap badges retained the design and shape of the crowned helmet plate; for instance, in the centre of the badge of the Devonshire Regiment is Exeter Castle. The cap badge of the Essex Regiment shows the castle and key of Gibraltar, an honour awarded to four regiments in 1784. The sphinx on a tablet inscribed 'Egypt' is a battle honour granted on 6 July 1802 to several regiments, including the Essex Regiment, that had taken part in the campaign against the French in Egypt. During the battle of Alexandria, on 21 March 1801, the 28th Foot beat off a French assault from the rear, and all ranks of the Gloucestershire Regiment have the unique privilege of wearing the sphinx at the front and at the back of their head–dress.

Two cap badges were changed during World War I. The 1st King's Dragoon Guards had borne the arms of the Empire of Austria, for Emperor Francis Joseph I was their Colonel-in-Chief between 1896 and 1914. The original badge had a scroll underneath, which was abandoned when the Austrian eagle was re-adopted in 1937. The second cap badge to change during World I was that of the 14th/20th King's Hussars, which depicts the Prussian eagle in honour of the Princess Royal of Prussia, who had married the Duke of York in 1791. It was abolished in 1915 and restored in 1931.

Several badges were modified in the 1920s, including that of the Cheshire Regiment, which lost its scroll. At the same time, the badge of The Queen's Royal Regiment lost its scroll and the shape of the flag was modified as well, while the horse and the inscription on

Examples of gilt and silver plated badges for officers: 1. The Derbyshire Yeomanry 2. The Devonshire Regiment 3. The Lancashire Fusiliers 4. 23rd County of London Regiment 5. The Buffs (Royal East Kent Regiment) 6. 14th/20th King's Hussars 7. 3rd King's Own Hussars, which in 1930 changed its title to 8. 3rd The King's Own Hussars 9. The Lanarkshire Yeomanry 10. The King's Shropshire Light Infantry 11. The Queen's Royal Regiment (West Surrey) 12. The Royal Hampshire Regiment 6th (Duke of Connaught's Own) Battalion. 13. The King's Own Yorkshire Light Infantry 14. The Royal Scots Fusiliers.

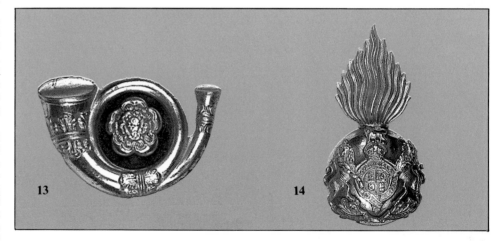

the scroll of the badge of the King's Regiment were modified. In 1937 the badge of the Royal Norfolk Regiment lost the laurel wreath and the scroll that had previously surrounded the figure of Britannia. The badge of the Manchester Regiment was later changed completely from the arms of the city of Manchester to a fleur-de-lis.

Occasionally, often because the title 'Royal' was granted to a regiment, the regimental title on the scroll was changed, as

The period in which these badges were used is primarily determined by the type of crown, but their pattern and type of metals further identify their age. No. 11 is a beret badge worn from 1949 to 1959/61, nos. 7 and 8 also differ in style – the horse is different and that of the first badge is made of stirling silver, a characteristic of pre-World War II badges, while the horse of the second badge is silver plated.

Most of these badges have two long shanks, for the split pin, at the back.

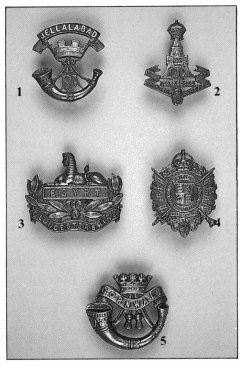

Above: Solid silver cap badges for officers: no. 3 is hallmarked 1918 and no. 5 is marked 1924.
1. The Somerset Light Infantry (Prince Albert's) 2. The Green Howards (Alexandra Princess of Wales's Own Yorkshire Regiment) 3. The Gloucestershire Regiment 4. 5th City of London Regiment 5. The Duke of Cornwall's Light Infantry.

Above: Officers' service dress cap badges adopted in 1902. They were initially made of bronze, later painted brown. The latter have bending blades at the back.
1. The Royal Warwickshire Regiment 2. The Cambridgeshire Regiment 3. The South Lancashire Regiment (The Prince of Wales's Volunteers) 4. The Essex Regiment 5. The Royal Leicestershire Regiment.

Above: 1. Grenadier Guards 2. The Queen's (Royal West Surrey Regiment) 3. The Royal Scots (The Royal Regt) 4. The King's Own Royal Regiment (Lancaster) 5. The Royal Fusiliers (City of London Regt) 6. The Royal Welch Fusiliers.

Below left: The King's (Liverpool Regt) 8. The West Yorkshire Regiment (The Prince of Wales's Own) 9. The Royal Berkshire Regiment (Princess Charlotte of Wales') 10. The Royal Inniskilling Fusiliers.

Below right: 13. The Manchester Regiment 14. As 13. 2nd pattern 15. The Lincolnshire Regiment 16. The Cheshire Regiment 17. The Shropshire Yeomanry.

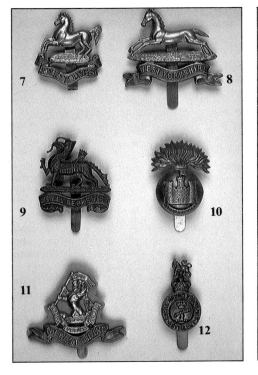

happened with the 3rd 'The' King's Own Hussars.

Large cap badges were awkward to wear on berets when they were adopted during World War II, and some regiments, therefore, wore a collar badge on their berets instead. After the war many regiments adopted small cap badges, with versions for officers and other ranks, especially for the beret.

The Volunteer Force existed until 1908, when it was reorganized to form the Territorial Army. The volunteers wore white metal badges and buttons, and their cap badges were generally similar in design to those of the regular army battalions to which they were affiliated. Many volunteer battalions carried

18. The Argyll and Sutherland Highlanders
(Princess Louise's) 19. The Loyal North
Lancashire Regiment 20. The East Yorkshire
Regiment (The Duke of York's Own) 21. The
Gloucestershire Regiment, back badge 22. As
16, 2nd pattern 23. The Herefordshire
Regiment 24. The City of London Yeomanry
(Rough Riders), beret badge 25. The Rifle
Brigade (Prince Consort's Own) 26. 11th
Hussars (Prince Albert's Own) 27. Liverpool
Scottish 28. The Wiltshire Regiment (Duke of
Edinburgh's) 29. The East Surrey Regiment
30. 15th & 16th County of London Regiments
31. The Royal Ulster Rifles 32. The South Wales
Borderers 33. The Royal Norfolk Regiment
34. The King's Royal Rifle Corps.

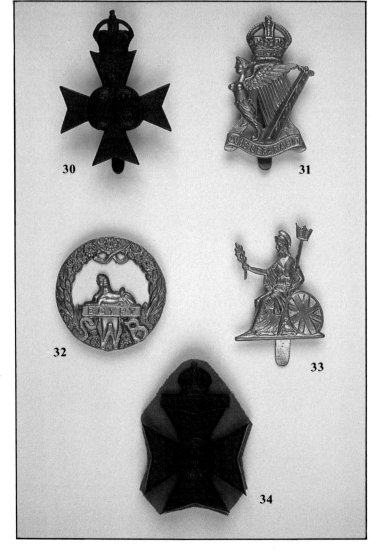

on a scroll or a tablet the battle honours of the battalions that had served in South Africa during the war against the Boers. Others obliterated the regular battalion's battle honours, holding the view that, as they were 'territorials', they did not strictly carry on the traditions of their predecessors.

Most volunteer badges were clearly identified by title scrolls or by initials.

As a general rule, after 1908 the 1st and 2nd battalions of each regiment were regular army battalions, the 3rd was a militia battalion, and the 4th, 5th and so on were territorial battalions.

In 1908 four independent territorial regiments were formed that had no affiliation to the regular army; their battalions were numbered from 1st onward. One was the Cambridgeshire Regiment and another the Monmouthshire Regiment.

The battle honours of territorial badges were modified, as were those of the volunteers. For example, the cap badge of the 4th Battalion, the Border Regiment displays only the battle honour 'South Africa 1900-1902' instead of the numerous battle honours appearing on the cap badge of the regulars. Battalions that traced their origins to rifle units wore blackened cap badges.

Because of the shortage of nickel, all-brass badges started to be issued to the troops in 1916, and during World War II plastic badges were adopted, also for reasons of economy. These cap badges were made in four colours — grey, grey-brown, light brown and dark brown (Bibl. 55).

Staybrite badges, made of anodized aluminium were introduced in 1952 for the use of other ranks. They do not need cleaning and are light in weight, but, although they are shiny, they tend to lose their glittering surface when exposed to constant light. Many regiments have been amalgamated and reorganized since staybrite badges were introduced (see page 000), and many new badges have been adopted. The new badges are often overloaded by the regimental devices of their predecessors, the titles of which usually appear on the scroll, almost unreadable amid the glitter.

Many old regiments did not adopt staybrite badges until the accession of Queen Elizabeth II and most badges, therefore, bear St Edward's Crown.

Below left: Cap badges of Volunteers: 1. 3rd Bn, The Devonshire Regiment 2. 3rd Bn, The Durham Light Infantry 3. 2nd Bn, The Manchester Regiment 4. 2nd Bn, The Duke of Wellington's (West Riding Regiment) 5. 2nd Bn, The York and Lancaster Regiment 6. 4th Bn, The Border Regiment.

Below: Territorial cap badges: 1. The Buckinghamshire Battalion 2. 8th (Irish) Bn, King's Liverpool Regiment 3. 6th Bn, The Durham Light Infantry 4. 1st Bn, The Monmouthshire Regiment 5. As 4, 2nd pattern

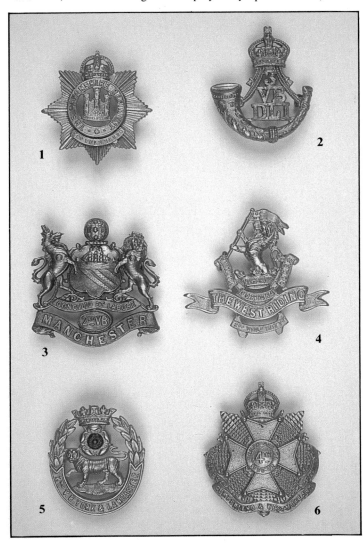

After World War II the regular regiments of the army lost their 2nd battalion, and in 1947 all the battalions were organized into Training Brigade Groups (*see* Formation sign), each battalion representing its regiment. Following the recommendations of the 1957 White Paper, all infantry regiments were grouped into 14 brigades, and as there were too many battalions to fit into 14 brigades, a number of regimental amalgamations were necessary.

The personnel of the remaining battalions wore brigade cap badges and regimental collar badges, so it was possible for entirely new head-dress badges to be adopted without upsetting the feelings of the 'traditionalists'.

The badges of the Scottish brigades were unmistakably Scottish, and the choice of device for the Fusilier, Welsh, Light Infantry and for the North Irish brigades was not difficult. The Lancastrian and Yorkshire brigades were identified by their own roses and the Wessex Brigade by the wyvern (*see* Formation sign). The badges of the East Anglian, Forester and Green Jackets brigades incorporated old regimental motifs, and Saxon crowns were displayed in the cap badges of the Home Counties and Mercian brigades.

All Gurkha regiments, apart from the 2nd, can be identified by the presence of *kukris* in their insignia. The officers usually wear a miniature version of the cap badge fitted on a coloured boss.

The first three Gurkha regiments trace their origins to 1815, and, after many redesignations, the 1st, 2nd and the 4th became affiliated to King Edward VII, after which the plume became part of their badges.

The 3rd Queen Alexandra's Own Gurkha Rifles adopted the crowned initials of Queen Alexandra in their badge. The 5th Royal Gurkha Rifles (Frontier Force) was a 'royal' regiment, and the Royal Crest therefore surmounted the regimental number. The 6th, 7th, 8th, 9th and 10th regiments were designated Gurkha Rifles, but in 1949 the 10th Regiment became the 10th Princess Mary's Own Gurkha Rifles. In 1959 the 6th Regiment was redesignated the 6th Queen Elizabeth's Own Gurkha Rifles and the 7th became the 7th Duke of Edinburgh's Own Gurkha Rifles. The royal crown and the Duke of Edinburgh's cypher, respectively, were added to the insignia of the two regiments.

In 1947 eight battalions of Gurkhas, from the 2nd, 6th, 7th and 10th regiments, became part of the British Army, and they later formed their own support units, engineers, signals and the Gurkha Transport Regiment.

The Royal Marines were granted the globe by King George IV in 1827 when they claimed 106 battle honours for the new colour; the globe was appropriate because the honours had been won in battles all over the world.

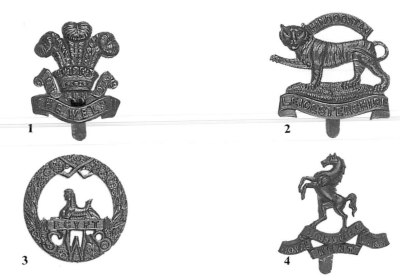

Brass badges used during World War I: 1. The Welsh Regiment 2. The Leicestershire Regiment 3. The South Wales Borderers 4. The Queen's Own Royal West Kent Regiment.

Plastic badges used in World War II: 1. The Royal Ulster Rifles 2. The Duke of Wellington's Regiment (West Riding) 3. The Parachute Regiment 4. The Wiltshire Regiment (Duke of Edinburgh's) 5. The Rifle Brigade (Prince Consort's Own).

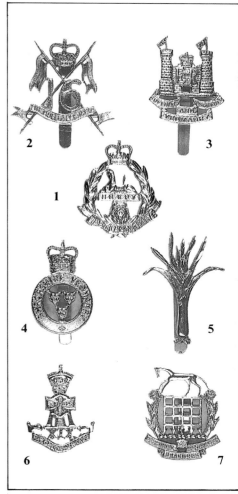

Staybrite badges worn after 1952: 1. The East Lancashire Regiment 2. 16th/5th The Queen's Royal Lancers 3. The Suffolk and Norfolk Yeomanry 4. The Shropshire Yeomanry 5. The Welsh Guards 6. The Green Howards (Alexandra Princess of Wales's Own Yorkshire Regt) 7. Berkshire and Westminster Dragoons.

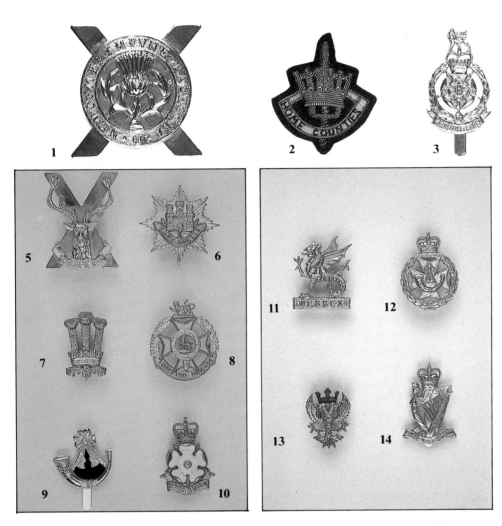

Brigades: 1. The Lowland Brigade 2. The Home Counties Brigade 3. The Lancastrian Brigade 4. The Fusilier Brigade 5. The Highland Brigade 6. The East Anglian Brigade 7. The Welsh Brigade 8. The Forester Brigade 9. The Light Infantry Brigade 10. The Yorkshire Brigade. 11. The Wessex Brigade 12. The Green Jackets Brigade 13. The Mercian Brigade 14. The Irish Brigade.

Royal Marines: 1. Officer's dress cap badge 2. Officer's service dress badge 3. Other ranks' cap badge 4. Other ranks' cap badge of the Royal Marines Light Infantry.

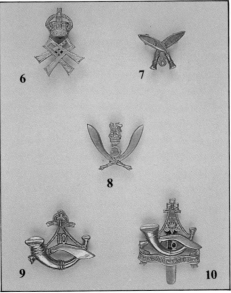

Gurkhas: 1. 1st King George V's Own Gurkha Rifles 2. 2nd King Edward VII's Own Gurkha Rifles 3, 8. 5th Royal Gurkha Rifles (Frontier Force) 4. 7th Gurkha Rifles 5, 7. 8th Gurkha Rifles 6. 3rd Queen Alexandra's Own Gurkha Rifles 9, 10. 10th Gurkha Rifles.

The officers, warrant officers and quartermaster sergeants have cap badges in two pieces. The officers' dress badge is made of gilt except for the globe, which is in silver with gilded continents, while the dress badge of the warrant officers and quartermaster sergeants is entirely in gilt. The other ranks wear a badge made in one piece of gilding metal. Bronze badges are worn by officers, warrant officers and quartermaster sergeants on the service dress.

The above badge was used by the Royal Marines Light Infantry until 1923 instead of the royal crest; the Royal Marines Artillery used a grenade (Bibl. 55 *interalia*).

As the cap badges of the corps and departments follow the pattern of those of the cavalry and infantry regiments, examples of the different types are illustrated together.

The Royal Artillery has four badges: the embroidered grenade and scroll are worn on the forage cap; the 'gun' badge in gilt is worn on the peaked cap and in embroidery on the beret; and the plastic collar badge was used on the beret by other ranks during World War II.

The Royal Army Service Corps, now the Royal Corps of Transport, the Corps of Royal Engineers and the Corps of Military Police, now 'Royal', have the monarch's cypher in the centre; it changes according to the sovereign.

The badges of the Corps of Military Police, Royal Artillery, Army Air Corps and Army Physical Training Corps, which are made of plastic, were used during World War II. The Army Air Corps was formed by the Parachute Regiment and by the Glider Pilot Regiment; it was disbanded in 1950, only to be re-formed with a different badge in 1957.

The Royal Army Ordnance Corps has worn four badges; illustrated are the second pattern for officers' service dress, which was changed in 1947 and again in 1949. Also illustrated are two versions of the badge of the Royal Electrical and Mechanical Engineers, and of the Royal Army Medical Corps, the latter with differing scrolls. The badge of the Royal Armoured Corps for other ranks was used until 1941, while the embroidered badge for officers was worn from 1941 on. The Royal Tank Corps and the Reconnaissance Regiment were part of the Royal Armoured Corps.

The Army Pay Corps wore the initials APC below the crown; in 1920 the Corps became 'Royal', and the initials were changed to RAPC. The badge illustrated has been worn since 1929.

The royal arms were used as the badge of the General Service Corps, the royal crest above crossed swords was worn by the infantry of the Junior Leaders Training Regiments.

Corps and Departments: 1, 3, 5, 13. Royal Regiment of Artillery 2. Royal Army Service Corps 4. Royal Army Chaplain's Department 6. 11, 24. Royal Army Ordnance Corps 7, 17. Royal Electrical and Mechanical Engineers 8, 16. Royal Armoured Corps 9, 19. Royal Army Medical Corps 10. Intelligence Corps 12, Corps of Military Police 14, 20. Army Air Corps 15. Royal Corps of Signals 18. Corps of Royal Engineers 21. Royal Pioneer Corps 22. Royal Army Dental Corps 23. Army Physical Training Corps 25. Royal Tank Regiment 26. Army Catering Corps 27. Junior Leaders Training Regiment, Infantry 28. General Service Corps 29. Royal Army Pay Corps 30. Reconnaissance Corps.

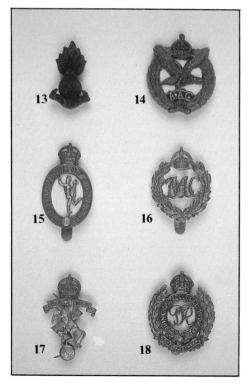

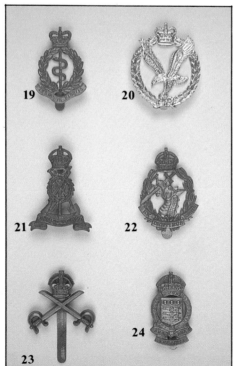

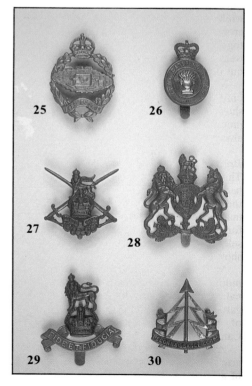

Royal Air Force : The Royal Air Force was formed on 1 April 1918 by the amalgamation of the Royal Flying Corps and the Royal Naval Air Service. The blue-grey uniforms were introduced in September 1919, and during the following months the cap badges were adopted that, although with a different crown, are still in use today.

The cap badge of officers of air rank depicts the RAF eagle on a laurel wreath ensigned by the royal crest. The other officers have the eagle, a four-leaf wreath and the royal crown, while the airmen wore the same type of cap badge as previously worn by the Royal Flying Corps but with the initials RAF instead of RFC. The same badge is still in use, but it bears St Edward's Crown and is made of anodized metal.

Chaplains have a special badge — a winged cross *patté* in metal below the crown. On the full dress busby the officers wear the original emblem of the Royal Air Force: an eagle superimposed upon a circlet bearing the motto *Per Ardua ad Astra* and surmounted by the crown (Bibl. 28, 60).

The same basic types of cap badges were adopted by the air forces of the Dominions, later the Commonwealth, although the initials in the centre of the airmen's badges varied: Canadians had the initials RCAF, New Zealanders RNZAF and Australians RAAF and a different wreath; South African airmen had an entirely different badge.

Officers have always worn large badges on their peaked caps and smaller versions on their berets. The officers of air rank wear the same badge on the side cap and on the beret, while the other officers have the eagle and crown on the side cap, in two pieces held together by a back plate. Warrant officers wear badges of the same pattern as officers but made of metal.

Metal badges were used by the officers only during World War II. The example shown, which is on a black felt backing, is mounted on a metal back plate. The eagle is always made of gilded brass.

British Commonwealth of Nations
This book describes the different patterns of badges used during this century, and, since the same basic types of cap badges, mainly made of metal, were used by all the armed forced of the British Commonwealth, only a selection of badges from these nations is shown.

Many of these badges display national motifs associated with the fauna or flora of the nation or continent; for example, the kangaroo and the swan of Australia, the fern leaf of New Zealand and the maple leaf of Canada.

At the beginning of the 20th century, the armed forces of these nations consisted largely of a militia force led by a very small regular army. Later all went through the same processes or reorganization at about the same time.

1

2

3

Royal Air Force:
1. Field service cap badge for officers of air rank
2. Badge for officer's peaked cap
3. Officer's beret badge
4. Royal Flying Corps
5. Royal Air Force
6. Royal Australian Air Force
7. Field service cap badge for officers.

4

5

6

7

Australia : The cap badge of the 18th Australia Light Horse (Western Australia Mounted Infantry), which was worn between 1900 and 1912, and the badge of the 10th Light Horse, which was adopted in 1953, depict the black swan of Western Australia.

In 1912 the programme known as 'universal training' began for the units of the Australian Citizen Forces. By this programme, 43 battalions were formed from the existing units, many other battalions being formed during World War I. The cap badges of the pre-1912 regiments were replaced by battalion numbers, and the personnel of the units that went abroad were issued with the General Service badge, known as the badge of the Australian Commonwealth Military Forces, which was also used during World War II.

The General Service badge does not, as it is popularly supposed, represent the rising sun. In fact, it originated as a trophy of swords and bayonets surrounding the crown, and it was the insignia of the first regiment to serve in the South African war (Bibl. 61).

The next five badges illustrated were worn between 1930 and 1942.

The kangaroo formed the centrepiece of the cap badge of the 12th Australian Light Horse (New England Light Horse). The badges of the 22nd Infantry Battalion (The Richmond Battalion) and the 46th Infantry Battalion (The Brighton Rifles) followed the pattern of the General Service badge.

The officers of the 60th Infantry Battalion (The Heidelberg Regt) wore an enamelled cap badge. The shape of this badge and its motto, *Celer et Audax*, derived from the cap badge of the British King's Royal Rifle Corps, formerly the 60th Royal American Regiment.

The last badge to be illustrated is made of anodized aluminium; it is worn by the other ranks of the Australian Army Aviation Corps.

Canada : The first five of the badges illustrated come from the pre-World War I period; all were modified or changed in the 1920s.

The cap badge of the Governor General's Foot Guards still exists, but in 1922 the regimental motto, *Civitas et Princeps Cura Nostra*, replaced the title around the cross.

The badge of the 5th Regiment (Royal

Australia: 1. 18th Australian Light Horse (Western Australia Mounted Infantry) 2. 12th Australian Light Horse (New England Light Horse) 3. 13th Light Horse Regiment 4. 22nd Infantry Battalion (The Richmond Bn) 5. 46th Infantry Battalion (The Brighton Rifles) 6. General Service 7. The Heidelberg Regiment 8. 10th Light Horse 9. Australian Army Aviation Corps.

Scots of Canada) changed in 1922 when the regiment became the Royal Highlanders of Canada (Black Watch), and it changed yet again in 1936, when the regiment became the Black Watch of Canada (Royal Highlanders).

The 8th Royal Rifles of Canada dropped the regimental number, and in 1928 a bugle was placed in the centre of the badge, surrounded by the regimental title.

The cap badge of the 50th Militia (Gordons of Canada) was abolished in 1928 when the regiment was redesignated the Canadian Scottish Regiment and obtained an entirely different cap badge.

The 57th Peterborough Rangers lost its number in 1925, and the Roman numerals LVII were removed from the insignia.

During World War I the Canadian Expeditionary Force was created from existing Canadian units to form the contingent that was sent overseas. The CEF was divided into battalions, and the battalion number was displayed on the cap badge.

Three examples are shown: the officers' badge of the 28th Battalion, the other ranks' badge of the 72nd (of which the stag's head and scroll were later used by the Seaforth Highlanders of Canada and by the Pictou Highlanders), and the cap badge of the 151st Central Alberta Battalion.

A major reorganization in the 1920s led to the changing of many regimental insignia and titles.

In 1922 the 31st Horse became the British Columbia Light Horse, which was redesignated British Columbia Hussars in 1933. These badges prove that the trophy of arms, popularly known as the 'rising sun', was not an exclusively Australian insignia.

Also in 1922 the 18th Mounted Rifles became the Manitoba Mounted Rifles, and the Ottawa Regiment became the Ottawa Highlanders, changing their insignia and designation once again in 1939.

The Essex Fusiliers were redesignated Essex Scottish in 1927, and in 1928 the North Waterloo Regiment was redesignated the Scots Fusiliers of Canada.

A new phase of reorganization took place in the late 1930s. The 5th Dragoon Guards, which had been redesignated Princess Louise's Dragoon Guards in the 1920s, was numbered 4th in 1939, and the regimental number was added in the cap badge. The 2nd Armoured Car Regiment was formed from the former 2nd Motor Machine Gun Brigade in 1938, and the New Brunswick Tank Regiment was formed in 1939.

The 8th Reconnaissance Regiment, of which an officers' cap badge is shown, was raised in 1942, and the Lake Superior Regiment, which was raised in 1943, existed until 1950. The Yukon Regiment, a post-World War II unit, still exists. (Bibl. 80).

1. The Governor General's Foot Guards 2. 5th Regiment (Royal Scots of Canada) 3. 8th Royal Rifles of Canada 4. 50th Militia (Gordons of Canada) 5. 57th Peterborough Rangers 6. 28th Battalion CEF 7. 72nd Battalion CEF 8. 151st Central Alberta Battalion CEF 9. 5th British Columbia Light Horse 10. The Manitoba Mounted Rifles 11. The British Columbia Hussars 12. The Ottawa Highlanders 13. The Essex Scottish 14. The North Waterloo Regiment 15. 4th Princess Louise's Dragoon Guards 16. 2nd Armoured Car Regiment 17. The New Brunswick Tank Regiment 18. 8th Reconnaissance Regiment 19. The Lake Superior Regiment 20. The Cameron Highlanders of Ottawa (MG) 21. The Yukon Regiment.

New Zealand : The 1st Regiment Otago Mounted Rifles existed between 1901 and 1911, when it was redesignated the 5th Mounted Rifles (Otago Hussars) and new insignia were adopted. In 1911 the New Zealand Forces were reorganized into 17 infantry regiments and 12 regiments of mounted rifles.

The 8th (South Canterbury) Mounted Rifles was one of the new regiments, and the badge displayed the arms of the Earl of Ranfurly. In 1921 the 8th and the 1st Mounted Rifles amalgamated to form the 1st New Zealand Mounted Rifles (Canterbury Yeomanry Cavalry).

In 1916 the personnel of the New Zealand Machine Gun Corps were issued with conventional British machine gunner's cap badges,

but with additional initials NZ.

During World War I two main training camps operated in New Zealand, at Trentham and at Featherstone, both supervised by the Camp Military Police; the badge of Trentham is shown. The cap badge known as 'Correction 1' of the Featherstone Camp derives from the system of graduation of the recruits, who went form A to D. Grade C1 meant 'likely to become fit for active service after special training'.

A typical Scottish cap badge was adopted by the 1st Armoured Car Regiment (New Zealand Scottish), which was formed in 1939 as the 1st Battalion New Zealand and Scottish. It was re-formed after the war as the 1st Divisional Regiment RNZAC (New Zealand

Scottish) and still exists under its original name (Bibl. 81).

British paramilitary forces
The formation of a Control Commission for the administration of occupied Germany was devised in November 1943, and its organization was gradually built up before the actual invasion of Germany. It was an Anglo-American establishment, the British element of which wore a special cap badge and identifying badges on the shoulder straps (*see* Slip-on).

Another interesting organization was created by the Allies in the region of Venezia Giulia in north-eastern Italy. When this area was occupied by the British 13th Corps on

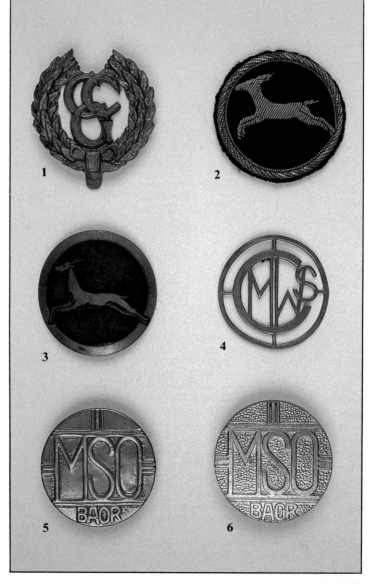

New Zealand: 1. 1st Regiment Otago Mounted Rifles 2. 8th (South Canterbury) Mounted Rifles 3. NZ Machine Gun Corps 4. Trentham Camp Military Police 5. 1st Armoured Car Regiment (NZ Scottish) 6. Featherstone Camp Correction.

1. Control Commission Germany 2, 3. Civil Police Venezia Giulia 4. Civil Mixed Watchmen Service 5, 6. Mixed Service Organisation.

1 May 1945, a territorial dispute ensued with the Yugoslav Army. Therefore, instead of installing the usual Allied Military Government (AMG) with the support of Italian police, a new administrative organization was formed, the AMG–VG (Allied Military Government–Venezia Giulia), and a special police force was raised locally.

The emblem on the police cap badge was the gazelle of 13th Corps. It was embroidered in silver for the officers, and made in white metal and blue enamel for the policemen.

The Mixed Service Organization (MSO) was formed in Germany in 1946 from refugees and expatriated persons. It had two branches, the Civil Mixed Watchmen Service (CMWS), which consisted of armed guards deployed around military installations, and the Civil Mixed Labour Organization (CMLO). The MSO men wore dark blue uniforms and special badges. The personnel of the CMWS wore a round cap badge, with the initials of the organization; after 1953 it bore the initials MSO.

The MSO still exists, although it now has a different role and different badges. For many years its personnel have been in charge of the transportation of tanks and heavy vehicles, and they wear the cap badge of the Royal Transport Corps with the initials MSO in its centre.

China, Republic of

The white sun on a blue round background, which is the main emblem of China, was worn by all ranks on the head-dress before and during World War II.

The badge existed in different patterns, in different sizes and with different fittings at the back. During World War II a 'sun' flanked by two gold wings was adopted for the officers of the air force, but the army officers continued to wear the round badge alone until the 1950s.

All ranks wear the 'sun' only on the field cap; officers and non-commissioned officers who are entitled to wear the peaked cap have the badge surrounded by a gold or silver wreath, according to their class of rank. Smaller versions of the peaked cap badge are worn on the left side of the garrison cap.

The wreath of the modern army badge depicts plum blossom and leaves, as the plum's flower is a traditional Chinese emblem. Wheat leaves and ears form the wreath of the navy and of the marines, which have the anchor and the anchor and globe in the centre respectively. Aviators wear the badge with the wings that was adopted during the war.

Czechoslovakia

The lion and the lime leaves, the emblems of Czechoslovakia, always appear on military uniforms.

Even before World War II the Czech lion was displayed on the head-dress. The rank

and file wore it embossed on a bronze shield; non-commissioned officers wore it on a silver shield and officers on a gilt shield, both superimposed upon a diamond-shaped base. Combatant corps wear the whole device above crossed swords.

Although Czechoslovakia was the first nation to be invaded during the war, Czechoslovaks continued to fight in units attached to the British Army in the west and to the Soviet Army in the east. In both cases, the Czech lion was worn.

When Czechoslovakia was partly annexed to Germany and the remaining territory divided between the new state of Slovakia and the German Protectorate of Bohemia and Moravia, new cap badges were adopted for the armies of these states. The Slovaks wore on their peaked caps a spread eagle of Germanic appearance, perched on a wreath with crossed swords in its centre. On the eagle's chest was the emblem of Slovakia. In the Protectorate two badges were worn on the peaked cap — a blue, white and red cockade on the crown, and crossed swords above a wreath of lime leaves on the cap band, above the chinstrap.

After the war the pre-war cap badges continued to be worn until 1948.

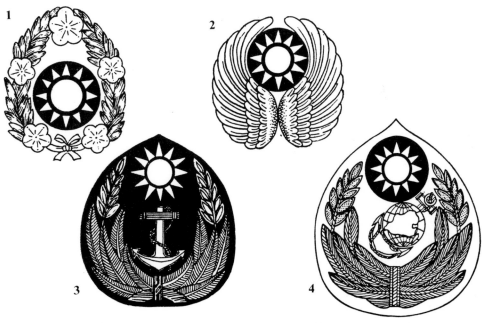

Chinese officer's cap badges: 1. Army 2. Air force 3. Navy 4. Marines, taken from the dress regulations.

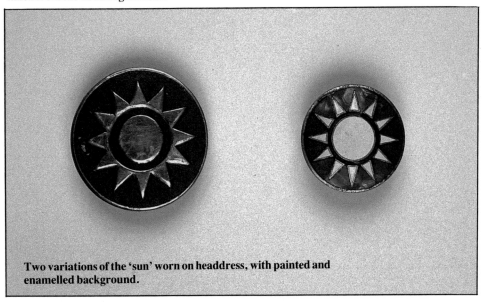

Two variations of the 'sun' worn on headdress, with painted and enamelled background.

Czechoslovakia, Socialist Republic of : On 25 February 1948 Czechoslovakia became a socialist nation, and the Czech lion was placed in the centre of the red star. After 1955, to match the Soviet officers' new cap badges, the star was mounted on an oval, Russian-style metal base.

Since the star was higher than it was wide, when its five points were joined a pentagon was formed, and this was the shape of the cap badge next adopted. It was available in gold, silver and bronze, according to class of rank, and the Czech lion was placed in the pentagon on a red background, ensigned by the red star. Generals wore a golden wreath at the bottom of the badge.

Recently the emblem on the chest of the lion has been changed from the cross to a flame on a red and blue background, and a gold or silver backing device has been added to the pentagonal badge. This new badge is worn by officers on their peaked caps only; the brown pentagonal badges are used by all ranks on the field cap.

Air force personnel wear the star and wings on their peaked caps above the main badge, as is customary in all other Warsaw Pact nations.

Denmark

The army dress regulations published in 1923 prescribed three types of head-dress: the peaked cap, the forage cap and the steel helmet. Each carried different badges.

The peaked cap was used by officers who were wearing service dress. It was khaki and displayed an oval red, white and red cockade on the crown and an embroidered badge on the silk woven cap band. The same type of silk woven lace was sewn around the forage cap, which had the national cockade at the front. The lace was light brown (later grey) for officers and cadets and dark brown for administrative officials and sergeants (*see* Distinction lace). A metal badge was worn on the helmet.

The white ring of the officers' and sergeants' cockade was originally embroidered in silver, but after World War II the ring was made of white metal, in imitation of embroidery. The cockade of the rank and file was made of felt and later of plastic.

The insignia on the cap band was made in two parts: the central button was of gilded metal with three blue lions and nine hearts enamelled on it. The cluster of oak leaves was embroidered in gold wire, the leaves and the acorns identifying class of rank as follows:

Generals	2 × 4 oak leaves
	2 × 3 acorns
Field officers	2 × 3 oak leaves
	2 × 2 acorns
Company officers	2 × 2 oak leaves
Officials	2 × 1 acorns

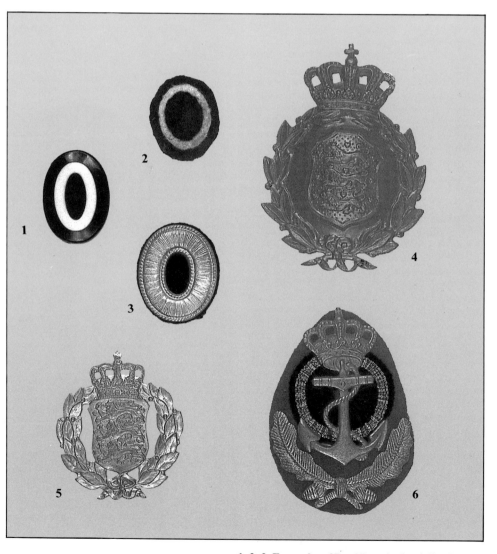

1, 2. Czechoslovak Forces in Britain
3. Protectorate of Bohemia and Moravia
4. Air force officers of the Socialist Republic
5. Officers' cap badge, 2nd pattern
6, 7. Officers' and NCOs' badges, 3rd pattern.

1, 2, 3. Examples of Danish cockades 4. Steel helmet badge used before 1940 5. Post World War II beret badge 6. Petty officers' badge used until the late 1960s.

The officer cadets and sergeants wore a badge made of gilded brass, which had two leaves and two acorns, one on each side and, in the centre, a regimental button, instead of the national button used by officers.

A beret badge was introduced in 1948. It was a smaller replica of the pre-war badge worn on the steel helmet, and it was made of gilded metal for officers and in brass for the other ranks. Branch-of-service and regimental collar badges were adopted at the same time and became very popular with the troops. Subsequently, a third collar badge, which faced to the right, was worn on the beret.

A few years later a beret badge was adopted for the personnel of the air force, and it is still used today. It depicts a small, crowned shield above two wings, the whole set on a round cockade.

The Royal Danish Navy used the typical naval pattern of cap badges, the crown and wreath with the **foul anchor** above, and the national cockade in the centre. The number of oak leaves and acorns identified class of rank as in the army.

The air force did not exist as a separate service until the 1950s, and air crews wore wings on khaki or navy blue uniforms, according to which service they belonged.

When the Royal Danish Air Force was instituted in the middle 1950s, cap badges of the three services were standardized on the pattern used by the navy, that is, by incorporating the national cockade above the wreath and adding the crown on the top.

The three services were, and are still today, distinguished by a device placed in the cockade's centre: the shield bearing the lions and hearts identifies the army, the foul anchor identifies the navy, and a winged shield ensigned by the crown identifies the air force.

Three new badges were devised for each service. All the officers had the same cap badge, which had six, later seven, oak leaves on each side of the cockade; the two *Fenrick* ranks wore a badge with two oak leaves at each side of the cockade, and the sergeant major, sergeant and corporal had one leaf at either side at the base of the cockade.

The non-commissioned officers ranks were modified in 1970. The ranks of *Overfenrik* and *Fenrik* were abolished, together with their cap badges with four oak leaves. In the navy, the petty officers' badge was replaced by a badge with an oval cockade above the oak leaves, and another badge was adopted that had no oak leaves at all.

At the time of writing, dress regulations show one army badge only for the peaked cap, the officers' type, two cockades and the beret badge.

Finland
Until 1949 only small, round cap badges were used by the Finnish Army. Regular officers had a semi-spherical badge depicting the Finnish lion in gilt on red enamel, which was worn in combination with a white, light blue and white enamelled cockade on those head-dresses that required two badges. On the fur hats, for instance, the national cockade was worn above the Finnish lion, while only the lion was worn on the cap band of the peaked caps and on the upper front of the forage caps.

Sergeants had their own version of the Finnish lion badge, which took the form of a metal button and was worn with the enamelled national cockade. The rank and file wore the cockade only, painted in the national colours.

These badges are still in use today, although the cockade of the rank and file is now made of coloured plastic; new badges for the peaked cap were adopted in 1949 and are still in use. These badges have a gold embroidered laurel wreath around the Finnish lion. Army officers' badges have the Finnish lion placed on a backing of branch-of-service colour; air force officers' cap badges display a gold metal eagle; naval officers' badges are distinguished by the **foul anchor**.

The aviation officers used the wreath and eagle badge during the war, but that badge was in two parts — the lion and wreath were placed on the cap band and the eagle, higher up on the crown.

A smaller badge with a gold wreath was introduced for non-commissioned officers, but later abolished, as they now use the same badges as the officers.

1. Finnish Air Force officer's badge

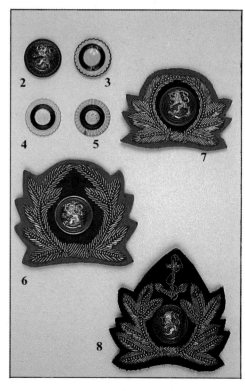

2. National insignia 3, 4, 5. Examples of enamelled, painted and plastic cockades
6. Army officers, Engineers 7. Army NCOs, Services 8. Naval officers.

7. Guards Hussars 8. Jutland Dragoons
9. Chief petty officers

1. French Air Force cap badge for rank and file

2. Air force helmet badge

3. North-East Fortress units beret badge

4. Marine Commandos.

Post World War II beret badges

5. Infantry

6. 'Chasseurs'

7. Marine units

8. Parachutists

9. Signals

10. Transportation.

France

The kepi is the traditional head-dress of the French Army, and the modern pattern derives from the model described in the 1919 regulations. It is now worn only by officers and sergeants.

Badges or regimental numbers have always been worn half way up the front of the kepi, between the rank stripes and the chinstrap. Embroidered devices are stitched directly on to the kepi. In 1939 the officers and non-commissioned officers of the infantry of the line, *zouaves*, Algerian and Tunisian rifles and *spahis*, and the artillery and engineers had gold embroidered badges. Officers and non-commissioned officers of the cavalry, armour, *chasseurs* on foot, African *chasseurs* and supply train had silver badges. Services used gold or silver according to branch.

The rank and file had badges or numbers cut out from coloured felt and attached to their kepis and berets.

Mountain troops, fortress troops and tank-men wore berets. All ranks of the *Chasseurs Alpins* (the mountain and fortress units of the Alps) had dark blue, very large berets, with

the bugle for the *chasseurs* and a flaming grenade for the others. The bugles of the rank and file were made of yellow felt; those used by the ranks from sergeant upward were embroidered in silver. The flaming grenade worn on the Alpine berets was in madder red felt for infantrymen, scarlet felt for gunners and in gold embroidery for their officers and non-commissioned officers (Bibl. 98).

The personnel of the 'fortress units north-east' wore a smaller khaki beret with a white metal badge. Tankmen had dark blue berets with a white metal badge depicting a knight's helmet above two crossed cannon barrels.

A set of 15 round metal badges was worn on the steel helmets by army personnel, and a further badge, adopted in 1924, was used by air force personnel. All ranks of the air force wore wings on their blue peaked caps. The wings were embroidered in gold down to the rank of chief corporal and in orange cotton for the others. Mechanic and specialist officers had their wings embroidered on violet velvet and administrative officers' wings were on brown velvet; all other wings were embroidered on black felt.

The officers of air rank wore rank insignia in the form of small, five-pointed stars above the wings, while the other officers displayed the branch insignia — a star for staff, a crescent for the North African and an anchor for the colonial branch — combined with the formation number. The number alone was worn by the officers of the metropolitan (France) branch. The rank and file wore the number, in orange, below the wings.

The **foul anchor** within a laurel wreath embroidered in gold was, and is still, worn by naval officers.

The kepi is now worn only with dress and walking-out uniforms by officers and non-commissioned officers of the army. Berets are worn at all other times, and the beret is also the standard head-dress of the rank and file of all corps, except the Foreign Legion, which still makes extensive use of the kepi.

Round metal badges are worn on the berets. Since the 1940s several different beret badges have been worn by special units; the Marine Commandos, for example, adopted their own badge in 1943.

Germany

Germany, Empire of : The main head-dress badges worn by all ranks were two cockades: one, bearing the Imperial national colours of black, white and red, was used by all units from 1897; the other displayed the colours of the regional state from which the unit originated.

Large cockades, 50mm (2in) in diameter, were worn on the sides of the *pickelhaube* or similar head-dress as an ornament below the attachments of the chinstrap; the national cockade was worn on the right, the state's cockade on the left. The officers wore enamelled cockades, but those of the other ranks were painted.

The spiked *pickelhaube*, the helmet of the *cuirassiers* and the lancers, the hussars' busby and the shako of the *jäger* battalions displayed the state's emblem or a large metal regimental badge at the front. The lancers' *czapka*, the hussars' busby and the shako carried the state's colours in the form of a large oval boss above the cap badge.

Officers and senior non-commissioned officers wore the peaked cap as service head-dress, and the other ranks had a similar type of cap but without a visor. All ranks wore both cockades at the front, the national cockade on the crown and the state's cockade on the cap band. These were about 25mm (1in) in diameter or smaller, enamelled and protruding for officers, and made of painted metal for the other ranks.

The following were the colours of the cockades:

National	black—white—red
Anhalt	green
Baden	yellow—red—yellow
Bavaria	white—light blue—white
Bremen	white—red—white
Braunschweig	light blue—yellow—light blue
Hamburg	white with red cross
Hessen	white—double red ring—white
Lippe	yellow—red
Lubeck	white with red Maltese cross
Mecklenburg	blue—yellow—red
Oldenburg	light blue—red—light blue
Prussia	black—white—black
Sachsen-Koburg-Meiningen	green—white—green
Sachsen-Weimar	green—yellow—black
Schaumburg-Lippe	white—red—blue
Swartzburg-Rudolfstadt	blue—white—blue
Swartzburg-Sonderhousen	white—blue—white
Waldeck-Reuss	yellow—red—black
Württemburg	black—red—black

(Bibl. 17, 99)

Third Reich After the NSDAP (German National Socialist Workers' Party) came to power a new national emblem was adopted for use on uniforms. Although the black, white and red *Reichskokarde* was retained as a secondary insignia, it was subordinated in 1935 to the eagle clutching the swastika.

Both badges were worn on the cap by all the armed forces personnel; sizes and patterns differed according to the type of head-dress and to the class of rank.

The badges varied from service to service. The army and navy used the same type of eagle, but in white and yellow, respectively; the air force used an eagle in flight, and the *Waffen* SS wore a white eagle, similar to the army pattern, but with slightly different wings.

Army officers, except generals, wore a silver eagle on the peaked cap (generals wore a gold eagle), above the cockade, which was surrounded by a silver wreath of oak leaves.

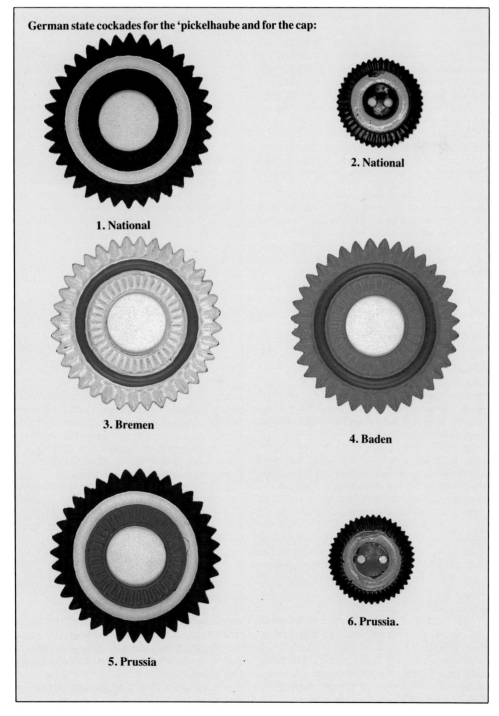

German state cockades for the 'pickelhaube and for the cap:

1. National
2. National
3. Bremen
4. Baden
5. Prussia
6. Prussia.

The officers' eagle and cockade were usually made of metal, and the wreath was of silver embroidery. The cockade could also be embroidered; alternatively, the cockade and wreath could both be of metal. Towards the end of the war officers also wore embroidered eagles. All the badges of the other ranks' peaked cap were made of white metal.

A variety of smaller hand-embroidered or machine-embroidered badges, according to class of rank, was used on other types of caps.

On the peaked cap all ranks of the air force wore the eagle in flight clutching the swastika above the cockade and wreath (which were slightly different from the army pattern), and they were set above two stylized wings on the cap band. The officers of air rank had gold badges, other officers had silver badges, and the other ranks had white metal cap badges.

The same varieties of badge existed for the air force as for the army.

Mountain troops wore the edelweiss on the left side of the field cap, and the flowers only, without the stem and leaves, on the peaked cap below the eagle but above the cap band.

Germany, Federal Republic of : When the *Bundeswehr* was formed in 1955 entirely new badges were adopted that broke with the traditions of the past. The wreath of oak leaves that remained on the cap badges had never previously had any political significance.

The colours of the cockade were changed to yellow, red and black, and were made in gold and coloured thread for officers, and either of metal or woven for the other ranks.

With minor modifications, the same type of cap badges are still in use today. The symbolism of the badges is straightforward: army personnel wear crossed swords, airmen wear wings and naval personnel wear the **foul anchor** (Bibl. 118).

The badges worn on peaked caps display the swords, wings and anchor combined with the wreath; silver embroidery is used for the officers of the army and air force, and gold embroidery is used for naval officers, while metal is used for the other ranks. The national cockade, either embroidered or in metal, is worn above the arm-of-service badge.

The crossed swords or the wings below the cockade were worn on field caps from 1956 and, later, on the beret. They were worn as separate metal pieces or woven as one badge. However, forage caps are now worn, on which the cockade only is displayed.

In 1972 three beret badges were adopted for tank troops, parachutists and *Jäger*, and in November 1978 a set of 20 new beret badges was adopted, for all the branches of service of the *Bundeswehr*. There is a small national flag at the bottom of each badge.

The mountain troops still wear the edelweiss on the left side of the field cap.

1. 3rd Reich Army officers' badges for the peaked cap
2. 3rd Reich Army officers' badges for the peaked cap
3. Air force eagle
4. 'Edelweiss' for mountain troops of the Waffen SS.

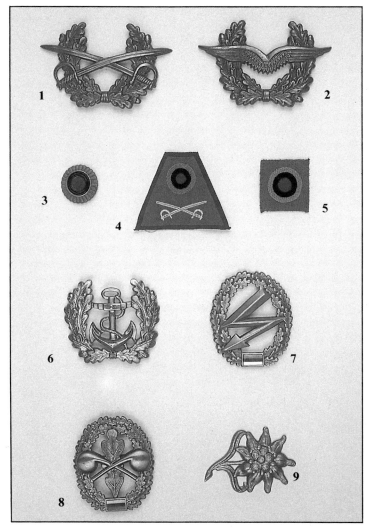

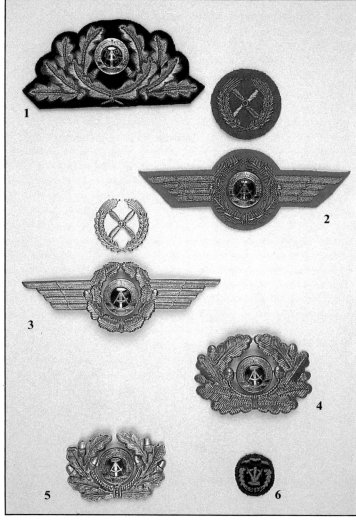

1, 2, 6. Other ranks' badges of the army, air force and navy of the 'Bundeswehr' 3, 4, 5. Examples of different 'cockades' 7, 8. Beret badges of Signals and ABC 9. 'Edelweiss' of the mountain troops.

1, 4, 5. Peaked cap badges for generals, officers and other ranks of the 'Volksarmee', army 2, 3. Air force generals and officers 6. Seamen.

German Democratic Republic : The armed forces of the GDR were formed in 1956, and, contrary to the policy adopted by the Federal Republic, traditional German insignia were introduced. However, the national cockade was not used, a black, red and yellow cockade being chosen initially but later changed to the coat of arms of the GDR.

The armed forces consist of four services: the army, navy, air force and anti-aircraft defence. The Border Guard is an autonomous branch of the army.

The generals of the army and the border guards and the flag officers of the navy use the same type of cap badge, but it is embroidered on red, green and black backgrounds respectively. Air force personnel wear a dual badge on peaked caps, a four-bladed propeller within two wheat ears is worn on the crown, and a wreath of oak leaves set on two wings and with the cockade in its centre is displayed

on the cap band. The officers of air rank have gold-embroidered cap badges, the officers have white metal badges and the other ranks' badges are made of aluminium.

The personnel of the army, border guards and anti-aircraft defence have the same design of cap badges. There are two patterns according to class of rank, the officers wearing white metal badges and the other ranks having aluminium cap badges.

Seamen wear brass or embroidered cockades.

Holland
Before World War II the armed forces of the Netherlands were divided into two separate organizations, one in Holland and the other in the Dutch East Indies. Each had different uniforms and, to a certain extent, different badges. The main cap badge of both organizations was an oval **boss** with orange centre,

but the Royal Netherlands Indian Army also used a round cockade.

The national cockade of the Netherlands is orange. In the cap badges, the boss, which surrounded the national colour, was intended purely as a service distinction, being gold or silver according to rank insignia. Gold was used by all corps except the Royal Constabulary, cavalry, pay corps, veterinaries and pharmacists, who had a silver boss and silver rank insignia.

Generals wore peaked caps when in service dress, with a small boss within sprigs of oak and of laurel embroidered on the cap band. Cavalrymen wore the busby in all uniforms except field, and the personnel of all other branches wore kepis, on which the boss had a loop underneath and a button displaying the lion of Nassau. The boss of the cavalry was larger than average and did not have a loop.

The boss worn by officers and warrant officers was made of gold or silver wire; the boss worn by sergeants was made of yellow or white silk; while that of the rank and file was made of metal, its centre painted orange.

Aviation personnel wore army uniforms and insignia, with blue branch-of-service piping and Army Air Service qualification badges.

After the German invasion of Holland the Dutch armed forces were reconstructed in Britain, America and Australia. The traditional cap badges were replaced by the lion of Nassau, or Netherlands lion, which, according to the regulations, was embroidered in gold on a black background for colonels and ranks above, in gilt for lieutenant colonels and majors, in bronze for company and warrant officers, *vaandrigs* and *kornetten*, and in brass for the other ranks (*see* Backing).

Regimental and branch-of-service badges for use on the beret were adopted from 1950 onwards. They are about 50 × 60mm

(2 × 2½in), with shanks for the split pin or bending blades at the back. The regimental or branch-of-service emblem is displayed on a standard background, and each badge is mounted on a felt backing that matches the colour of the collar patches (*see* Backing).

The Jager Guards Regiment was formed in 1829 but traces its origins to the Aquila Regiment, which was raised in 1665. The youngest regiment is the Fusiliers Guards Regiment *Princess Irene*, which was formed in Britain on 11 January 1941 under the name of Royal Nederland Brigade. The Infantry Regiment *Chassé* formerly the 7th Infantry Regiment, traces its origins to a battalion of marines raised in 1772.

The infantry of the line has poppy red backing under a different badges, while cavalry regiments wear the same badge but with different backings.

All the other badges are self explanatory: anti-aircraft, engineers, signals, supply corps and lastly, the badge of the medical corps.

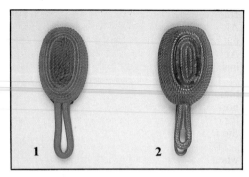

1, 2. Dutch badges for sergeants and for rank and file used until 1940.

Post-World War II beret badges: 3. Jager Guards Regiment 4. Fusiliers Guards Regiment 'Princes Irene' 5. Infantry Regiment 'Chassé' 6. Hussars 'van Boreel' 7. Anti-Aircraft 8. Engineers 9. Signals 10. Supply Corps 11. Medical Corps.

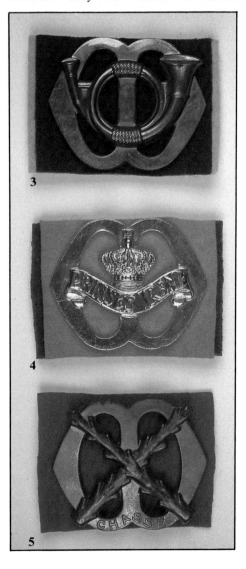

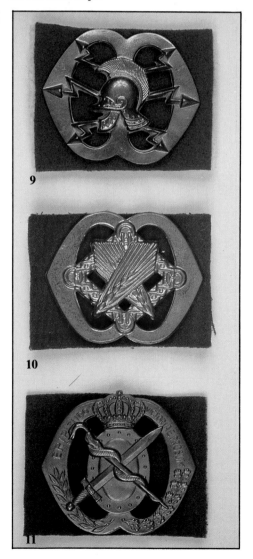

Hungary

Although Hungary became an independent nation after World War I, it retained the old Austrian 'flair' in its post-war uniforms and insignia.

The main cap badge was a **boss** with the national colours, green, white and red, placed horizontally in its centre. The boss was of gold for officers, silver for sergeants and bronze for the rank and file.

These cap badges were used until 1949, when two new patterns were introduced: the national coat of arms for officers, and the crossed hammer and wheat ear within the red star, surrounded by the national colours, for the other ranks.

New badges were again adopted in 1958, and they are still in use today. Made of metal and enamel, with a plastic, translucent red star in the centre, they are enclosed in an oval frame, which resembles a boss, in gold for officers, silver for sergeants and bronze for the rank and file.

According to Warsaw Pact custom, airmen are identified by the star and wings in the same colour as the frame of the main cap badge (Bibl. 123).

Ireland, Republic of

All ranks of the army of the Irish Defence Force wear the same type of cap badge, which was adopted in 1922. Although the basic design has remained the same since that time, there are many variations for, even as early as 1923, two special badges were adopted, one with red enamel embellishments for the staff officers of general headquarters and one with blue enamel embellishments for the staff officers of the commands. In the following year gold embroidered cap badges, on a red backing, but without the flames behind the star, were adopted for the generals. Colonels wore gold plated badges, and the other officers had bronze cap badges.

The full dress uniform was adopted in 1935, when new cap badges for the dress cap were introduced. They were embroidered in gold or silver on different backings according to the facings (Bibl. 125).

Gold embroidered cap badges on scarlet are still worn today in officers' dress uniform.

Black painted badges were also used, as were brass and staybrite cap badges; the staybrite badges are the latest pattern for the other ranks. Two examples are shown: an officer's bronze cap badge and a brass badge for other ranks.

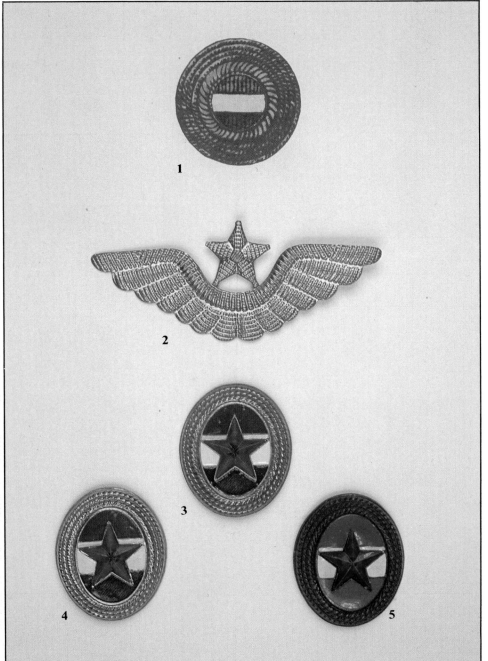

Above: 1, 2. Irish bronze and brass insignia.

Left: 1. Hungarian pre-World War II officers' cap badge, used until 1949 2, 3. Air force officers 3, 4, 5. Army officers, NCOs and other ranks.

Italy

Kingdom of Italy : The generals of the army wore the eagle of Savoy on the head-dress from 1872 to 1946. The eagle was in gold or silver and on different coloured backgrounds according to rules that were changed several times during the period of its use.

Until 1934 the infantry (all arms and corps except *Bersaglieri*), the cavalry and the medical and veterinary corps wore silver badges; the personnel of the other branches had gold badges. In 1934, however, gold badges were adopted for all.

The badges of colonels in command of a regiment or an equivalent organization were embroidered on deep red felt, while the badges for all the other officers were embroidered on felt that matched the colour of the cap. Officers, warrant officers and sergeants had the same type of badges, but after 1934 cap badges of officers and warrant officers had the central disc made of black velvet, while the sergeants' badges had a grey-green or khaki disc, according to the colour of the uniform.

The regimental number or, for unassigned personnel, serving at headquarters and depots, a cross, was shown in the disc.

In April 1915 insignia for officers and warrant officers were embroidered in grey-green silk or in grey-green wool, and, following an Army Order of June 1916, black cap badges were introduced for all ranks.

Until 1923 the rank and file of the infantry wore on their kepis the regimental number, 25mm (1in) high, ensigned by the crown; thereafter they wore the standard infantry cap badge, embroidered in black wool and later in rayon.

In 1934 the peaked cap replaced the kepi, and a new pattern of forage cap was introduced for all ranks. Corporals and soldiers who were issued with the peaked cap initially wore a brass badge on it; later they wore a black embroidered badge, the same as that previously worn on the kepi but with the regimental number or cross in yellow metal. Smaller badges were embroidered in gold on forage caps for ranks down to the class of sergeants; for the rank and file the badges were machine embroidered in black rayon.

In 1940 officers, warrant officers and sergeants were ordered to have black badges on all head-dresses worn with field uniform, and large and small badges, embroidered in black rayon, therefore appeared. These badges were hand embroidered on the dark grey-green cloth of rank and file pattern. The crown was embroidered separately and stitched on the badges.

Before World War I metal badges were worn by all ranks on the dress kepi, on the colonial helmet and, in the 1920s, on the steel helmet.

Some corps entitled to wear a metal head-

dress wore a metal badge on it. The *Alpini* (mountain infantry) had a tall bowler hat of black felt with a large white metal badge at the front. Before World War I this hat was replaced by a more sombre grey-green hat with a feather on the left side and an embroidered cap badge.

The first companies of *Bersaglieri* (rifle troops) were formed in 1836, and even today they wear the wide brimmed hat with cockerel feathers that was first adopted 150 years ago. A brass badge on a tri-coloured cockade is worn at the front.

Several different types of infantry metal

cap badges have been used. The officers' badges were smaller than the other ranks' pattern, and they had the regimental number engraved on the disc. Brass badges were always used by the artillery and engineers and, after 1934, by all branches of service.

The dragoons had a special dress helmet with high crest and the cross of Savoy on the front; they wore the metal cap badge on the colonial helmet. The lancers and the light cavalry were distinguished by the busby, on the front of which they wore a badge, of white metal before 1934 and afterwards of brass.

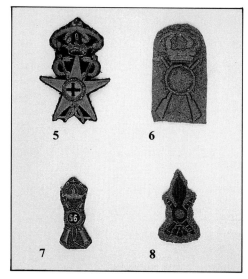

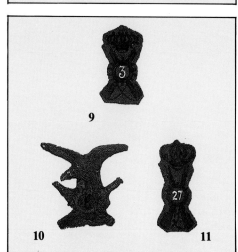

1. Infantry officers, c.1910 2. Army generals 3. Infantry officers 1934-46 4. 'Bersaglieri' officers, c.1910 5. Medical Corps officers 1934-46 6. Infantry officers M.1915 7. Infantry officers for forage cap. 8. Tank Corps rank and file for forage cap 9. Infantry rank and file 1923-34 10. 'Alpini' all ranks, World War I 11. Infantry officers M.1940.
12. Infantry officers pre-1934 13. 'Alpini' 1880-1915 14. Dragoons post-1934 15. Infantry other ranks pre-1934 16. As 15 but post-1934.

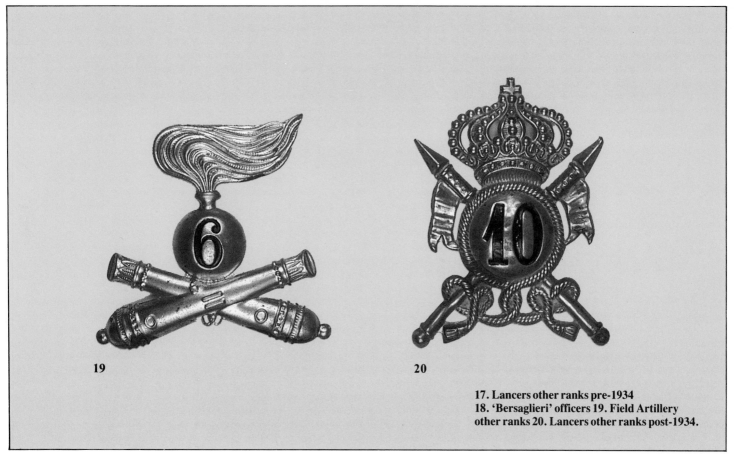

17. Lancers other ranks pre-1934
18. 'Bersaglieri' officers 19. Field Artillery
other ranks 20. Lancers other ranks post-1934.

Fascism : The term derives from the fasces (*il fascio*), the bundle of rods and an axe head fastened together by a tie, and originally carried by the *lictors* in ancient Rome. It was the emblem of the Italian Fascists and became the emblem of the *Milizia Volontaria per la Sicurezza Nazionale* (MVSN) when this organization was formed in 1923.

Initially the fasces had the axe head on the top below a star, but, before the issuing of written regulations, the star was often embroidered on the centre of the fasces, because, when it was in its proper position, the badge was too tall. In 1927, therefore, the axe head was moved to the side of the rods. Warrant officers wore silver badges with a star; sergeants also wore silver badges but without a star. The 'black shirts' wore brass badges.

The MVSN had some Special Detachments deployed on particular tasks — the Anti-aircraft Militia, for example. All ranks wore a winged cannon on the fasces from 1931 to 1935, and crossed cannon barrels and wings between the fasces and the disc from 1935 to 1938. The Colonial Militia, which operated in Libya, was distinguished by the fasces and the bugle. In 1934 special cap badges were adopted for the battalions that were sent to East Africa to invade Ethiopia; these badges were embroidered in gold or silver or made of brass as usual.

MVSN generals wore the Roman eagle, which should not be confused with the Roman eagle that was used by the officials of the National Fascist Party or the eagle that was used by the officials of the civil service (*see* Backing).

By an order issued in 1938 all existing MVSN badges had to have four laurel leaves added to each side of the disc to form a wreath, and all badges were changed (Bibl. 140).

The personnel of the Fascist youth organizations were distinguished by a round shield worn upon the fasces: the leaders wore embroidered cap badges while the youngsters wore white metal badges, which, from 1930 to 1937, bore the initials FGC; later they had the initials GIL.

Different cap badges were used by the Libyan branch of the Fascist youth: young children wore the fasces above a square shield bearing the unit's number; older members wore the shield placed above crossed rifles (Bibl. 143, 146).

1, 2. MVSN officers' badges used before 1927 3. 'Capo Squadra' 4. Rank and file 5. Officers M.1927 6. Colonial Militia other ranks 7. MVSN officers M.1938. 8. Fascist Youth leaders 9. Anti-Aircraft Militia other ranks 1931-35 10. MVSN Generals 11. Fascist Youth members 1930-37 12. Black Shirts Bns in Ethiopia, other ranks

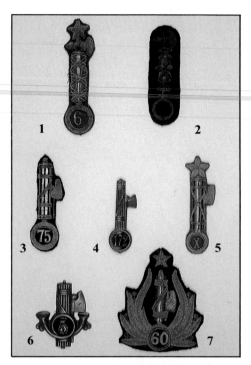

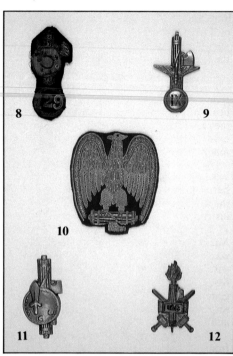

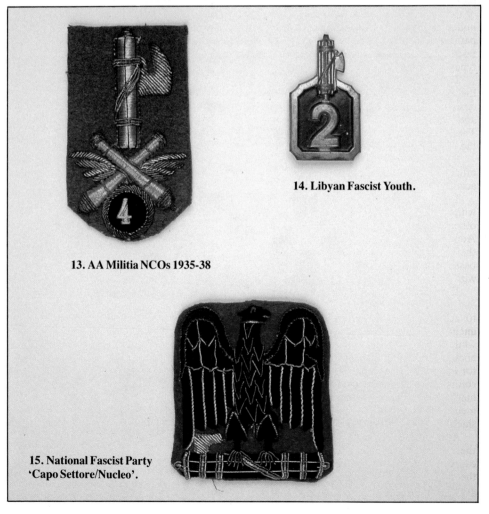

13. AA Militia NCOs 1935-38

14. Libyan Fascist Youth.

15. National Fascist Party 'Capo Settore/Nucleo'.

Italian Social Republic : After the Armistice of 8 September 1943 the Italian armed forces were reorganized in the north of Italy under the supervision of the Germans.

All the emblems of the House of Savoy, from the crown to the white metal stars, were removed from the uniforms of the new republican armed forces. In some instances this meant that the crown was cut off from an existing badge or completely new badges were made.

New dress regulations published in 1944 sanctioned the adoption of new cap badges, but lack of materials and ultimately the end of the war prevented the mass production of new insignia.

The MVSN was re-named *Guardia Nazionale Repubblicana*. A new cap badge was adopted, which depicted the old fasces with the axe head on the top flanked by two Ms; the badge was in gold and silver for generals, silver for warrant officers and sergeants and embroidered in red for the rank and file.

The Black Brigades were formed in 1944 from Fascist volunteers, and they were employed in anti-partisan warfare until the end of the war. The men did not wear a standard uniform as each brigade favoured a different pattern, and cap badges varied, ranging from fasces of different colours to skulls of different types and sizes.

The officers' cap badges of the navy and of the air force were similar in style, the basic design of both consisting of six leaves of laurel and four berries, surmounted by the crown. The centrepiece of the badges differed, as did the colour of the felt background.

A complete set of Royal Italian naval officers' cap badges consists of 14 pieces, according to class of rank and corps.

The Great Admiral had the royal crown with a gold cushion and purple base; flag officers with the rank of Admiral of Fleet or Admiral of Squad in command of a fleet had the crown with a purple cushion and purple base, and all the other officers had the crown with a blue cushion and base.

The badge in the centre of the oval shield and the colour of the shield varied according to corps. Officers of the line had the **foul anchor** on a blue velvet oval background, while officers of the naval corps wore the anchor combined with the corps emblem — for example, a gold five-pointed star for the commissariat, a three-bladed propeller for the mechanical engineers, a red cross for the medical corps — which was worn on an oval shield, the colour varying according to corps.

Although there were eight naval corps, there were only seven different badges because the officers of the port captaincy wore the foul anchor of the line, but on a grey-green shield.

The air force cap badge was adopted in 1923. Officers, warrant officers and sergeants had two sizes — large for wearing on peaked caps and small for the forage caps.

Generals, from the rank of General of Air Squad and above, and the Inspector General of the Aviation Engineers wore badges with a purple cushion in the crown, all the other officers, except chaplains, had a blue cushion. The chaplains had a violet cushion in the crown and a red cross on the chest of the eagle.

Flying personnel had cap badges with a plain laurel wreath, while the ground specialists had a disc below the eagle in which was displayed the speciality device. The engineers, for instance, had a Roman helmet and technical engineering assistants had the Roman helmet above a crossed hammer and axe.

Airmen's badges were embroidered in yellow silk, with and without the specialists' disc. The badges with the disc were abolished during World War II.

1. Commissariat officers for forage cap
2. Airmen 3. 'Guardia Nazionale Republicana' officers 4, 5. Black Brigades

1. Naval officers, Line 2. Air force officers, Air Crew 3. As 2, but for field service cap.

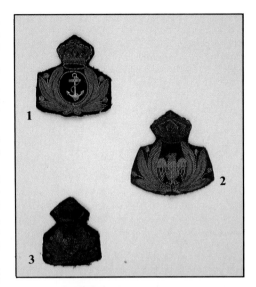

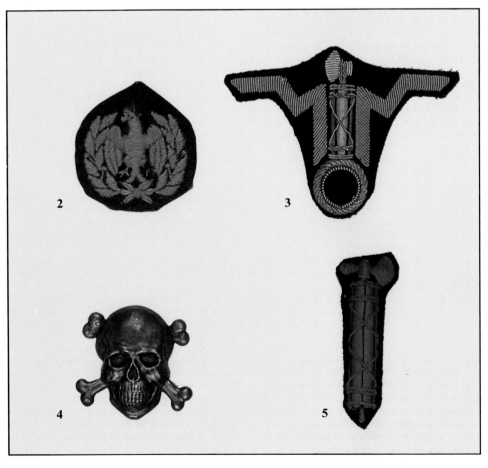

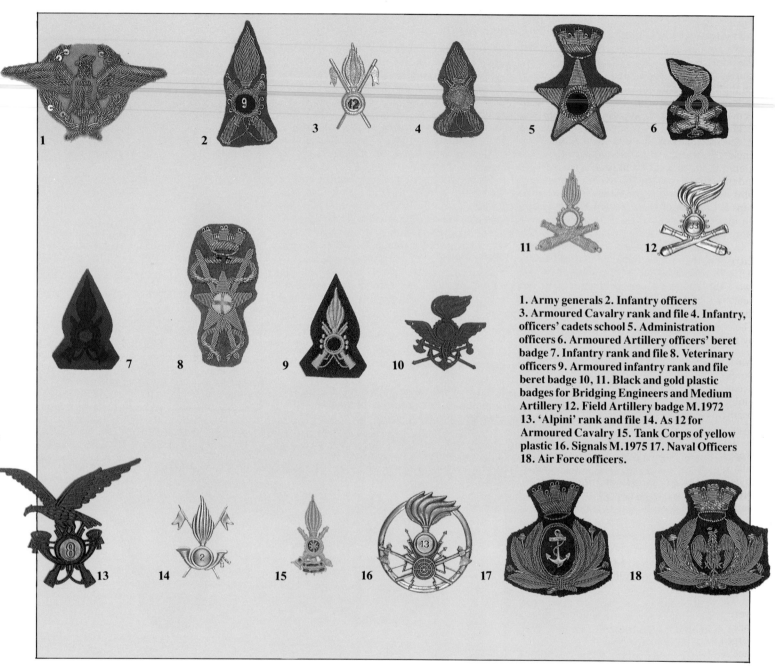

1. Army generals 2. Infantry officers
3. Armoured Cavalry rank and file 4. Infantry, officers' cadets school 5. Administration officers 6. Armoured Artillery officers' beret badge 7. Infantry rank and file 8. Veterinary officers 9. Armoured infantry rank and file beret badge 10, 11. Black and gold plastic badges for Bridging Engineers and Medium Artillery 12. Field Artillery badge M.1972 13. 'Alpini' rank and file 14. As 12 for Armoured Cavalry 15. Tank Corps of yellow plastic 16. Signals M.1975 17. Naval Officers 18. Air Force officers.

Italy, Republic of : After the 1946 referendum, Italy became a republic, and, in theory, all the royal emblems were abolished. However, no specific orders were issued to the armed forces until February 1948, when a few badge was introduced for generals and for the infantry, which had a straight flame in place of the crown. The crown was removed from all the badges that had one, and a new cap badge was adopted for the armoured cavalry. Subsequent instructions replaced the royal crown with the mural crown of the republic.

Officers, warrant officers and sergeants wore a large cap badge embroidered in gold on the peaked caps, with a smaller version for forage caps or berets. Armoured and motorized troops wore black berets with a gold or yellow badge on a black background. Until the early 1950s, the officers and warrant officers were still distinguished by a black disc under the regimental number, a custom that was later abandoned.

The cap badges of the rank and file were metal or machine embroidered in black on khaki or in yellow on black felt, according to the colour of the head-dress. Plastic cap badges appeared in the early 1950s, with three finishes, black, gold and yellow. A period of great confusion ensued, as battalions of the same regiment wore different types of cap badge until 1972, when white metal badges were adopted and the use of all previous badges was forbidden.

For the first time, the artillery, engineers and *Bersaglieri* were given 'white' badges. New badges, for all ranks, were adopted in 1975: these were larger and enclosed within a ring; initially they were made of white metal although later they were made of polished aluminium.

Except for the crown, the naval and air force cap badges have not changed. Plastic badges are used by airmen on their peaked caps and machine-embroidered badges are worn on the forage caps.

Japan

All ranks of the Imperial Japanese Army wore a five-pointed star on the head-dress, except the Imperial Guards, who had the star above a laurel wreath. A brass star was always worn on the peaked caps, and yellow cloth stars, of different manufacture, sewn on a round or pentagonal cloth backing, were worn on the field caps.

The naval officers wore the **foul anchor**, enclosed in a ring and surrounded by a gold embroidered laurel wreath, the whole surmounted by silver cherry blossom. The cherry blossom upon the anchor was used on field caps by officers and ratings; petty officers had an oval ring around the anchor; and seamen wore the anchor alone.

Luxembourg

All ranks of the Army of Luxembourg wear two crossed Cs ensigned by a crown on the head-dress. The initial stands for Charlotte, the former Grand Duchess of Luxembourg. The officers' cap badge is larger than that used by the other ranks.

Norway

A dual device, the national colours and, according to class of rank, the national emblem or a branch-of-service button were used by the Norwegian Army before World War I.

The blue, white and red national colours were in the form of a proper cockade, made of silk for officers and, although in the same style, larger and made of metal, painted in blue, white and red, for the other ranks. The national emblem, a lion holding an axe, is also shown on the button of the infantry. The Norwegian lion, which is used by officers, was and still is mounted on a semi-spherical, red background, but the cockade has developed into a metal roundel in enamelled or painted colours.

The two devices of generals and officers were joined by vertical strips of gold or silver lace, respectively; the devices worn by the sergeants were joined by strips of dark red lace up to 1934, later of green lace; while the rank and file wore the national colours and the branch-of-service button without any adjoining lace.

After World War II the Norwegian Army adopted the battledress and khaki beret on which all ranks wore the King's cypher within an oak wreath. The beret badges depict the cypher of King Haakon VII and of King Olaf V, in gilt for officers and white metal for other ranks.

Officers continued to wear the national colours and the Norwegian lion on the peaked cap of the service dress until the late 1950s, when a new cap badge was adopted: the lion surrounded by a wreath, the whole ensigned by the royal crown.

Japanese badge for the peaked cap

Officers' badge of the Luxembourg Army.

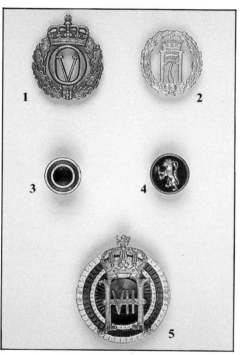

1, 2. Beret badge with the cyphers of King Olaf V and Haakon VII 3. National cockade 4. National insignia 5. Old cap badge with metal cockade.

The officers of the navy wear conventional naval cap badges — the anchor within a wreath surmounted by the crown. Petty officers have the crown above the **foul anchor**.

Poland

The white eagle has been the emblem of Poland since the late 18th century, and it is depicted in the centre of the cross of the *Virtuti Militari*, an order that was instituted in 1792 and still exists today. It appeared in various forms, and after 1807 the eagle was combined with the 'Amazon' shield for wearing on the *czapka* in the army of the Grand

1, 2. Examples of World War I badges 3. Pre-World War II badge 4. Cap badge made in Egypt 5, 6. Badges made in Britain.

Duchy of Warsaw.

The eagle perched on the shield reappeared during World War I, when it was worn as a cap badge by the various Polish legions in France, Russia and Austria. Until 1919 the shield was used to display regimental numbers, initials or other devices of the units it represented. However, the first Polish dress regulations, published in 1919, introduced the eagle on a blank 'Amazon' shield as the standard cap badge for all units.

Although the badge always depicts the eagle perched on the shield, there are innumerable different types, made in several countries including Poland, England and Egypt.

19, 20, 21. Examples of other Polish units' badges worn on the beret.

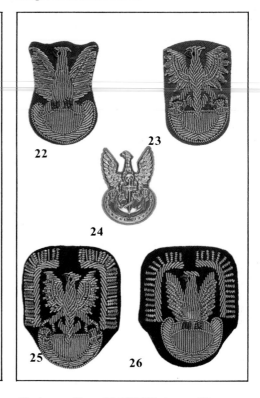

7. Woven cap badge 8, 9, 10. Examples of machine embroidered badges 11. Air force badge 12. 2nd Rifle Battalion.

13. 2nd Corps 14. HQ 1st Carpathian Rifle Brigade 15. 5th Battalion 2nd Carpathian Rifle Brigade 16. 8th Battalion 17. 9th Battalion.

22. Army officers M.1957 23. Army officers M.1970 24. Seamen 25, 26. As 22, 23 but air force.

Some eagles are fatter than others; some have a longer neck; some look to their right while others look upwards; some stand on the shield and others sit on it; and there are many variations in the wings.

When British Army badges were made in plastic during World War II, a plastic eagle was made for the Polish Army in Britain. Cloth badges made for use on the berets were machine embroidered in grey cotton on khaki for the khaki beret, in grey on black for the black beret or woven in grey on black silk.

A white metal badge was made in Britain during World War II for the Polish Air Force serving with the RAF. It is 46mm (1¾in) high, while the air force cap badge made in Poland according to the 1936 regulations was 60mm (2¼in) high.

After the German occupation of Poland a new Polish Army was formed in France, and two separate Polish armed forces were later organized, one, composed of refugees from Poland and France and volunteers from abroad, was organized by the British, the other, formed by ex-prisoners of war and volunteers, was organized in the Soviet Union. The men of both organizations wore 'foreign' uniforms, British or Russian, but with Polish insignia, and the army in the east gradually re-adopted Polish uniforms until, in 1945, except for minor details, officers and men wore the same uniforms as before the

war (Bibl. 156).

The army in the east adopted a new cap badge in 1943; it depicted the Polish spread eagle as shown on the flags, but without the crown. The old badge continued to be worn by the Poles in the west on the front of the head-dress, and many regiments and battalions also adopted a unit's insignia, which was usually worn on the left side of the forage cap or beret.

The personnel of the 2nd Rifle Battalion of the 1st Corps, which was based in Scotland, adopted a white metal badge on a patch of tartan. In 1946 a special badge was made in Italy for the personnel of 2nd Corps and for almost every battalion of the formations still in existence.

The headquarters of the 1st Carpathian Rifle Brigade, for instance, wore an edelweiss, and the 1st, 2nd and 3rd battalions of the brigade had the number 1, 2 and 3 on the stem of the edelweiss.

The headquarters of the 2nd Carpathian Rifle Brigade wore the badge illustrated, but with the centre blank, and the 4th, 5th and 6th battalions had the number in the centre of the badge. There was no cap badge for the 3rd brigade's headquarters, but the three battalions had their own badges: those of the 7th and 8th were similar, except for the number, which was all in white metal for the 7th battalion. The 9th battalion's badge depicted

the Polish eagle in flight and the arms of the city of Bologna, which the battalion entered first in 1945.

There are many other badges for different branches of service, often with coloured backings, and for the divisional support units. Many are self-explanatory. Most were made in 1946 and were used for a short time before the Polish Army's disbandment

People's Republic of Poland The present Polish armed forces are descended from the units raised in the Soviet Union during the war. Although the pre-war state was a republic, the conventional crowned eagle was retained, although after World War II the crown was abolished.

All ranks wore white metal badges until 1957, when embroidered cap badges were adopted for officers. In that year the traditional air force badge was reinstated, replacing the earlier, different badge, which had had a golden wreath.

A different type of embroidered cap badge was introduced in 1970 for the regular officers, although reserve officers continued to wear the 1957 pattern.

Naval officers wear the eagle on the 'Amazon' shield above a golden wreath of laurel, and the **foul anchor** on the shield. Seamen have the anchor on the Polish eagle, without the wreath, in metal (Bibl. 157).

Russia, Empire of
An oval cockade made of metal was used as a cap badge by all ranks of the regular army until 1917. It consisted of concentric rings of black and orange, the imperial colours taken from the ribbon of the Order of St George. The type and size of the cockades varied according to class of rank, but they were usually small, with or without an outer metal ring, for the soldiers.

Territorial troops, however, wore a cross, the arms of which were embossed with the motto 'For Faith, Tsar and Country' and which had the cypher of Tsar Nicholas II in the centre.

Serbia
Only officers wore cap badges, which took the form of an oval cockade made of metal and enamel. The colours were those of the Serbian flag — white, blue and red — and they were also used as the ribbon of several decorations and medals. The cypher of King Peter I was displayed in the centre of the cockade.

Spain
Until the end of the Civil War the branch-of-service badge worn by officers was the same as the badge worn on the collar, on the crown of the peaked cap and the rank insignia on the cap band.

During the Civil War, most units of the Republican Army wore the red star on the crown of the cap, and the branch-of-service badge was, therefore, moved to the cap band, where it was worn between two sets of rank stripes.

Many different types and sizes of branch-of-service insignia have been used, especially by the infantry; two different badges were worn by airmen, the first illustrated being used by the Republicans.

After the Civil War, a national type of cap badge, the same for all ranks of all branches of service was adopted; a large version was available for the officers' peaked cap, a smaller one for the other ranks.

Sweden
The Swedish armed forces are divided into four services: the army, the navy, the coast artillery and the air force. The army consists of field units, local units and the home guard.

The main head-dress insignia are the national cockade and the national button, both of which were adopted in 1865 and are known today as model 1865-1960. There are two cockades. One displays the national colours — yellow, light blue and yellow — and is made of enamel for officers or painted metal for the rank and file. The other is made of gilded brass, which is always worn in combination with the national button by the personnel of the army and coast artillery. The two

devices are joined by a gilded double bar, which is of a scalloped design for generals but plain for officers and other ranks down the rank of *Furir*. On their forage caps the *Korpral* and privates wear the national colours above the button or a disc displaying the company's number but without the adjoining bar. The colours of the disc and of the number identify the branch of service:

	Disc	Number
Infantry	yellow	gold
Cavalry	white	gold
Armour	yellow	black
Field Artillery	red	gold
Air Defence Artillery	light red	gold
Engineers	black	gold
Signals	green	gold
Transportation Supply	blue	gold

Some regiments are entitled to wear the 'straw garland' around the disc. This garland is a yellow ring, in the form of a woven garland of straw, 5mm (¼in) wide, which protrudes around the edges of the disc. It was adopted in 1833 in honour of the memory of the battle of Lund, fought against the Danes in 1676.

The buttons used by officers are semi-spherical and made of blue enamel with a gilt base and three gilt crowns. The buttons worn by the warrant officer and sergeants are silvered and those used by the *Oberfurir* and *Furir* are made of gilded brass.

Regimental badges are worn on the left side of the forage cap, 45mm (1¾in) from the front and 20mm (¾in) from the top edge of the curtain.

A special version of the cockade and button badges is used on the cap of field

1. Russian Army NCOs' cockade 2. Cap badge of territorial troops.

1, 5. Infantry 2, 3. Badges for peaked cap and forage cap 6. Aviation.

uniforms by all except the rank and file, who wear no badges at all on this type of head-dress. Generals have the same badges as on the forage caps.

Between 1952 and 1960 different badges were worn on the field and fatigue caps. The national cockade in colour and the national button, the pattern varying according to class of rank, were placed upon an oval patch of cloth. Rank insignia was also shown on the patch in the form of chevrons for the officers, warrant officers and sergeants, and in the form of short stripes for the others.

Army personnel entitled to wear peaked caps have a badge on the cap band. Illustrated is the pattern worn by warrant officers and sergeants; the officers' badge is similar, but it has the blue enamel button in the centre, while the cap badges of the *Oberfurir* and *Furir* have a gilt button and do not carry a wreath.

Before 1952 the badges were generally made of bronze, and these badges were different in style as modifications to insignia were made in 1952, and in 1960 further changes were introduced.

The personnel of the coast artillery wear different insignia, but, as they use the same type of head-dresses as the army, their cap badges vary according to class of rank as do those of the army.

Navy personnel wear the typical naval cap insignia — the foul anchor within a wreath, the whole ensigned by the crown. Petty officers wear the usual oval ring instead of the wreath. Swedish navy badges are distinguished by three small crowns, one of which is worn at each side and one at the bottom of the anchor.

All ranks of the air force wear the peaked cap and the forage cap with a winged, two-bladed propeller at the front, ensigned by the crown (Bibl. 160).

7. 14th Infantry regiment 'Kungl Halsigne Regt' 8. 19th Infantry Regiment 'Kungl Norrobottins Regt' 9. M.1952 field/fatigue cap badge of 2nd Lieutenant.

Turkey
The Turkish cap badges depict the star and crescent as on the national flag.

Officers' badges display a wreath of oak leaves below the crescent, and air force officers have a white metal eagle inserted into the crescent, under the star.

The other ranks' badges have the crescent and star only, and could be made of metal or embroidered on to a backing in branch-of-service colour.

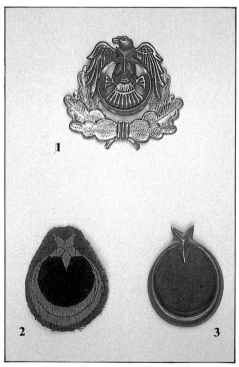

1. Air force officers 2, 3. Army other ranks badges in cloth (Artillery – Engineers) and metal (Infantry).

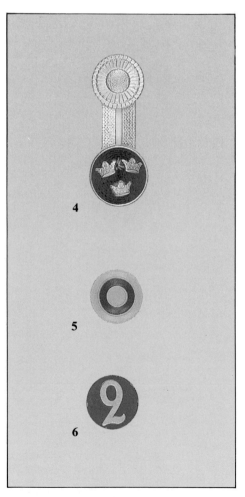

1. Army warrant officer and sergeants' pre-1952 2. Coast artillery officers pre-1952 3. Army warrant officer and sergeants 4. Officers' forage cap badge 5, 6. Privates' forage cap badges

1. Army officers 2. Army enlisted men 3. West Point Academy 4. Marine Corps officers 5. Coast Guard Cadet.

1. M.1922 Red Army cap badge 2. Aviation wings 3. M.1955 Soviet Army officers 4, 6. Other ranks 5. Naval officers.

United States of America

The officers and enlisted men of the US Army and Air Force wear on the peaked cap the American eagle as it appears in the coat of arms of the United States.

Officers have used several different types of badge, varying in size up to a maximum height of 75mm (2¾in) and slightly differing in design. The badges are made of brass or gilded brass for the US Army and the US Army Air Force, and, more recently, of white metal for the officers of the US Air Force.

Enlisted men wear the eagle on a brass disc, and since the air force became an independent service, airmen have worn the eagle in white metal within a narrow outer ring.

The cadets of the West Point Academy wear the Academy's coat of arms on the head-dress and on the lapels of the collar. On their peaked caps bandsmen wear the lyre surrounded by a wreath of laurel.

The emblem of the US Marine Corps was introduced in 1868. The officers' cap badges have the rope of the anchor made of twisted metal wires, while the rope of the badges worn by enlisted men is struck as part of the badge. When worn on the blue and white peaked caps, officers' badges are made of silver and gilt, but dress cap badges of enlisted men are made of brass, while the badges used on the service dress cap by both officers and enlisted men are made of bronze.

Naval officers wear a two-metal cap badge, which depicts the spread eagle of the US Navy above the stars and stripes, which are superimposed upon two crossed **foul anchors.**

There are many other naval cap badges, including those of the US Coast Guard, and those for warrant officers, petty officers, mid-shipmen and cadets of both the US Navy and the Coast Guard. The cap badge of a cadet of the US Coast Guard is illustrated.

Soviet Union

The phrase 'Red Army' was the usual abbreviation for the Red Army of Workers and Peasants, which was its official title until 1946 when it was changed to Soviet Army. Initially, the red star displayed in its centre the hammer and plough. The plough was changed to the sickle in 1922, however, and was used as a cap badge by all ranks until 1940.

In 1940 a special badge was introduced for the Marshal of the Soviet Union and for the generals. This new badge depicted a smaller star mounted in the centre of a round gold **boss.** Aviators had an additional wreath of gold laurel leaves around the boss, and the star and wings on the crown of the peaked cap. All the other ranks continued to wear the red star until the 1950s.

From 1943 onwards embroidered oak or laurel leaves were worn on the dress cap by marshals and generals, respectively. In 1949

7. Soviet Navy petty officers

the use of the boss within the laurel wreath was extended to officers of the air force for wearing both in dress and ordinary uniforms.

A series of modifications, which led to the introduction of the modern insignia still used today, began in 1955 with the adoption of the oval cap badge for all officers. The new badge was, and is still, worn on the dress cap in combination with different types of metal backings, in imitation of embroidery; the backings vary according to service and class of rank. Air force officers retained the laurel wreath around the new badge when it was worn on the peaked cap of the ordinary uniform.

In 1958 the use of the wreath, which is similar to that used by naval officers, was extended to the officers and senior non-commissioned officers for the cap of the dress uniform, and an oxidized cap badge, greenish-khaki in colour, was adopted for the cap of the officers' field uniform. A gold wreath was later added to the red star of the rank and file for wearing in dress and walking out uniforms.

Modern cap badges are now made of anodized aluminium. The difference between the modern red star and the star used 40 years ago should be noted.

On their peaked caps, naval officers wear the foul anchor on a boss, surrounded by a wreath of laurel leaves and ensigned by the red star. Gold badges are used by officers of the sea branch, and silver badges by those of the services. Petty officers have the anchor enclosed in an oval ring, ensigned by the red star.

The naval red star has a white centre, on which stands the hammer and sickle.

Yugoslavia

Kingdom of Yugoslavia The Kingdom of Serbs, Croats and Slovenes became an independent nation after World War I. As Serbia, the leading partner among the three territories, was already an independent state, a Serbian type of cap badge, but with inverted colours, was adopted for the armed forces. The colours of the Serbian cockade were, from the outer ring, white, blue and red, while the colours of the Yugoslav cockade were red, white and blue.

The **cypher** of King Peter I was used on the Serbian cockade; Yugoslav cockades bore the Yugoslav eagle or the cypher of the reigning sovereign. Officers wore cockades made of metal and enamel with the cypher or the eagle; non-commissioned officers wore a padded cockade made of cloth and embroidered without any additional device; the rank and file did not wear cap insignia.

In 1941 Yugoslavia was invaded by the German and Italian armies, and King Peter II formed a provisional Yugoslav government in Britain. Meanwhile Colonel D. Mihailovic, later a general, began the resistance movement in Yugoslavia in competition with the Communist organization led by J. Broz, later to become known as Marshal Tito.

A new Yugoslav Army was organized in Britain by the government in exile, and Mihailovic's men, who were known as *Chetniks*, became officially the Royal Yugoslav Army 'at home'.

The government in Britain issued dress regulations by which new cap badges were adopted. These badges depicted the two-headed Yugoslav eagle ensigned by the crown, within a wreath for officers and without the wreath for other ranks.

The badges made in Britain had the king's cypher on the chest of the eagle, while those used by the army 'at home' did not. Coloured patches of cloth or velvet were placed behind the cap badges to identify branch of service:

Generals	light grey-blue
General Staff	red
Infantry	deep red
Cavalry	blue
Artillery	black
Engineers	plum violet
Economic Service	green
Doctors and Veterinaries	brown

These branch-of-service colours were used by the Yugoslav Army before the war.

As the supplies directed to the *Chetniks* dwindled during the course of the war, they wore whatever uniforms were available, often without any insignia, even wearing civilian clothes. Toward the end of the war, the *Chetnik* cavalry favoured fur hats with the skull and crossbones of the *Waffen* SS at the

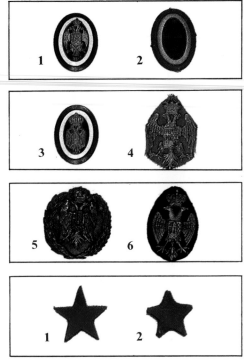

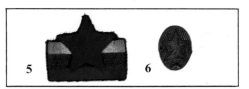

1, 3. Officers 2. NCOs 4, 5, 6. Wartime badges
1, 2, 3, 4. Yugoslav red stars of wartime
5. Slovenian units 6. Police 7, 10 Army officers
of proletarian formations, for peaked cap and
for forage cap 9, 12. As 7, 10 but of normal
formations 8, 11. Large stars for other ranks
14. Generals' badge for forage cap 13, 15, 16,
18. Small stars for other ranks' forage cap
17. Air force officers.

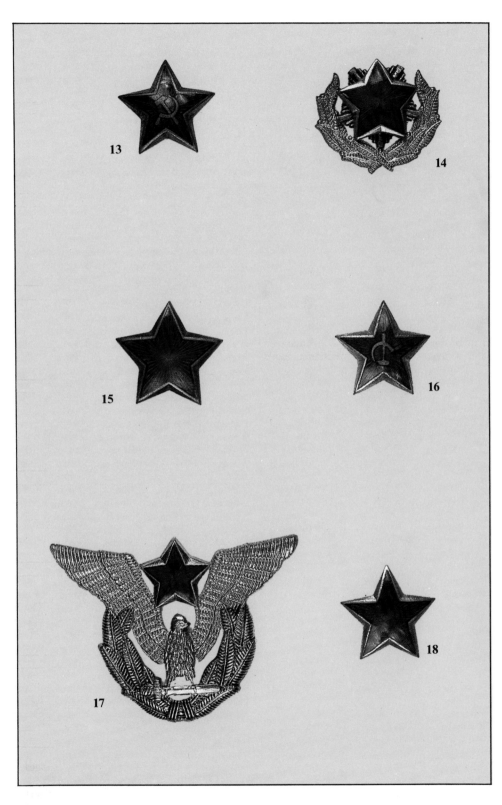

divisions, and divisions joined to form army corps, which were grouped into armies. Nevertheless, few formations were issued with standard uniforms until the end of the war, and although the first official insignia were adopted in November 1941, all these badges were made locally, cut out from felt.

All ranks wore the red star on the head-dress, the commissars (political officers) having the hammer and sickle embroidered in its centre. Red stars, often with uneven points, were usually stitched directly on the cap; others were sewn on a thick felt backing; and some were even padded underneath the red cloth. Some units wore the star above a small regional flag.

Metal badges appeared toward the end of the war, and were often roughly made, consisting, for example, of a metal base covered with some sort of red paste.

For a short time after the war, army and police personnel wore the red star on an oval cockade, but the cockade was discarded in favour of the plain star for other ranks and the star on an ornamental base for the officers. The generals obtained the officers' badge within a wreath of gold laurel leaves.

Some army formations deriving from proletarian brigades and divisions that fought with distinction during the war obtained, and still retain today, the prefix 'proletarian' as a special honour, and all ranks wear the hammer and sickle in the centre of the red star.

There are now four basic types of cap badges: the large badges are worn on peaked caps by officers or other ranks qualifying for this head-dress; the small pattern for officers is used on the forage cap; and the small stars, on either a brass or white metal base, are worn on the forage caps by soldiers.

On their peaked caps the officers of the air force wear an eagle holding a sword above a laurel wreath, the whole ensigned by the red star. Navy officers and petty officers wear conventional naval cap badges, the foul anchor and wreath or anchor within the oval ring, respectively, both surmounted by the red star.

CAP BAND The phrase is generally used to refer to the lower part of the peaked cap. The band may be plain, made of the same cloth as the rest of the cap or covered by another 'band' of cloth or woven material. Coloured cap bands may identify a class of rank or a branch of service.

British Army generals, for instance, wear scarlet cap bands, while the border guards of the German Democratic Republic have green cap bands.

Coloured piping may serve the same purpose, and stripes (*see* Distinction lace) or other devices may be placed on the cap band to identify rank or class of rank.

front.
Federal Socialist Republic of Yugoslavia : On 4 July 1941 the Central Committee of the Yugoslav Communist Party launched the 'armed struggle against the Axis occupation

forces', which marked the constitution of the first units of the Partisans' Army. These first units grew into battalions, and on 21 December 1941 the 1st Proletarian Brigade was formed. Brigades were later grouped into

1. Chevron of 'Caporal-chef' of the French Foreign Legion, for right sleeve 2. British Army Corporal or Bombardier 3. US Army Corporal M.1948 4. Italian Sergeant, World War II pattern made of metal 5. USAAF Airman 1st Class 6. Italian Fascist Youth 'Giovane Fascista Scolto' 1938-41.

CHEVRON In heraldic terms, a chevron is a figure on a shield representing two rafters that meet at the top. In a military context, the word refers to the rank insignia often used to identify the ranks of non-commissioned officers, usually the sergeants and corporals. Chevrons could also identify, according to national customs, re-enlistment periods, long service, wounds, periods of overseas duties or special appointments.

As only the chevron that is pointing upward may correctly be called a chevron, the other type should be called a V or inverted chevron. The French and the US Armies use chevrons to identify sergeants and corporals. The French Army used **bars**, which are still worn in certain circumstances, but after the adoption of the **branch-of-service insignia** on the sleeve, chevrons that fit above the diamond-shaped insignia on the left sleeve have been introduced, and they are worn on their own on the right sleeve.

Sergeants and *marechals des logis* have chevrons of gold or silver lace, according to branch of service, and the corporal chief, or *brigadier chef*, wears two coloured chevrons and a gold or silver one above them. Corporals and privates 1st class wear one and two coloured chevrons, respectively. (It should be noted that the hierarchy of the lower ranks is constantly developing, and the ranks mentioned may not be in use in future years.)

In the US Army both the chevrons and the hierarchy of rank have been modified several times since 1945. At that time, the chevrons of the olive drab (khaki) uniforms were embroidered on dark blue felt, and embroidered or woven in light sandy colour on a dark blue background for the summer shirt. By the late 1940s, the chevrons were machine embroidered on twill material. By the time of the Korean War, however, smaller chevrons woven in dark blue on yellow were used, and yellow chevrons on army green background were adopted in 1957 when the new army green uniforms were introduced.

The technicians' chevrons were abolished in 1948 and replaced by specialists' chevrons, which were also modified and later changed twice.

When the US Army Air Force became an independent service and adopted blue grey uniforms, it adopted new rank insignia for enlisted men.

The Turks use the same type of rounded V chevrons, but with the star and crescent in the centre and of different manufacture, in yellow on khaki for the non-commissioned officers of the regular army and in red on khaki for conscripted personnel.

The familiar British V chevrons, which were worn in two world wars, were changed in the 1960s to a smaller size and to a new pattern, machine embroidered on felt. Smal-

7. US Army Technician 5th Grade, World War
II 8. Irish Army Company Sergeant M.1963
9. Conscripted seamen of the German
Democratic Republic 10. Turkish Army
Sergeant Major 11. US Army Sergeant 1st Class
M.1957.

ler chevrons of anodized metal are used on the summer shirt.

Italian sergeants wear one large together with one narrow stripe of gold lace; sergeant majors wear one large and two narrow stripes. Corporal and corporal majors wear one large and one or two narrow stripes of black or, in 1939-45, red lace. The chevron illustrated was made of brass. The *Carabinieri*, who are deployed as civil and military police, always had silver or red chevrons, of the same type as the army, but in addition the rank of private 1st class was indicated by one narrow red chevron.

The traditional colours of the city of Rome — crimson and golden yellow — were adopted by the Fascist youth organization in the 1930s, and they were often shown in the badges. The V-shaped chevron illustrated was used from 1938 to 1941 (Bibl. 143).

The 'winged' Irish chevrons were adopted in the early 1950s, and they were originally slightly larger, 12mm (½in), than the pattern shown. The hierarchy of rank was also modified in 1961: the battalion sergeant major and quartermaster sergeant obtained red bands on the shoulder straps, thereby simplifying the rank insignia of the lower ranks. The private of 1st, 2nd and 3rd class wears embroidered red stars edged in yellow (Bibl. 125).

The regular seamen of the German Democratic Republic wear two yellow V chevrons on the forearm; conscripted seamen wear one only.

CHINSTRAP A chinstrap is a strap attached to the lower sides of the head-dress and worn under the chin to keep the head-dress in place. The chinstrap may be shortened by means of two sliding buckles and may be worn horizontally on the front of the head-dress.

The helmets worn in the 19th century were often fitted with chinstrap scales, chains or coloured chinstrap cords that had a purely decorative purpose, and a separate leather chinstrap was often used as well, either underneath the decorative device or placed inside the head-dress.

Plain leather chinstraps were adopted at the beginning of the 20th century by most armies for the cap of the field uniform, but even the leather chinstrap became merely a fitting of the cap and served no useful purpose.

Some organizations opted for chinstrap cords, which varied according to class of rank. These are divided into two patterns — single or double. The manufacture of the individual cord varies from the twisted type to plain woven cord, and the chinstrap cords may be flat or round.

The type of the Italian officers' chinstraps identifies class of rank, and the lace stripes on both outer ends identify individual rank.

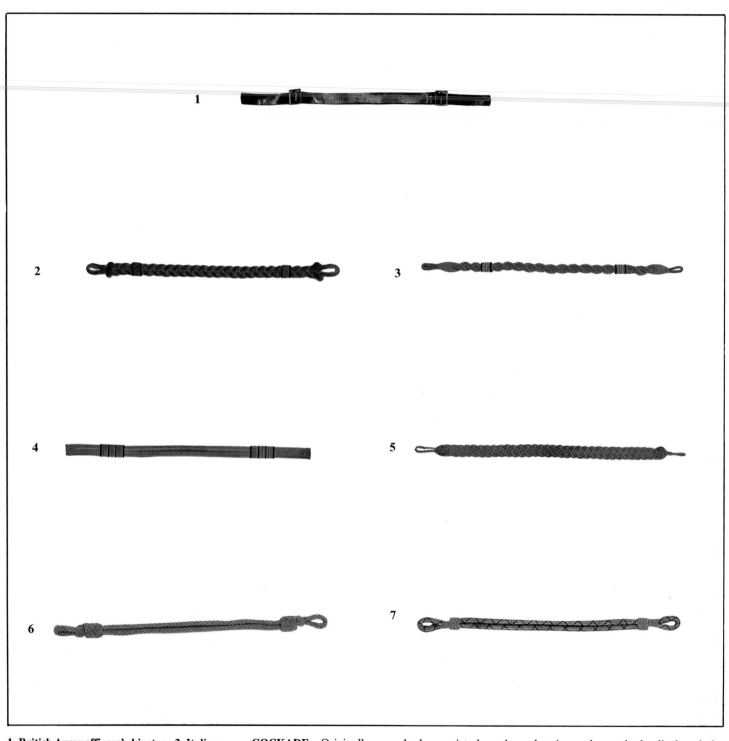

1. British Army officers' chinstrap 2. Italian Army Brigadier General 3. As 2 but for Major 4. As 3 but for Captain 5. Yugoslav 6. Officers 'Volksarmee' 7. Italian.

COCKADE Originally a cockade consisted of a bundle of coloured ribbons worn on the head-dress and resembling a cock's comb, from which it takes its name. Toward the end of the 18th century, the cockade developed into a round, pleated device, which was obtained by gathering together a strip of ribbon on one side only and stretching it on the other, thus forming a round or oval shape. If the cockade was made of ribbon with horizontal coloured stripes, the cockade displayed the colours in the form of concentric rings.

Cockades have been made of cloth, silk and leather; they may be round or oval in shape; and imitations of pleated cockades have been made of painted metal or metal and coloured enamels. Metal and enamel badges are now widely replaced by plastic and other synthetic materials.

COLLAR INSIGNIA Until the end of the 19th century most armies displayed coloured collars that identified the branch of service of the wearer. It was the penultimate stage in the evolution of the field of branch-of-service identification, the last stage being the adoption of collar patches, or collar badges, which permitted the mass production of uniforms that were the same for all soldiers.

In many countries, according to national custom, rank badges were also worn on the coloured collar, and in this case the rank badges were later transferred on to the collar patches (*see* Rank insignia).

Austria-Hungary

The Austro-Hungarian Army's rank insignia and regimental- and branch-of-service insignia were worn on the collar and are practically indivisible.

The peace-time establishment of the infantry of the line consisted of 102 regiments, which were identified by their facing colour, *Egalisierungs-farbe*, combined with that of the buttons:

Facing colour	Button colour			
	Austrian Regiments		Hungarian Regiments	
	Yellow	White	Yellow	White
black	14	58	26	38
white	94	92	—	—
dark brown	93	7	12	83
reddish brown	55	17	68	78
light brown	100	98	—	—
madder	15	74	44	34
dark red	1	18	52	53
carmine red	84	81	96	82
amaranth red	90	95	86	—
cherry red	73	77	43	23
Bordeaux red	89	88	—	—
scarlet red	45	80	37	39
lobster red	35	20	71	67
light red	57	36	65	66
pink	13	97	5	6
orange yellow	59	42	64	63
yellow	27	22	2	31
sulphur yellow	99	41	16	101
steel green	56	47	48	60
grass green	8	28	61	62
apple green	9	54	85	79
seaweed green	102	—	—	—
sea green	21	87	70	25
parrot green	91	10	46	50
sky blue	4	3	32	19
light blue	40	75	72	29
pike grey	30	49	76	69
ash grey	11	24	51	33

According to this scheme, only four regiments wore the same colour of facing, two with yellow and two with white buttons, and therefore only one Austrian and one Hun-

garian regiment had the same facing colour and the same colour of button; they could be distinguished by the different cap badges and details of the uniforms and, of course, by the language the soldiers spoke.

All infantry regiments raised after the drafting of this scheme wore light blue facing colour and white buttons. The other branches had the following colours:

Branch	Facing	Button
Generals	scarlet red	gold
General Staff	black velvet with red stripe at the end of the patch	gold
Jäger	grass green	yellow
Schützen	grass green	white
Artillery	scarlet red	yellow
Engineers	cherry red	yellow
Train	light blue	white
Medical	madder	yellow
Signals	black	silver

After the introduction of the pike grey (light blueish grey) field uniform in 1909, the facing colours on the collar, cuffs and piping of the blue tunic were reduced to the form of patches, worn on the front of the collar of the new tunic in combination with rank insignia. Initially this tunic had a stand collar, but later stand-and-fall collars were introduced, and they required a larger patch. The collars had concealed buttons but, as the officers' and non-commissioned officers' rank insignia were based on the colour of the button, the regimental number could still be identified. The lace on the collars of the field officers and non-commissioned officers and the stars worn by the other officers were gold or silver according to the colour of the buttons (*see* Rank insignia).

Some special devices were worn on the collar behind the rank insignia: for example, signalmen had a winged wheel, mountain troops had an aluminium edelweiss and bandsmen wore the lyre, but at the front of the collar, before the rank insignia.

In 1915 the colour of the field uniform was changed to field grey, and by 1917, because of the shortage of materials, collar patches were replaced by strips of coloured cloth sewn vertically behind the rank insignia.

All ranks had spearhead-shaped patches in branch-of-service colour on the collar of the greatcoat; the officers' pattern was worn with a button, the other ranks without.

Austria

1933-1938 : The uniforms of the Bundeswehr

of the Republic of Austria were similar in style to those of the former Imperial Army. Coloured patches, which, as before, identified the branch of service, were sewn on the collar of the tunic together with stripes of lace and stars that identified the rank of the wearer. The colours of the patches did not change, although black was added for the tank troops.

1955-1986 : The jacket of the modern Austrian uniform has an open collar, and new patches shaped to fit the angles of the collar are therefore worn.

The collar patches identify branch of service and rank as before, and a strand of twisted gold or silver cord around the outer edges of the patch identify the officers' or non-commissioned officers' class, respectively (*see* Rank insignia). This edging is displayed on the spearhead collar patches worn on the greatcoat, and a button is worn by all ranks.

Only two badges are worn on the collar patches of the jacket — the lyre of the bandmaster and the cross of the chaplain — and both are appointment badges, used in lieu of rank insignia. In some cases one colour is superimposed upon another, leaving an 8mm (⅓in) wide chevron of a different colour at the top of the patch. This secondary colour is called piping.

The plain collar patches worn by privates are shown to illustrate the type and shape of the patches only. Their colours, in relation to branch of service, are as follows:

Branch	Patch	Piping
Generals	scarlet red	—
Artillery		
Air Force (Ground)		
Guards Battalion	scarlet red	white
Tank Troops	black	—
General Staff	black (velvet)	scarlet red
Doctors	black	light blue
Veterinaries	black	madder
Pharmacists	black	cherry red
Infantry	grass green	—
Armoured Infantry	pink	—
Reconnaissance	golden yellow	—
Air Force (Flyers)	cherry red	—
Engineers	steel green	—
Signals	brown	—
Medical	light blue	—
Supply	dark blue	—
NBC	pike grey	—
Commissariat	carmine red	green
Administration	light blue	cherry red
Technicians	dark red	brown
Chaplain	violet	black

Belgium

After the introduction of khaki uniforms in 1915, the coloured collars, strips and piping previously worn were simplified into collar patches, which had, and still have, the dual purpose of identifying the branch of service and the rank of the wearer (*see* Rank insignia).

The shapes of the collar patches depend on the type of collar on which they are placed: rectangular patches were worn on the stand collar of old tunics, and they are still worn on the collar of the modern dress tunic; pentagonal patches fit the open collar of the jacket; and diamond-shaped patches were used on the stand-and-fall collars seen on the British-style battledress.

The collar patches, taken in conjunction with a series of metal or embroidered devices — badges, initials and numbers — worn on the collar and on the shoulder straps of the tunic and of the greatcoat, identified also the regiment or unit and, often, the higher formation to which the unit may be attached.

Only metal or embroidered badges were worn on the collar of the greatcoat, but these were necessarily also worn on the tunic collar, where the colours of the patch already served the same purpose.

The rules related to the displaying of insignia have been modified several times during this century. The following scheme lists the collar patches prescribed by the 1939 Regulations (Bibl. 42).

Generals of arms wore black collar patches with amaranth piping and the *foudre* above rank insignia, while generals of the services had the patches and badges (instead of the *foudre*) of their own branches of service. General staff officers wore the *demi-foudre* above rank insignia on patches of their own branches of service.

	Patch	Piping
Infantry of the Line	scarlet	royal blue
Grenadiers	scarlet	royal blue
Carabiniers	deep green	yellow
Chasseurs on Foot	deep green	yellow
Chasseurs Ardennais	deep green	scarlet
Carabiniers Cyclists	deep green	yellow
Frontier Cyclists	scarlet	royal blue
Guides	amaranth	green
Lancers	white	royal blue
Chasseurs on Horse	yellow	royal blue
Light Regiments	royal blue	scarlet
Artillery	royal blue	scarlet
Engineers	black	scarlet

Chaplains did not wear collar patches; they wore only the badge of their faith on the collar of the tunic and of the greatcoat. Catholics wore the Latin cross, Protestants the Maltese cross, while Jewish rabbis had the Star of David.

The scheme lists only patches and devices that referred to a specific branch of service, but some branches included specialities. The gunners of the 7th (Motorized) Corps, for example, wore on the collar of their greatcoats a cog wheel set above crossed cannons, and those attached to cavalry or armoured formations wore the crossed cannon and a horse shoe. Anti-aircraft personnel had a special badge, which depicted a torch above crossed cannons and two wings as a background.

Ground personnel of the air force had a propeller on the collar of the greatcoat, and motor transport personnel wore a motor car wheel.

The end of World War II found the Belgian Army wearing British battledress and with a few new branches of service inherited from the British Army.

	Patch	Piping
Parachutists	maroon	sky blue
Commandos	black	white
Signals	black	green
RASC	ultramarine	orange
REME	black	orange
RAOC	grey	amaranth
Military Police	scarlet	white
Security Sections	deep green	black
Chaplains	purple	—
Royal Military School	royal blue (velvet)	scarlet
Cadets School	royal blue (velvet)	scarlet

The RASC, the REME and the RAOC were amalgamated to form the *Corps Logistique*, which wore light blue patches with amaranth piping, and more recently the medical corps of the three services have been amalgamated to form the *Service de Santé des*

Type of Austro-Hungarian Army collar patch for field uniform used during World War I and readopted after the war 2. Strip of regimental or branch − of − service colour used towards the end of World War I 3. Type of collar patch adopted in 1955 4. Great-coat collar patch.

Armées, the personnel of which wear bottle green uniforms and different insignia from the rest of the armed forces.

Branch-of-service badges are not now worn on the collar of the greatcoat.

Collar patches are issued in large format and then cut to a basic size of 50mm (2in) high, 30mm (1¼in) at the base and 35mm (1½in) at the widest point. Officers wear larger patches to accommodate stars and bars, and often a branch-of-service badge is worn as well, and a higher patch has to be wider to accommodate it (Bibl. 43).

The officers could wear either general issue or privately purchased patches, the latter usually padded and with embroidered rank devices.

1. Belgian Commandos 'Capitaine-Commandant' 2. Uncut collar patch as issued 3. Engineers Warrant Officer 4. Logistical Service 5. Infantry of the Line 6. Cyclists 7. 'Chasseur Ardennais'.

Britain

Illustrated is a set of metal collar badges of the North Staffordshire Regiment (The Prince of Wales's), which gives an indication of the numerous variations of badges that have been used by an average regiment of the British Army.

The first three badges on the left show the pattern used from 1895 to 1904 by regular officers, other ranks and militia, respectively. The militia was identified by badges in inverted metals, the volunteers by silver or white metal badges.

In 1904 the design of the regimental collar badges was changed. There were at least four variants of officers' badges in gilt and silver, with different types of knot, with solid or voided feathers and with silvered or gilded scrolls. Bronze badges were worn on the officers' khaki service dress. At first a larger badge was adopted that was similar in style to the other ranks' pattern, which is made of white metal and brass. By 1904 all metal badges worn by officers conformed to the same style; service dress badges were made initially of bronze, but later of brass and painted brown.

Until October 1880 officers wore rank insignia on the collars of their tunics and the other ranks had a plain collar in facing colours (Bibl. 60). In 1881 collar insignia as an alternative means of regimental and branch–of–service identification were adopted. At that time most regiments opted for collar badges displaying the main regimental device that was already shown on the cap badge, but a few took the opportunity to display a secondary device. The King's Regiment (Liverpool), for example, adopted the Lancashire rose, although in 1895 the device was changed to the horse of Hanover. The design was changed again in 1925, and in the 1950s the badges were made in anodized aluminium or staybrite. The Essex Regiment had two badges, one depicted the sea-axes from the country's coat of arms, and the other consisted of the eagle, which, in 1900, was worn by officers on the mess jacket (Bibl. 50).

In 1896 the magazine *The Regiment* published a list of regimental collar badges, and the Regulation of 1900 described them in detail. Different types of collar badges were used on different uniforms according to regimental custom. There were embroidered badges, often worn horizontally on the stand collar; for example, the badge of the Princess Victoria's (Royal Irish Fusiliers) consisted of two devices, the princess's coronet and the fusiliers' grenade. The officers wore also gilded and silver-plated badges, often made of solid silver or embellished with enamel details. In many regiments, the collar badge worn by officers on their service dress was as large as the cap badge.

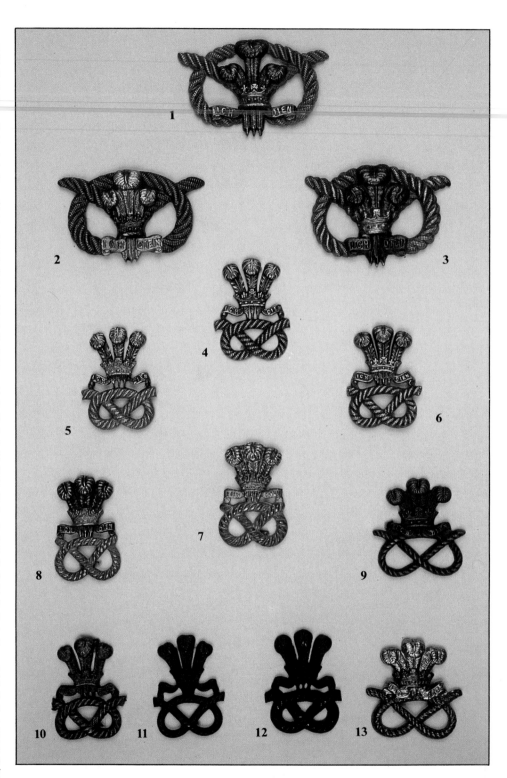

Collar badges of the North Staffordshire Regiment (The Prince of Wales's): 1, 2, 3. First pattern with the Prince of Wales's plume, 1895–1904 4. Volunteers 5, 6, 7, 8. Variants of officers' dress collar badges made of gilt and silver 9. Officers' khaki service dress badge, 1st pattern 10, 11, 12. Variants, and pattern 13. Other ranks' collar badge. The plain Stafford knot was worn before 1895 by the North and South Staffords and a new badge was adopted in 1959 after the amalgamation of the two regiments (see page 124).

1

19

29

2 3 4 5 6 8

24 25 26 27 28

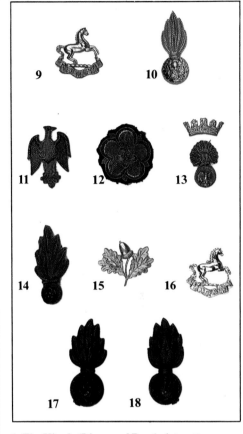

9 10 11 12 13 14 15 16 17 18

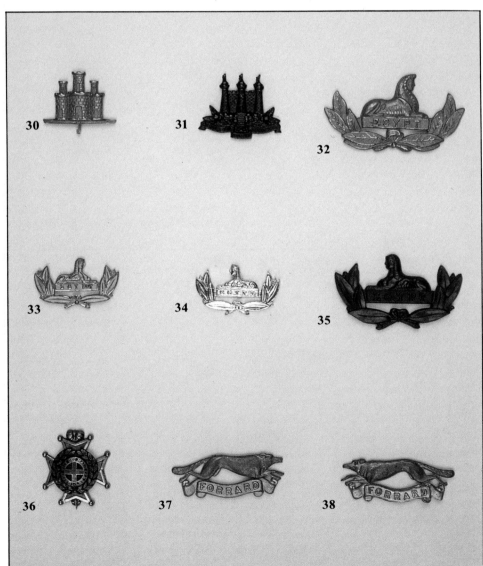

30 31 32 33 34 35 36 37 38

1. The King's (Liverpool Regt), 1st pattern
2. The Princess Victoria's (Royal Irish Fusiliers)
3. The Essex Regiment 4. The King's (Liverpool Regt), 2nd pattern 5. The King's Regiment (Liverpool), 3rd pattern 6. The West Yorkshire Regiment (The Prince of Wales's Own) 7. The Royal Hampshire Regiment 6th (Duke of Connaught's Own) Battalion 8. The Essex Regiment.

9. The King's Regiment (Liverpool) 10. The Royal Dragoons 11. 1st The Royal Dragoons 12. The Lancashire Hussars 13. The Princess Victoria's (Royal Irish Fusiliers) 14. The Royal Fusiliers (City of London Regt) 15. The South Nottinghamshire Hussars 16. The King's Regiment (Liverpool) 17, 18. The Royal Welch Fusiliers.

19. The Hampshire Regiment 20, 21, 22, 23. The Green Howards (Alexandra Princess of Wales's Own Yorkshire Regt) 24. The Buffs (Royal East Kent Regt) 25, 28. The Monmouthshire Regiment 26, 27. The Royal Berkshire Regiment (Princess Charlotte of Wales's).

29. The Cambridgeshire Regiment 30. The Suffolk Regiment 31. The King's Own Scottish Borderers 32, 33, 34, 35. The Gloucestershire Regiment 36. The Royal Sussex Regiment 37, 38. The East Riding Yeomanry.

123

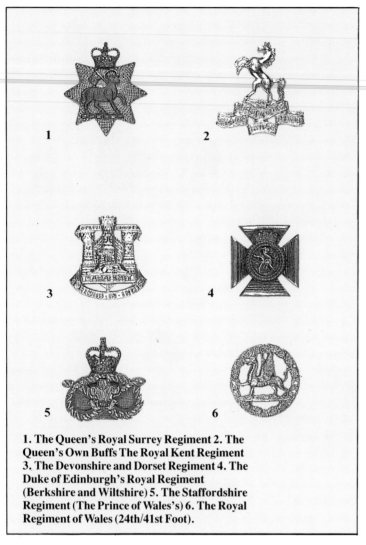

1. The Queen's Royal Surrey Regiment 2. The Queen's Own Buffs The Royal Kent Regiment 3. The Devonshire and Dorset Regiment 4. The Duke of Edinburgh's Royal Regiment (Berkshire and Wiltshire) 5. The Staffordshire Regiment (The Prince of Wales's) 6. The Royal Regiment of Wales (24th/41st Foot).

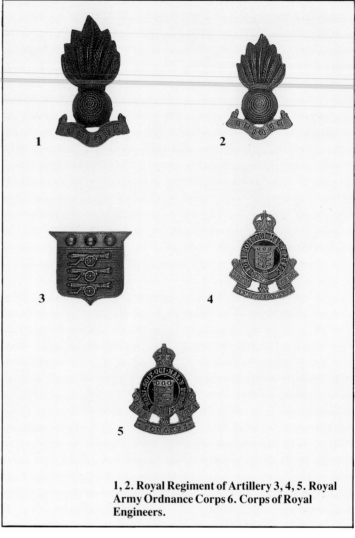

1, 2. Royal Regiment of Artillery 3, 4, 5. Royal Army Ordnance Corps 6. Corps of Royal Engineers.

Some badges may be difficult to identify. There were different types of dragons — the dragon of the Buffs (Royal East Kent Regt), the dragon of the Monmouthshire Regiment and the Chinese dragon worn by the Royal Berkshire Regiment (Princess Charlotte of Wales's). Some collar badges depicted castles — the castle and key of Gibraltar belong to the Suffolk Regiment, the castle bearing the arms of Ely belongs to the Cambridgeshire Regiment, and Edinburgh Castle was shown in the badges of the King's Own Scottish Borderers. The sphinx could be shown as a male or as a female.

A few examples of post-1958 collar badges are illustrated. All are regimental insignia, although some were worn in combination with a brigade's cap badge. The Queen's Royal Surrey Regiment was formed in 1959 by the amalgamation of the Queen's Royal Regiment (West Surrey) and the East Surrey Regiment. The officers' badge shows the lamb from the former regiment set on the crowned star background that belonged to the East Surreys.

The Queen's Own Buffs, the Royal Kent Regiment, was formed in 1961 by the amalgamation of The Buffs (Royal East Kent Regt) and the Queen's Own Royal West Kent Regiment. Buffs remained in the title, but their dragon disappeared, only to reappear in 1966 on the cap badge of the Queen's Regiment, which was formed from the battalions of the Home Counties Brigade. At that point, however, the lamb was sacrificed, and the new collar badge displays the prancing horse of Kent on the eight-pointed star above the Roussillon plume.

The next two badges were used as regimental collar badges by battalions of the Wessex Brigade; subsequently both became regiments of the Prince of Wales's Division, and the same devices, but larger, were adopted as their cap badges. The Devonshire and Dorset Regiment was formed in 1958 by the amalgamation of the Devonshire Regiment and the Dorset Regiment. The badge shows Exeter Castle of the Devons and the battle honours

of the Dorsetshire Regiment. The Duke of Edinburgh's Royal Regiment (Berkshire and Wiltshire) was formed in 1959 by the amalgamation of the Royal Berkshire Regiment (Princess Charlotte of Wales's) and the Wiltshire Regiment (Duke of Edinburgh's), and the badge displays the former officers' badge of the Royal Berkshires surmounted not by the crown but by the ducal coronet on the cross *patté* of the Wiltshires.

The Staffordshire Regiment (The Prince of Wales's), formed in 1959 by the amalgamation of the South Staffordshire Regiment and the North Staffordshire Regiment (The Prince of Wales's), was part of the Mercian Brigade, and later, as a regiment, it became part of the Prince of Wales's Division. The collar badge is still in use, and the cap badge depicts the Stafford knot surmounted by the Prince of Wales's plume.

Also illustrated is the collar badge of the Royal Regiment of Wales (24th/41st Foot), which was formed in 1969 by the amalgamation of the South Wales Borderers and the

7, 8. Corps of Royal Engineers 9. Special Air Service Regiment 10. Royal Army Pay Corps 11. Army Territorial Service 12. Army Educational Corps.

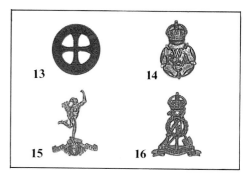

13. Women's Transport Service 14. Women's Royal Army Corps 15. Royal Corps of Signals 16. Royal Pioneer Corps.

Welch Regiment, from where it got the immortelles and the Welsh dragon. The regiment retained the cap badge of the Welsh Brigade.

The badges of the territorial infantry and yeomanry units have changed considerably since 1947, when the TA was re-formed following the reorganization and amalgamation of regiments. Many badges, both old and new, have disappeared.

The collar badges of both the Royal Regiment of Artillery and the Royal Corps of Engineers depict the flaming grenade, and the badges of both, especially those worn on officers' service dress, are similar in shape and size, except that the grenade of the gunners has seven flames while that of the sappers has nine.

The Royal Army Ordnance Corps had four types of badges: the Ordnance shield was used as a collar badge until 1920; the title scroll was carried at the bottom of the cap badge. The second and third patterns to be used are illustrated by the two dress collar badges worn by officers, while yet another pattern was adopted in 1949.

The badge of the Royal Army Pay Corps was adopted in 1920, and in 1929 it was changed to the Royal Crest above a title scroll. The Army Educational Corps was instituted in 1920 and wore the same badge, larger in size as a cap badge, from 1927 to 1951.

The women's organization, the First Aid Nursing Yeomanry (FANY), first raised in 1909, was redesignated Women's Transport Service in 1933 and absorbed in 1939 in the Auxiliary Territorial Service (ATS), which had been formed in 1938. In 1949 it was redesignated the Women's Royal Army Corps. The cap badge of the ATS displayed the initials surrounded by a laurel wreath and surmounted by the crown; the WRAC has the initials ATS replaced by a lioness.

The second pattern of the badges worn by the Royal Corps of Signals, which was used after 1947, and the collar badge of the Royal Pioneer Corps are illustrated.

Czechoslovakia

During World War I Czechoslovak volunteers fought for their country's independence in Russia, France and Italy, while most of their countrymen were drafted into the Austro-Hungarian Army. The first Czechoslovak units were formed in Russia and France from ex-prisoners of war. The 39th Czechoslovak Infantry Regiment was formed in Italy, and by 1918 two Czechoslovak divisions, the 6th and the 7th, operated on the Italian front.

These units wore different badges and several types of collar patches. The 21st Rifle Regiment in France had a blue patch edged in red, with the regimental number in gold for officers and in red for soldiers. White and red horizontal stripes in rectangular patches with blue edging all the way round were used in Italy, often with two crossed rifles at the front. Spearhead-type patches were worn by the units in Russia: cherry red for the infantry, scarlet for the artillery, orange for the intendants and white, edged in red, for the cavalry.

The post-1918 Czechoslovak Army wore khaki uniforms, and coloured patches were worn by all ranks on the tunic collar. Generals and general staff officers had two-pointed collar patches, generals having a device of lime leaves embroidered in gold wire. The lime leaves had previously adorned the collar patches of generals of the Czechoslovak units in France, and they were later displayed on the patches of the army of the Protectorate of Bohemia and Moravia and re-adopted in the army of the Socialist Republic after 1945. The chaplains had rectangular patches, rounded at the top back end, and all the others, officers and other ranks, wore smaller patches fitting on the front of the collar.

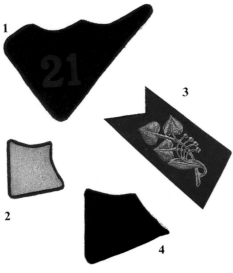

1. 21st Rifle Regiment, for greatcoat 2. Czechoslovak Cavalry in Russia 3. General of Arms, pre-World War II 4. Ordnance (Administrative) pre-World War II.

By the late 1930s the following patches were worn:

	Patch	Piping
Generals of Arms	carmine	—
Generals of Services	branch-of-service colour	—
General Staff	carmine	—
Infantry Mountain Infantry Frontier Troops Cyclists Tanks	cherry red	
Artillery Mountain Artillery Motorized Artillery	scarlet	
Cavalry Armoured Cars	yellow	—
Engineers Railway Engineers	dark brown	—
Signals	light brown	—
Doctors	black*	cherry red
Veterinary	black*	yellow
Pharmacist	black*	dark blue
Chaplains	black*	white
Commissariat	dark blue*	dark blue
Administration	dark blue*	brown
Supply	dark blue	—
Ordnance (Technical)	scarlet	grass green
Ordnance (Adminis- trative)	grass green	scarlet
Geographical Service	light green	—
Legal Service	violet*	—
Recruiting Service	yellow ochre	cherry red
Army Records	grey	yellow ochre
*denotes velvet		

The engineers of the Technical Service had grass green patches with dark brown piping, while the Service's signal officers had light brown piping around their grass green patches. The other ranks of the Ordnance wore the scarlet patches of the Artillery, and medical orderlies had plain black collar patches. Grey patches with different colours of piping were used by officers clerks; for instance, legal clerks and wardens had violet piping in accordance with the violet patch worn by the Legal Service.

The generals' device of lime leaves and another four badges were worn on collar

Modern collar badges: 1. Infantry 2. Artillery 3. Anti-Aircraft 4. Armour 5. Aviation 6. Parachutists 7. Engineers 8. Signals 9. Chemical 10. Motor Transport 11. Railway Transport 12. Road Service 13. Building Service 14. Topographical Service 15. Medical 16. Provisions and Fuel 17. Legal 18. Administrative 19. Military Music 20. Border Guards, in brass for officers, silver for NCOs and bronze for rank and file.

patches: an eagle on a cliff top by the mountain troops; a dog's head by the Frontier troops; a bicycle wheel by the cyclists; and an arrow within a ring by the tank troops. The badges were in gilt for officers, silver for non-commissioned officers and bronze for the rank and file. Several other branch-of-service badges and regimental numbers were worn farther back on the collar in line with the shoulder straps (Bibl. 26).

Socialist Republic of Czechoslovakia After 1948 the armed forces were reconstructed within the structure of the Warsaw Pact, and this called for a certain uniformity of insignia.

Collar badges were adopted to identify branch of service. The badges were in gold for officers, silver for warrant officers and sergeants and brown for the other ranks. In all there are 20 badges, one for each of the 19 branches of service, plus the badge of the Border Guards, an autonomous organization that still wears its pre-war insignia.

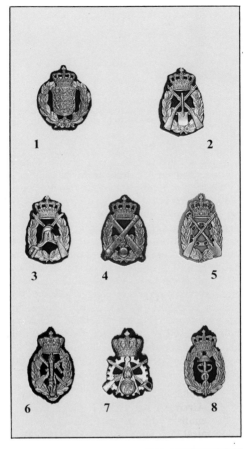

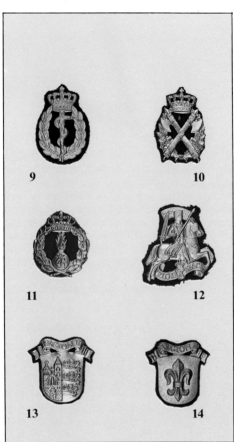

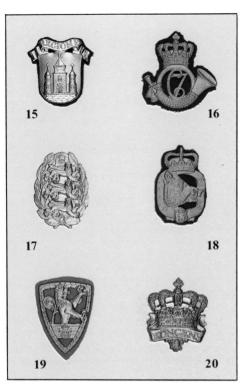

1. Generals 2. Inspector General of Infantry
3. Inspector General of Armour 4. Inspector
General of Infantry 5. Inspector General of
Engineers 6. Inspector General of the Home
Guard 7. Army Ordnance Corps 8. Finance &
Quartermaster Corps 9. Medical Corps
10. Legal Corps 11. Army Material Command
12. 3rd Division 13, 14, 15. 3rd, 4th and 6th
Home Guard Region 16. Rangers 17, 18, 19, 20,
21. 4th, 3rd, 5th, 9th and 10th Infantry
Regiment 22, 23, 24, 26. 1st, 2nd, 3rd and 4th
Field Artillery Regiment 26, 27. Jutland and
Zealand Anti-Aircraft Artillery Regiment 28,
29. Army Troops and Infantry at Bornholm 30,
31. Zealand and Jutland Engineers 32. Jutland
Transport.

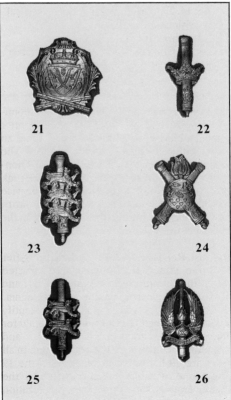

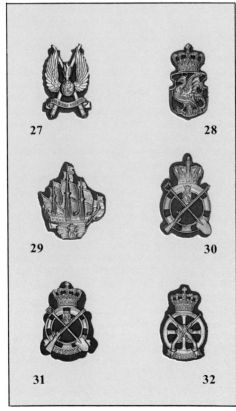

Denmark

Regimental and branch-of-service badges to
be worn on the collar by units already in
existence were introduced in 1948; others
were introduced as new units required badges.
Many are still in use today, although some
have been abolished or have changed their
unit's title following the reorganization of the
army.

The badges are of brass or gilding metal,
and they are worn on coloured felt backings
(*see* Backing) that vary according to the
precedence of the battalion or unit. Some are
made in pairs and face inwards; others are
identical and may be worn on either the right
or the left of the collar.

Generals wear a smaller version of the
beret badge on the collar of their jackets (*see*

Cap badge), and the inspector generals of the corps have their own collar badges, some examples of which are shown.

The personnel of divisional headquarters wear divisional badges on their collars. There are three divisions: the badge of the 2nd Division depicts St George killing the dragon; that of the 3rd Division depicts a knight in armour; and that of the 6th Division is a coat of arms.

Some branch-of-service badges are also shown.

Each of the eight home guard regions has a self-explanatory badge, the emblems on the shields being taken from local coats of arms; the emblem of the 3rd region, for instance, comes from the arms of Ribe; the fleur-de-lis of the 4th region from the arms of Odense; and the emblem of the 6th region is from the coat of arms of Copenhagen.

The Rangers wear the crowned bugle with the cypher of King Christian VII in the centre. The ten infantry regiments of the army were simply numbered from 1st to 10th and were not given any additional title. The badge of the 4th Infantry Regiment bears two cyphers, that of King Christian IV at the top and the cypher of Frederick VI at the bottom.

The four regiments of the field artillery, the 1st, 2nd, 3rd and 4th regiments, have different collar badges, as do the Anti-Aircraft Artillery Regiments of Zealand (Sjaelland) and of Jutland. The troops stationed on the island of Bornholm wear two collar badges, the Army Troops wear a griffin and the infantry have a galleon.

Each branch of the Engineers, Signals and Transport troops is divided into two regiments, of Zealand and Jutland. Therefore there is a badge for the Engineers Regiment of Zealand and another, which has the title *Jydske* in the scroll, for the regiment of Jutland.

The original titles of the units that have worn these badges is given; many are still in existence but others have been disbanded or converted to other roles. The badge of the 10th Infantry Regiment, for example, is now used by the staff of the 2nd Jutland Brigade, and the badge originally worn by the 1st Field Artillery Regiment is today worn by the *Kronens Artilleriregiment*. The badge of the 2nd regiment is now worn by the Zealand Artillery Regiment, those of the 3rd and 4th regiments are now used by the North and South Jutland Artillery Regiments respectively.

The anti-aircraft regiments no longer exist, but the same badges are still worn by the personnel of the anti-aircraft units stationed in Zealand and in Jutland.

The royal cyphers on the badges show under which king the regiment was created.

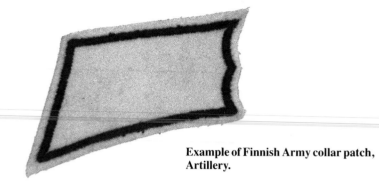

Example of Finnish Army collar patch, Artillery.

Finland

In the Finnish Army branch of service and rank are identified by collar patches. The colours of the patches, of their frame and additional embroidered devices — fir twigs for officers and senior sergeants — identify the branch of service. The type of frame and the presence or absence of embroidered fir twigs at the front of the patch identify class of rank (*see* Rank insignia).

The colours shown on the patches are as follows:

	Patch	Embroidery
General Staff	crimson	grey
Infantry	deep green	grey
Jägers	deep green	yellow
Cavalry	yellow	grey
Artillery	red	black
Engineers	purple	grey
Signals	purple	yellow
Armour	black	grey
Service Corps	blue	grey
Chaplains	black	gold or purple
Cadets	blue	yellow

These are the combinations of colours used by the main branches of service, some of which were changed after World War II. Tankmen, for instance, used to wear black patches with orange embroidery, and chaplains had black and grey patches. The coast artillery had black patches with red embroidery, and they have been abolished in favour of the basic artillery patches of red with black embroidery.

Officers of the services wore, and still wear, patches of the same colour as the unit to which they are attached, but their branch-of-service badge replaces the fir twigs. In the service corps this rule applies only to officers with a university degree.

Several patches of schools and other organizations have been abolished or changed, and some new ones have been recently adopted for the personnel of the battalions.

France

All ranks of the French Army displayed branch-of-service insignia, in the form of coloured patches, on their collars, until the post-World War II years, when diamond-shaped patches were adopted for use on the left sleeve by the other ranks. Officers and warrant officers now wear pentagonal patches on dress and service dress uniforms only.

The type of officers' collar patches worn before World War I was also used in the 1930s on dress uniforms. Generals were distinguished by gold or silver embroidery, which varied according to branch of service, and officers wore coloured patches that, in combination with the colour of the collar, identified the branch of the wearer. Gold or silver embroidered numbers or badges indicated the unit or speciality. Before World War I the same system of branch-of-service identification was used by the other ranks, but the numerals and badges were coloured.

New collar patches were adopted for the horizon blue field uniform that was introduced in 1915. The patches were similar in shape to the previous pattern, but, since the collar, like the rest of the uniform, was horizon blue, the colour of the patch and of the stripes of braid sewn on its outer end became the only means of branch-of-service identification. Infantrymen, who formed numerically the bulk of the army, wore their regimental number on horizon blue patches, which had dark blue stripes of braid (Bibl. 17).

The patches worn on the greatcoat were cut to fit the points of the collar. The regimental number or badge was set in the centre, and the braid above was in the form of a chevron, as were the patches illustrated, which, however, belong to a later period.

Khaki uniforms were adopted in November 1921 (Bibl. 98), but, as large stocks of horizon blue cloth were still available, the army was not fully clothed in khaki until 1937. Meanwhile, the pattern of the other ranks' field tunic was changed in 1920, the stand collar being replaced by a stand-and-fall collar so that the collar patches could be standardized to the shape already used on the greatcoat. A similar tunic, but khaki and with only six buttons at the front, was adopted in 1935.

The average size of the corporals' and privates' collar patches was 80 or 90mm (3¼–3½in) wide and 80mm (3¼in) high, and they were made of melton (a felt-like cloth) or of velvet with numbers or badges, or sometimes both, cut out from cloth or made of metal. The stripes were of woollen or rayon Russian braid, sewn at the top of the patch. Some patches had embroidered stripes, numbers and badges; the embroidery was usually machine work.

Most patches had two stripes of braid. However, those of the fortress units of the Alps, the motorized *cuirassiers* and dragoons, the reconnaissance groups and the artillery repair groups had three stripes. On the other hand, the patches worn by medical orderlies, administrative clerks, personnel of the supply train and of the cavalry remount and by the 'workers' of artillery and tank depots had no stripes of braid.

Certain branches of service were entitled to two or even three, different types of collar patches, according to the type of uniform on which they were worn. On their walking out tunics, for example, motorized dragoons wore patches with three stripes, two of white braid and one of violet, and a red number, while their field uniform patches had two white stripes, a white number and a white, five-pointed star at the bottom.

Officers, warrant officers and sergeants, who wore tunics with a narrower stand-and-fall collar, had narrower patches, and officers also wore an open-collar jacket on which they had pentagonal patches, with stripes of braid as the other ranks, but with gold or silver embroidered numerals, badges or numerals and badges.

Germany

Third Reich : The *Litzen* or double bars worn on the collar became standard insignia for all ranks of the German Army in May 1919, and they assumed particular importance during the period of the Third Reich as a means of branch-of-service identification.

The general officers of the army, except those of the *Wehrmachtbeamte*, wore the general's gold-embroidered device on a scarlet background; the generals of the *Wehrmachtbeamte* (administrative officials) had a dark green background to the embroidery and an additional colour in the form of an edging to the patch.

The double bars of the officers and of the other ranks were always placed upon a backing of cloth that fitted the front of the stand-and-fall collar in use at that time. These collar patches could be divided into two types. The dress uniform patches were embroidered in silver for all officers (except those of the *Oberkommando der Wehrmacht* (OKW) or *Oberkommando des Heeres* (OKH) staff), embroidered or in silver lace for other ranks, but always on a cloth backing in the branch-of-service colour. The undress patches for

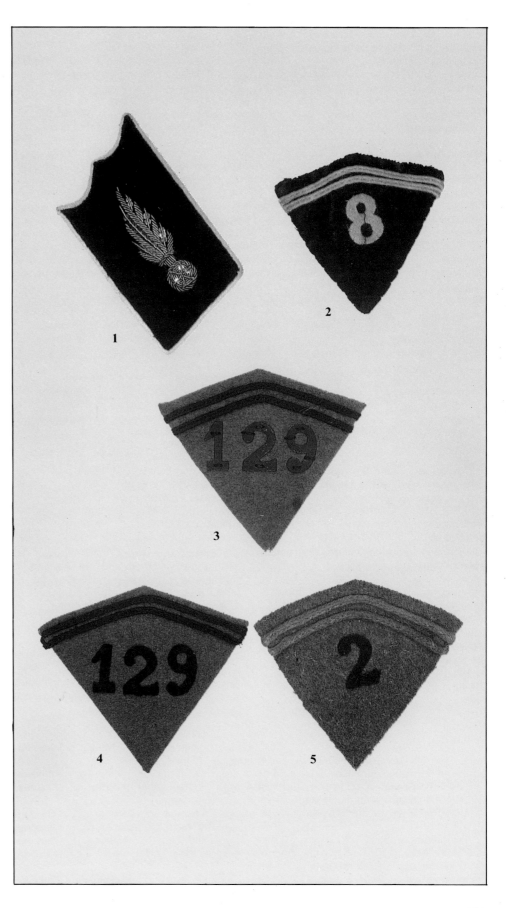

1. Engineers, Administrative officer, pre-World War I 2. 8th Engineers Regiment 3, 4. 129th Infantry Regiment, with metal or cloth number 5. 2nd African Light Infantry Regiment.

service or field uniform, which were embroidered in silver or in grey cotton, were on dark bluish-green backing.

Staff officers of the OKW and OKH had special collar patches embroidered in gold, and those of the general staff had special bars, but in silver.

The personnel of tank units wore a special style of black uniform; the black collar patches had a pink edging and the skull-and-crossbones badge.

The following branch-of-service colours were used by the regular army:

Infantry	white
Mountain Troops	green
Armoured Infantry	grass green
Cavalry	golden yellow
Artillery	scarlet
Engineers	black
Signals	lemon yellow
Armour/Anti-Tank	pink
Motorized Reconnaissance	brown
Smoke Troops (Chemical)	dark red
Medical	blue
Transport/Supply	light blue
Recruiting Service/Field Police	orange
Veterinary/General Staff	carmine
Specialist Officers	grey-blue

The officers of the *Wehrmachtbeamte* had dark green **Waffenfarbe** behind the double bars or generals' device, and an additional coloured edging, according to branch of service, at the sides and back of their collar patches.

The following secondary colours were used to identify the officials' branch:

carmine	Headquarters' Officials, Surveyors, Meteorologists, Archivists, etc.
white	Paymasters
golden yellow	Remount
scarlet	Administration
black	Engineering Technicians
pink	Supply of clothing
light brown	Training Specialists
dark red	Court Officials
light green	Pharmacists

Some colours corresponded to the main branch-of-service colours, blue being used by hospital officials and orange by recruiting staff officials. Chaplains' collar patches were violet with gold or silver double bars, according to class.

The quality of the collar patches, particularly those worn by the rank and file, deteriorated during the course of the war, until eventually plain grey woven double bars were

worn on a field grey patch or, more usually, sewn directly on the collar.

Naval detachments that served on land, at coastal defences or on other semi-permanent assignments wore field grey uniforms with double bars on the collar.

The collar patches worn by personnel of the air force identified branch of service and rank. Branch of service, except for the highest ranks, was shown by the colour of the patch, and rank was indicated by wreaths and other devices embroidered or pinned on to the patch.

All officers' collar patches had a narrow edging of twisted cords, which were of gold for generals and silver for the other officers, according to the colour, gold or silver, of the rank insignia they wore on the patch. Non-commissioned officers had a stripe of lace along the front and the outer side of the patch.

White was used to identify the class of rank of air marshals and generals, and it was also used by the personnel of the Hermann Göring Tank Division. Other branch-of-service colours were:

General Staff	carmine
Flying Personnel/ Parachutists	golden yellow
Signals	golden brown
Anti-Aircraft Artillery	scarlet
Medical Corps	dark blue
Air Ministry (until 1939)	black
Construction Troops (after 1939)	black
Air Traffic Control	light green
Engineering Corps	pink
Administrative Officials	dark green

The Hermann Göring Tank Division was part of the air force, and, as a tribute to Göring, the commander-in-chief of the air force, from April 1943 its personnel wore white collar patches with coloured piping around the edges as follows:

Rifle Regiments	grass green
Tank Troops	pink
Artillery	scarlet
Engineers	black
Signals	golden brown
Field Police	orange

Officers of the reserve had additional light blue piping around the collar patches and within the twisted cords.

Instead of the wings, other badges could be worn on the collar patches: three-pointed stars were worn by the administrative officials; two-, three- or four-bladed propellers were used by the personnel of the engineering corps; and the lyre, together with wings, was worn by the musicians of the air force.

National Socialism : During the 1930s the

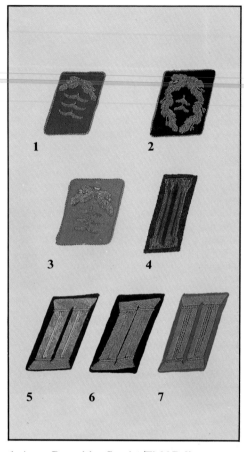

1. Army Recruiting Service/Field Police
2. Anti-Tank 3. Signals 4. Rank and file tattoo
World War II pattern 5. Air Force Flying
Personnel/Parachutists 6. Medical officer
7. Anti-Aircraft.

NSDAP (German National Socialist Workers' Party) embraced many affiliated organizations, including the structure of the state administration. Starting with the Hitler Youth and the German students' association, teachers' associations, women's associations, workers' associations and many others became part of the symbolic pyramid led by Adolf Hitler.

Uniforms and insignia proliferated, as every association wore its own, and collar patches, which usually identified the type of association or service and the appointment of the wearer, were particularly numerous.

The best known collar patches are those of the *Schutzstaffel*, an organization that traced its origins to the para-military squads raised in Germany in the early 1920s. Initially the SS was divided into two branches, the *Stabswache* (Staff Guard), which developed into the *Waffen* SS, and the *Totenkopfverbände* (Death's Head units), which became a political police. By 1939, however, the *Totenkopf-*

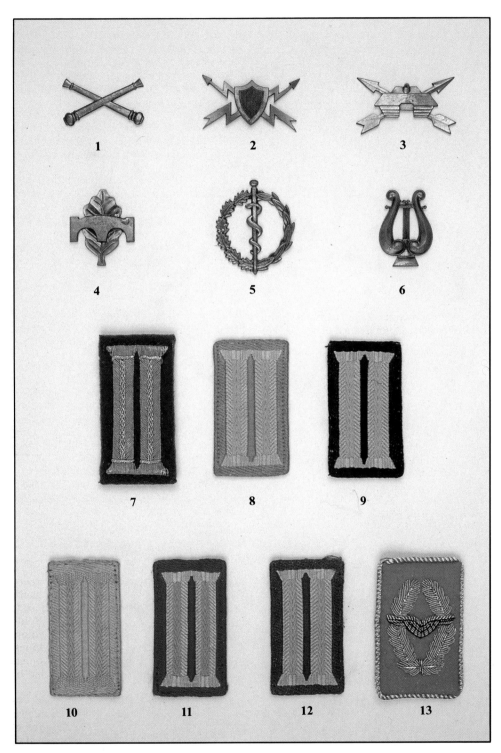

Examples of 'Bundeswehr' collar badges:
1. Artillery 2. Signals 3. 'Panzerjäger'
4. Engineers 5. Medical 6. Band. Collar
patches: 7. Armoured Infantry 8. Armour
9. Engineers 10. Signals 11. ABC Defence
12. Technical Troops 13. Air force.

1. National Railways 2, 3. SS and 'Totenkopf'
collar patches.

(*See* Rank insignia).

The patches were adopted in 1933, modified in 1934 and again in 1942. The latest pattern had an edging of twisted silver cords and silver embroidered devices for officers. The other ranks had no edging and grey machine-embroidered devices. The SS runes were worn on the right collar patch by most units, except for *Totenkopf* regiments and units composed of foreign volunteers, which displayed their own national devices.

Federal Republic of Germany : The dress regulations of July 1955 prescribed metal branch-of-service badges for the army personnel of the new *Bundeswehr*.

Generals retained their traditional gold embroidered patches, and double bars of general staff pattern were re-adopted for the staff officers, although they were embroidered on a rectangular grey, later carmine, background.

Collar badges were made of solid metal with a brownish, old gold finish. There were 14 in all, of self-explanatory design. The tank troops had a side-view of a tank, and medical personnel wore the caduceus on a wreath; both were made in pairs, so that the tanks and snakes would face outwards. All the other badges were made singly. Personnel of the armoured infantry should have worn a tank above crossed sabres, which should not be confused with *Panzerjäger*, and reconnaissance troops that had a shield on crossed lances, but as collar badges were used for only a short time these two badges were never worn.

verbände also provided a fighting formation, the *Totenkopf* Division. The organization was later definitively divided into the *Waffen* SS and the *Allgemeine* SS, which carried out territorial duties.

Collar patches on the right showed the unit while those on the left the rank, of the wearer. However, from the rank of colonel upward the rank insignia was displayed on both sides

The collar patches of the armoured infantry, anti-tank and quartermaster were subsequently abolished, as the first two branches became part of the infantry and adopted its patches. Green patches are also worn by rifle units, grenadiers and mountain and airborne troops.

The officers wear silver embroidered double bars, which are slightly longer than those of the other ranks and machine woven in grey directly on the coloured background (Bibl. 27).

Air force personnel wear 'grey-blue uniforms and air force insignia; their collar patch is yellow, with the air force's wing above a wreath.

Democratic Republic of Germany : All ranks of the *Nationale Volksarmee* wear collar patches of traditional German style.

Germans have the traditional gold embroidered devices; they are on a red background for those of the army and anti-aircraft defence, on green for the generals of the border guards and on bluish green for the officers of air rank of the air force.

All ranks of the ground forces wear on the collar of the tunic double bars set on a padded patch of cloth, the colour of which matches that of the uniform. The officers' double bars are made of white metal, finished in imitation of embroidery, with a **gimp** in branch-of-service colour in the centre of each bar. The other ranks wear woven patches, with silver bars and branch-of-service colour along the centre of each bar and in the space between the two bars. The colours of the branches of service are:

white	Motorized Rifles
red	Artillery and Rocket Troops
pink	Armour
black	Engineers, Chemical and Technical Services
yellow	Signals
dark green	Medical, Legal and other non-combatant services
olive green	Pioneers
grey	Anti-Aircraft Defence
green	Border Guards

Parachutists wear different patches, of air force shape but made of orange felt. The branch badge of all ranks is displayed on the patch in silver embroidery, but the officers' collar patches are distinguished by an additional edging of twisted silver cords.

The personnel of the air force wear bluish green patches that identify the class of rank. The patches worn by senior officers have a silver edging and a large wreath of oak leaves and a wing, both of white metal. Junior officers have a small wreath and a wing, and other ranks wear plain patches with one wing, of the same pattern as other ranks.

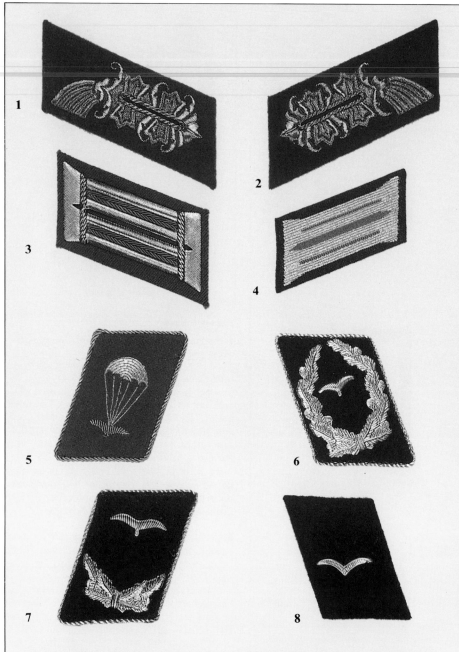

1, 2. Army and Air Force generals 3. Anti-Aircraft Defence officer 4. Army Signals other ranks 5. Parachutists officers 6, 7, 8. Air force patches for senior, junior officers and for other ranks.

On 1 January 1957 the traditional German double bars, embroidered on rectangular coloured patches, replaced the metal collar badges. The branch-of-service colours were:

Infantry	rifle-green
Armoured Infantry	grass green
Anti-Tank Units	dark green
Armour	pink
Armoured Reconnaissance	golden yellow
Artillery	scarlet
Anti-Aircraft	coral red
Engineers	black
Signals	lemon yellow
ABC Defence	Bordeaux red
Technical Troops	blue
Medical Troops	dark blue
Quartermaster	light blue
Military Police	orange
Army Aviation	light grey
Military Bands	white

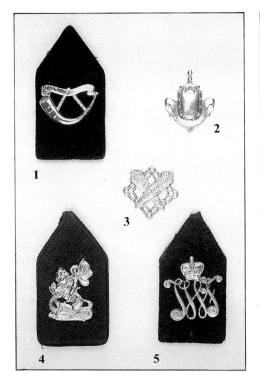

1, 5. Infantry Regiment 'Menno van Coehoorn' and 'Johan Willem Friso' 2. Infantry
badge 3. Hussars 'van Boreel' 4. Supply Corps.

Holland
Pentagonal collar patches were adopted in
1943 by the Netherlands Ministry of War,
which was based in London. Before 1939
branch of service was identified by coloured
collars, piping and badges, but, as these
insignia were not suitable for the British
uniform worn at the time by Dutch servicemen, an entirely new system was devised that
was based on the use of collar patches to
identify branch of service and rank.

Initially, many pre-war branch of service
colours were used — blue for the infantry,
black for the artillery, Bordeaux red for the
pay corps, crimson for the ordnance — but
some new colours were adopted, including
light blue for the cavalry and brown for the
engineers. Some colours were changed before
the end of the war, others were changed later.

In 1963 the rank insignia of officers and
warrant officers were transferred to the shoulder straps, and the branch-of-service badges,
previously worn on the shoulder straps, were
moved to the collar patches.

Poppy red patches are worn by the infantry
with either an infantry badge or a regimental
badge set in the centre. The cavalry regiments
have light blue patches surrounded by piping,
the colour of which varies according to the
regiment.

For further details on the colours of the
collar patches see Backing.

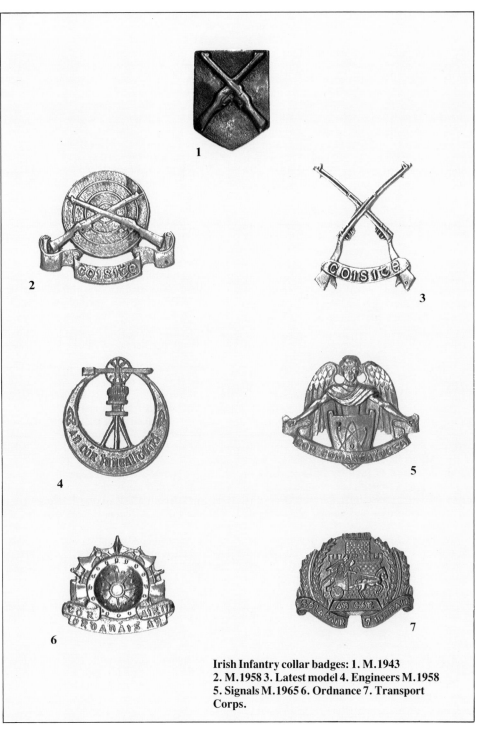

Irish Infantry collar badges: 1. M.1943
2. M.1958 3. Latest model 4. Engineers M.1958
5. Signals M.1965 6. Ordnance 7. Transport
Corps.

Ireland, Republic of
The army branches of the Irish Defence Force
are identified by metal collar badges, which
are now made of anodized metal. Since their
adoption in 1924, several badges have been
modified and others have been introduced for
newly formed services.

The infantry had six patterns of collar
badges, three of which are shown. The most
recent is similar to the earliest pattern, but it
does not have the regimental number, which,
in 1924, was worn on the joint of the rifle.

The engineers' badge has changed little
since 1924, but the inscription in the crescent
was modified in 1958. The signals' collar
badge illustrated was adopted in 1965.

There are several versions of the badge of
the ordnance, and that of the supply and
transport corps, which was adopted in 1931, is
still, in a staybrite version, in use today.

Italy

By the end of the last century the coloured piping of the army uniforms was replaced by collar patches known, because of their shape, as 'flames': the main body of the patch was at the front of the collar, below the white star, and ended at the back with one, two or three points.

A five-pointed star, in metal, embroidery or felt, according to class of rank, was adopted for wearing on the collar as the symbol of the Italian armed forces in 1871. The white felt stars of the rank and file were abolished in 1902, and, by 1914, metal badges were used by all ranks on all orders of dress.

All ranks of the special infantry corps — the *Bersaglieri* and the *Alpini* — wore, and still wear today, two-pointed patches made of crimson or green felt, respectively. In 1895 the infantry officers obtained two-pointed scarlet patches, while the men continued to wear the one-pointed black velvet patches edged with scarlet felt until 1902. The following one-pointed flames were still in use or had just been adopted in 1902:

	Patch	Piping
Infantry	black	scarlet
Artillery	black	golden yellow
Engineers	black	crimson
Medical	amaranth	— (1902)
Supply	black	light blue (1902)

In May 1902 coloured patches were adopted for the 47 infantry brigades then in existence; each brigade was composed of two infantry regiments, which were numbered in chronological order and named after regions and towns.

These patches were made of woven silk. They were 32mm (1⅓in) wide and 120mm (4¾in) long for the collar of the tunic, and 32mm by 100mm (1⅓in by 4in) for the collar of the greatcoat. The star was always worn at the front, near the opening of the collar, and there was a small button at the back where the patch was cut to form a point. No collar patches were worn on the grey-green greatcoat of the field uniform that was adopted in 1909.

In 1915 25 brigades of the mobile militia were called to active service, and another 17 brigades were formed during the following year. The mobile militia was distinguished by collar patches that were divided longitudinally in two colours; the brigades formed in 1916 had patches divided vertically in two colours. Because the infantry suffered appalling losses, another 26 brigades were formed by 1917; these brigades wore collar patches divided vertically in three colours.

The machine gunners' collar patches had three vertical white stripes on a blue (St Etienne), red (Fiat) or green background (Maxim).

Most infantry brigades were disbanded after 1918, but those that remained continued to wear the old patches, although shortened to 100mm (4in) in length. In 1934, however, jackets with an open collar were adopted for all ranks. Initially shorter, rectangular collar patches were adopted for officers and warrant officers only. These patches were 60mm (2¼in) long and the same width as before.

The stars grew smaller after the war, and had a decorated surface for officers and plain surface for the other ranks.

In 1938 the width of the collar patches was reduced to 26mm (1in), but, following the constitution of the divisional services in 1940, the wider patches were re-adopted for all ranks (*see* Backing).

The jacket introduced in 1934 for the rank and file and the post-war battledress blouse had pointed collars, and pointed patches as well as rectangular ones were used.

Plastic collar badges of various types appeared in the late 1940s; medium size patches for the jacket, large for the khaki greatcoat or small for the collar of the summer shirt. A series of small patches was also made in metal and enamel.

After World War II, the brigades were abolished, as one regiment of each was disbanded, the majority of those that remained becoming recruit training centres.

All types and sizes of collar patches were used in the 1960s. The woven pattern, made of felt or plastic, was used until 1975, when the 'universal' pattern, made of metal and coloured enamels, was introduced and made obligatory for all ranks and for wearing on all uniforms. About 150 'universal' patches are in use, one for each regiment and corps of the army.

The personnel of most service corps wore hand-made, one-pointed flames before the introduction of plastic and metal and enamel badges.

The pre-war chemical service was distinguished by an extraordinary patch, which, in a smaller version, is still used today by the NBC service.

Parachute units, a speciality of the infantry, wore the winged sword, which now has a parachute in the background.

The Grenadiers of Sardinia wore scarlet collars. Officers and warrant officers had silver embroidered double bars, and other ranks had a single bar embroidered in white thread. On the grey-green field uniform and post-World War II khaki uniforms all ranks wore as collar patches the bars on a scarlet backing.

Before World War I Italy had 30 cavalry regiments; 11 were distinguished by coloured collars, 18 had three-pointed flames on coloured collars and one had a coloured collar with additional piping (Bibl. 10). The flames distinguished the light horse regiments, while

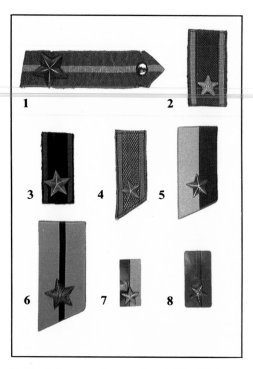

Italian Infantry collar patches: 1. 53rd/54th World War I 2. 79th/80th, 60mm length 3. 1st/2nd, 26mm width 4. 21st/22nd, World War II and post-war 5. 114th, plastic for jacket 6. 17th, plastic for greatcoat 7, 8. 114th and 59th, for summer shirt.

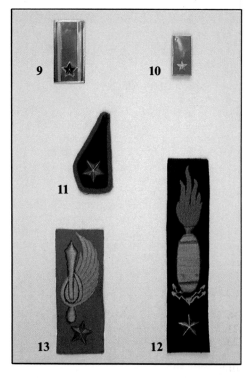

9. 79th/80th, M.1975 10. 52nd, enamel for summer shirt 11. Engineers 12. Chemical 13. Parachutists.

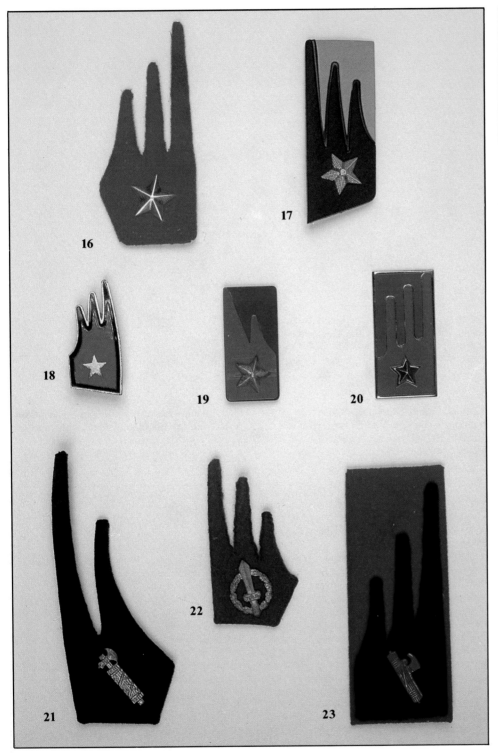

16. 2nd Dragoons 17. 12th Light Horse 18. 8th Lancers 19. Tank Corps 20. 28th Light Horse
21. MVSN 22. Italian Social Republic, 'Alpini'
23. 'Aldo Resega' Black Brigade.

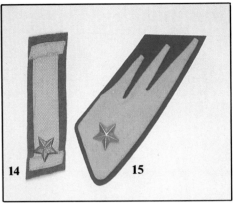

14. Grenadiers 15. 19th Guide.

This form of regimental identification still exists, and, as the cavalry patches went through the same phases of development as those of the other corps, several variations could be found made of felt, plastic, metal and enamel for the shirt's collar and the 'universal' pattern used now.

The tank corps was a speciality of the infantry, and it was identified by scarlet, two-pointed flames on a blue collar, which, in 1940, were reduced to red flames on a blue background.

All personnel of the Fascist Militia (MVSN) wore two-pointed black flames on which the fasces was displayed, in metal or in gold and silver embroidery.

Italian Social Republic : In September 1944 the republican government issued new dress regulations by which new badges were introduced, but lack of resources meant that the regulations were never fully implemented.

All combat units were ordered to wear three-pointed flames and service units to wear one-pointed flames, thus abolishing all the regimental collar patches. The new colours were:

Infantry	scarlet
Cavalry	white
Armour	blue
Artillery	golden yellow
Mountain Artillery	as above but with green piping
Chemical	plum red
Motor Transport	olive green

Bersaglieri, Alpini and the engineers retained their old colours. The star was replaced by a new badge.

In 1944-5 many independent units were formed, and they adopted their own individual badges. All were deployed in anti-partisan warfare. The best known are the Black Brigades, of which there were about forty, but their varying badges have never been fully recorded.

dragoons and lancers wore plain coloured collars. When coloured collars were finally abolished in 1940, 115 regiments then in existence were ordered to wear the three-pointed flames. For dragoons and lancers, it was plain or edged with additional coloured piping, while for the light horse regiments it was placed on a rectangular coloured backing.

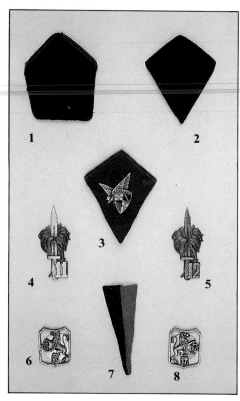

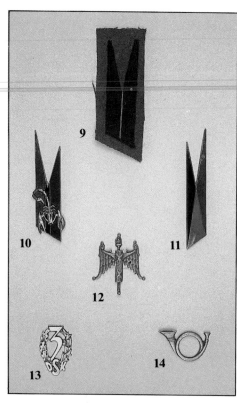

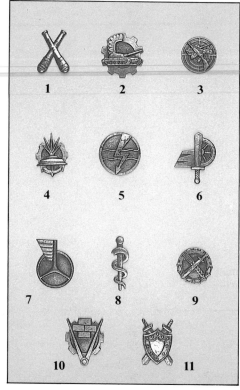

1. Signals 2. Field Artillery 3. 9th Carpathian Rifle Battalion 'Bolonski' 4, 5. 11th and 12th Battalions 'Wolyński' Infantry Brigade 6, 8. 16th and 17th Battalion 'Lwow' Infantry Brigade 7. Tank units.

9, 10, 11. Examples of Armoured Cavalry 'pennon' collar patches 12. Commissariat 13. 3rd Carpathian Rifle Division 14. 2nd Rifle Division, France 1940.

Collar badges M.1961: 1. Artillery 2. Armour 3. Mechanical Infantry 4. Engineers 5. Signals 6. Military Transport 7. Motor Transport 8. Medical 9. Supplies 10. Building Engineers 11. Legal

Poland

One of the outstanding features of the pre-World War II Polish uniform was the zigzag ornament (see Rank insignia) worn by all ranks on the collar patches or, in the case of mounted troops, around the front edges of the tunic collar. On the collar of their tunics and greatcoats, mounted troops wore coloured pennons, miniature replicas of the pennons of the cavalry lances.

Armoured troops had a triangular black and orange pennon. The branches of service of the rest of the army were identified by patches that covered the front of the collar ending at the rear with three points. The branch-of-service colours were displayed on the greatcoat collar in the form of two, 5mm (¼in) stripes, by all units apart from those that had pennons. The patch was distinguished by the stripe at the bottom, the piping by the stripe on the top (Bibl. 25, 156, 158).

After the German invasion of Poland and France, new Polish armed forces, formed in Britain and in Egypt, developed into the 1st and 2nd Polish army corps, respectively. In 1941 the Polish Ministry of War in London published new dress regulations, which re-established the use of pennons and adopted new collar patches for the rest of the army (Bibl. 155).

The army personnel obtained pentagonal patches to wear on the collar of the service dress jacket, and diamond-shaped, pointed patches for the battle dress. Badges could be worn on the collar patches, and by the end of the war many were in use, particularly by the troops of the 2nd corps (Bibl. 158).

The armoured cavalry regiments had the traditional pennons on the collar of all uniforms. They were made of felt, painted metal or metal and enamel. The pre-war triangular black and orange pennon identified tank units. Many regiments wore a pennon on the left side of the beret, behind the cap badge.

Innumerable badges were worn on the collar patches before and during World War II, some to identify a branch of service, a regiment or a battalion, others, which identified divisions, were worn by divisional headquarters staff.

People's Republic of Poland : The pre-war collar patches and zigzag devices were re-adopted in 1949, but the pennons were abolished because tank troops were distinguished by special blue-grey uniforms, and any further distinction became irrelevant. The new collar patches were all carmine, with a piping in branch-of-service colour at the rear.

Collar patches of a new shape were adopted in 1952 for the newly adopted open-collar jacket. Armoured troops now had black patches with light carmine piping; the personnel of the 1st Warsaw Infantry Division wore yellow patches with dark blue piping, and the remainder of the army personnel had light carmine patches with coloured piping at the top end and branch-of-service badges pinned on the patches.

In 1960 the collar patches were abolished, and in 1961 new collar badges were adopted for wearing directly on the collar of the jacket (Bibl. 27).

Most of these badges are self-explanatory, except for the badges used by the personnel of mechanized units and by engineers; military transport in general had the same badge, although the steering wheel identifies the personnel of the motor transport corps.

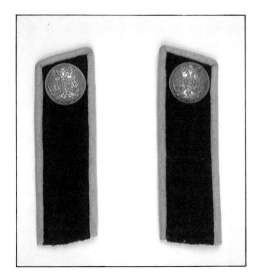

Imperial Russian patches for greatcoat, Artillery and Engineers.

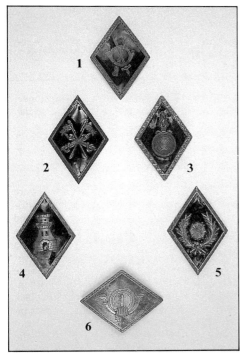

1. Infantry 2. Cavalry 3. Artillery 4. Engineers 5. 'Intendencia' 6. Mountain troops.

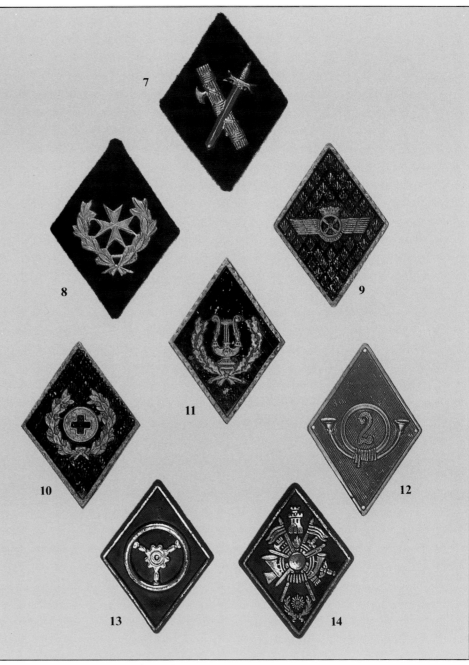

7. 'Guardia Civil' 8. Medical 9. Air Force 10. Red Cross 11. Military Band 12. 2nd Mountain Battalion 13. Drivers.

Russia, Empire of
The insignia displayed on the shoulder boards were the main form of branch-of-service and regimental identification. Collar patches were worn only on the greatcoat to identify branch of service or the numerical order of the infantry regiments within a division. The 1st, 2nd, 3rd and 4th regiments of each division wore, respectively, red, blue, white and green patches. Rifle regiments had green patches with crimson piping, and, as technical corps, the artillery and engineers had velvet black patches with red piping and, for officers only, a large gilt button. A great variety of coloured patches was worn by the guards units (Bibl. 17).

These relatively simple yet effective patches were copied by several other countries, and were re-adopted in 1943 by the Red Army.

Spain
Diamond-shaped collar badges are worn by the Spanish Army to identify branch of service; the type of badge identifies rank. Although there are felt badges, most are made of metal or plastic, and they are, therefore, badges not patches.

The branch-of-service insignia is represented by the central device; the background colour, usually red, refers to the specialist; the outer frame is purely ornamental.

Officers wear metal and enamel badges, and the other ranks wear painted metal or plastic badges.

1. Engineers

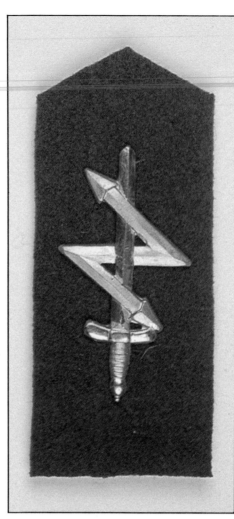

2. Signals

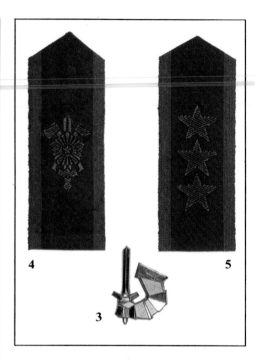

3. Armour. Collar patches for field uniform:
4. Engineers 5. Captain.

Black collar patches are used by generals, who have a laurel branch, general staff officers, who have an edelweiss, general staff secretaries and administration personnel, who have a quill pen, personnel of the legal service, who have the scales of justice, and chaplains, who have a cross.

The other patches display a speciality badge on branch-of-service colour: for instance, the dark green patch with crossed rifles identifies fusiliers, crossed machine guns below a grenade identify machine gunners, and crossed guns identify gunners attached to an infantry unit.

Several other patches are worn by infantry specialists: grenadiers display a flaming grenade, drivers display a steering wheel and signallers have a flash of lightning on dark green patches. However, all drivers attached to different branches of service wear the steering wheel but on different coloured background. The driver in charge of a vehicle of the signals corps wears a steering wheel on a light grey patch, while the signaller attached to an artillery or air defence unit has a flash of lightning on dark red background.

Tankmen display a tank on a yellow patch, while the personnel of self-propelled guns have a tank on the artillery's dark red patch.

The dark blue patch with winged propellers is used by aviation personnel and parachutists. A wheatsheaf is the emblem of the supply corps, and six cannon balls, in a pyramid on a green background, identify the ordnance (Bibl. 161).

Sweden
Army personnel wear regimental or branch-of-service badges on the collar of the service dress jacket. Some badges are placed on oblong pentagonal felt patches of different colours:

Air Defence Artillery	light red
Engineers	black
Signals	green
Transportation	blue

The field artillery badge, a flaming grenade, is mounted on a coloured backing of medium blue, white, orange, green, yellow or grey cloth, the colour of the cloth serving to identify the unit. All the other badges are pinned directly on to the collar.

Woven collar patches are worn on the collar of the field uniform. The right-hand patch identifies the branch of service, and the left-hand patch identifies rank. Privates wear the branch insignia on both sides of the collar.

Switzerland
The collar patches of the Swiss Army identify the speciality and the branch of service of the wearer in the form of a badge embroidered on a coloured felt patch. The branch-of-service colours are:

Infantry	dark green
Aviation	dark blue
Artillery Air Defence	dark red
Light Mechanized Troops	yellow
Engineers	black
Signals	light grey
Medical	blue
Supply Ordnance Catering	green
Transportation Repairs	crimson
NBC	greenish yellow
Territorial Units	light red

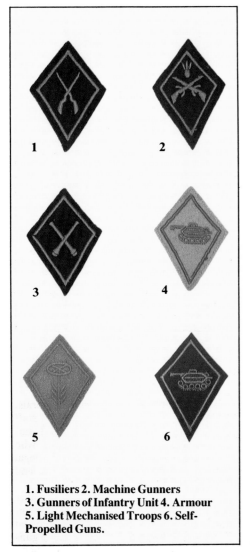

1. Fusiliers 2. Machine Gunners
3. Gunners of Infantry Unit 4. Armour
5. Light Mechanised Troops 6. Self-
Propelled Guns.

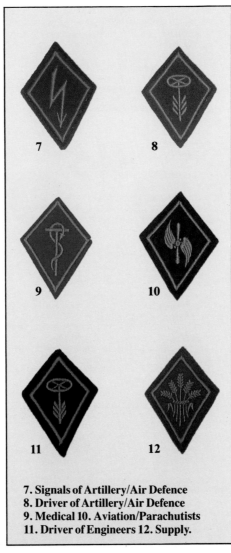

7. Signals of Artillery/Air Defence
8. Driver of Artillery/Air Defence
9. Medical 10. Aviation/Parachutists
11. Driver of Engineers 12. Supply.

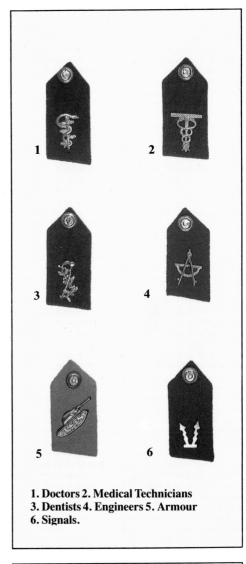

1. Doctors 2. Medical Technicians
3. Dentists 4. Engineers 5. Armour
6. Signals.

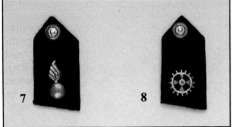

7. Ordnance 8. Mechanical Engineers

9. Chaplains 10. Educational Staff

11. Legal 12. Transport Corps.

Turkey
Coloured patches made of felt or velvet are worn on the collar by all ranks of the Turkish Army as branch-of-service identification. A small brass button decorates the top, pointed part of the patch. Some corps are identified by the colour of the patch only. Infantrymen have dark green and gunners blue collar patches, for instance, but most corps also have a branch-of-service badge.

All the medical personnel wear crimson patches, with different badges according to speciality; pharmacists have a snake and a wreath of laurel on each side of a goblet.

Engineers, signalmen and the personnel of the transport corps have blue collar patches with the appropriate branch-of-service badges. The badge worn by the transport corps and that worn by the ordnance, a flaming grenade, are the same as those used by the US Army. Teachers of the educational staff wear green patches with the torch of learning superimposed upon an open book, and the judges, advocates and clerks of the legal service wear the scales of justice on green and red patches. Military policemen are identified by blue patches edged in red.

Bronze collar badges: 1. US Army Officers 2. US Army Enlisted Men 3. Medical 4. US Marine Corps Officers 5. Signals 6. US Marine Corps Enlisted Men Brass collar badges: 7. US Army Officers 8. 28th Infantry Regiment 9. Sanitary 10. 251st Coast Artillery Regiment.

11. 44th Engineers Regiment 12. Specialists' Reserve 13. Signals 14, 15, 16. US Army Enlisted Men 17. Divisional Headquarters Staff.

18. Military Police 19. 351st Infantry Regiment 20. Army Air Force 21. Ordnance 22. Armoured Force 23. Adjutant General's Department 24. Detached Enlisted Men 25. US Air Force Enlisted Men.

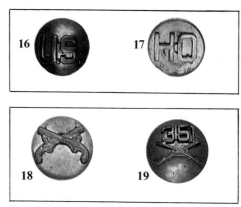

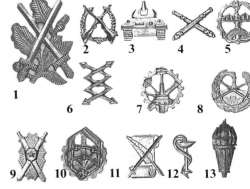

1. Generals 2. Infantry 3. Armour 4. Artillery 5. Engineers 6. Signals 7. Technical 8. Quartermaster 9. Finance 10. NBC 11. Administration 12. Medical 13. Legal.

United States of America
The regulations published in December 1902 established that army officers had to wear the national coat of arms on both sides of the front of the collar and the branch insignia behind the coat of arms; enlisted men had the initials US followed by the branch badge (Bibl. 171).

Later, the national coat of arms was relegated to the head-dress, and replaced on the collar by the initials US for officers, and the initials US in the centre of a disc for enlisted men, followed by the branch insignia.

Bronze badges were used on the service dress until the end of 1924; they were replaced by gilded or polished brass badges, in the appropriate patterns for officers or enlisted men, that for the latter depicting the insignia set on a disc. Marines kept bronze collar badges on their service dress; the officers' badge has a detached rope, while the rope is part of the badge in the enlisted men's insignia.

After the adoption of jackets with open collars, the officers wore the US national insignia on the collar and the branch-of-service insignia on both lapels. Enlisted men had the US disc on the right and branch-of-service insignia on the left side of the collar, and **distinctive insignia** on the lapels.

Unit numbers, initials and subsidiary badges used to be combined with the branch insignia or with the national insignia, in accordance with the regulations. In the early 1940s, the personnel of the National Guard could wear the unit's number, the State's abbreviation or both, combined with the national insignia, a custom that was abolished during the war. Nevertheless, regimental numbers were worn on the branch-of-service badge by some officers throughout the war. The Medical Corps wore its badge on its own or with a number of letters in black enamel, later in maroon enamel, superimposed above it. Officers not part of a branch of service wore the national coat of arms within a ring.

Several types of discs have been used for enlisted men: the flat, solid disc with removable national or branch-of-service insignia, with national or branch insignia embossed on the disc, or with removable insignia on a curved disc.

As an independent service, the US Air Force is distinguished by white metal collar insignia.

Yugoslavia, Federal Socialist Republic of
The uniforms of the Yugoslav Army changed drastically in 1953, when jackets with open collars were adopted: **rank insignia** previously worn on stiff shoulder boards were transferred to the **shoulder straps,** and the badges of branch that had previously adorned the officers' shoulder boards were moved to the collar of the jacket. In addition, new badges were adopted, because the branches of service were reorganized at the same time.

Two crossed swords on a branch of oak leaves, in gilt, were adopted as the generals' collar badge, together with a series of 21 branch-of-service badges, several of which were later modified. Most of the badges illustrated are self explanatory.

COMBAT LEADER IDENTIFICATION A **slip-on** or loop of green cloth worn in the middle of both shoulder straps by commanders of the US Regular Army, Reserve and National Guard units is used as a means of combat leader identification when these units' mission is to combat the enemy by direct means or methods. It is also used by commanders of units at corps level or below, whose mission is to control or directly support such units (Bibl. 163).

The combat leader identification insignia shown bears the **distinctive insignia** of the 349th Infantry Regiment.

COMMEMORATIVE INSIGNIA Insignia that preserve the memory of a specific event, battle or campaign are known as commemorative insignia. They are divided into two categories: badges awarded to individuals or units that took part in the event, and souvenirs of the event. The difference between them is that souvenirs were usually unofficial.

In the Austro-Hungarian Army it was common practice to wear on the field cap, metal badges that commemorated leaders, formations or campaigns connected with the wearer's war service.

Similar badges were worn by the Poles to commemorate the battles that led to their national independence, although these, being larger than the Austrian badges, assumed the status of formal decorations.

A series of shields to be worn on the left upper sleeve was officially instituted in Germany during World War II to award servicemen who had taken part in eight major engagements (Bibl. 114). The Narvik Shield was instituted in 1940 as an award for all German troops who participated in the battle of Narvik. The brass shield was worn by naval personnel, and a grey metal version was worn by army and air force personnel.

The bronze 'Krimea' Shield was awarded to all ranks who participated in the battle of Crimea, between September 1941 and July 1942.

Italian troops who fought in the Russian campaign obtained a breast badge, which depicts two crossed Cossack swords within a wreath. A small replica of this badge is still listed in the 1971 dress regulations under 'souvenir' badges.

After World War II, the Yugoslavs who fought in the ranks of the partisan brigades received an award in the form of a special badge and an individual certificate. This badge should be classed as a decoration.

In April 1951 the Border Regiment, the South Staffordshire Regiment and the Glider Pilot Regiment were authorized to wear

Combat Leader Identification.

2　　　　　3

1, 2, 3. World War I Austro-Hungarian badges.

4　　　　　5

4, 5, 6, 7. Polish badges 1918-21.

6　　　　　7

10

8

9

8, 9. German 'Narvik' and 'Krimea' shields.

11

10. Italian 'Russian Front' badge 11. Yugoslav World War II Partisan Award.

special shoulder titles to commemorate their participation in the first British airborne operation, which took place in Sicily on 10 July 1943.

After the regimental reorganization of 1959, the glider continued to be worn by the King's Own Royal Border Regiment and by the Staffordshire Regiment (The Prince of Wales's) but on its own and on regimental coloured background. The Staffords wore a brass glider on the upper right sleeve of their tropical dress (Bibl. 54).

Joint manoeuvres of the Warsaw Pact armies are always commemorated by special badges, the badges usually displaying the flags of the participant armies (Bibl. 5). The last flag is that of the nation that issued the badge. Some badges differ — for instance, the 'Vltava 1966' badge commemorates the Czecho-Soviet manoeuvres on the river Vltava, which was not a joint Warsaw Pact exercise.

CROWN The head-dress worn by kings and queens as a sign of sovereignty, is traditionally displayed on the top of insignia pertaining to the armed forces of monarchic nations. Several different types of royal crowns have appeared on insignia, but the most common pattern, and that still used in Belgium, Denmark and other countries, has five arches.

The British crown always has three arches, and, on its own or in combination with other devices, was and is still used as a **rank insignia**. Three crowns have been used this century: the Victorian Crown until 1901, the Tudor or Imperial Crown until 1953 and St Edward's Crown during the reign of Queen Elizabeth II.

The mural crown — from the Latin *murus* (a wall) — depicts a turreted fortress and, according to early history, the mural crown was awarded to the Roman soldiers who first stormed over the walls of a beseiged fortress. The mural crown has been used on cap insignia in Italy since 1948, and as a form of rank insignia from 1975.

CUFF INSIGNIA Two important types of insignia are displayed on the cuffs — patches and titles — and both are used in Germany.

Before World War II all ranks of the German Army wore two rectangular patches, in branch-of-service colour, on each cuff of the dress tunic. The generals' emblem or the double bars, embroidered or in lace according to class of rank, and a button were displayed on these patches.

The German Democratic Republic has reinstated the use of these traditional insignia. Now, however, there is no button and, on a rectangular patch of cloth matching that of the uniform, officers wear double bars made of metal, separated by a **gimp** in branch-of-service colour, while the other ranks wear

12. Shoulder title of the Border Regiment used until 1959 13. Badge of the Staffordshire Regiment (The Prince of Wales's) after 1959.

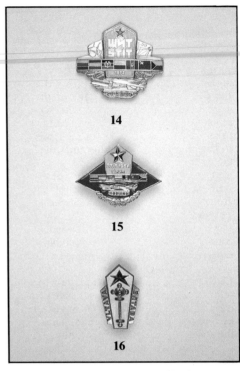

Czechoslovak 'joint manoeuvres' badges: 14. Shield 1972 15. Shield 1984 16. Vltava 1966.

1. Belgian crown 2. Danish crown 3, 4, 5. British Victorian, Imperial and the St. Edward's crown 6. Italian mural crown.

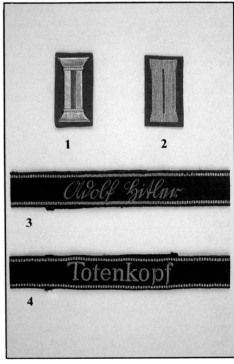

Two cuff patches of the 'Volksarmee': 1. Air Force officers 2. Artillery other ranks. Examples of cuff titles: 3. 1st SS Armoured Division 'Leibstandarte SS Adolf Hitler' 4. 3rd Armoured Division 'Totenkopf'.

bars that are machine woven in silver.

Three types of cuff titles were used until 1945. The first group was those awarded to troops and worn in lieu of a campaign medal, such as the cuff titles inscribed *Kreta, Kurland* and so forth. The second category comprised the titles of certain élite units of the army, such as *Grossdeutschland, Brandenburg* and so on, and of the SS, which used many cuff titles, ranging from those of high commands to those worn by small units and often manufactured in a variety of ways.

Two examples are shown: one of the 1st SS Armoured Division *Leibstandarte SS Adolf Hitler* and one of the 3rd Armoured Division *Totenkopf.*

For further information the reader should consult the volumes listed in the bibliography, especially number 103 and numbers 108-17.

CURL In naval terminology the word 'curl' refers to the round ornament usually worn by navy officers on the **distinction lace.** It is made by twisting the centre of the top stripe, or of the stripe if one only is worn, into a circle.

The curl of a Danish naval officer of the fleet air arm is shown as an example.

CYPHER A cypher is a monogram or literal device, usually formed by the intertwined initials of a person's name and often combined with crowns, coronets or other emblems.

The best known cyphers are those of kings and princes, which adorned the shoulder straps of many European regiments at the beginning of the 20th century. The monarch or prince, or sometimes a foreign monarch, was the colonel-in-chief of the regiment; alternatively the regiment could have been named after the monarch.

Cyphers may be used as individual badges, or worn on the head-dress, the breast of the jacket, the collar or the shoulder straps, according to national custom.

In Britain, besides being worn in the centre of many army badges, the royal cypher could be worn on its own or below the crown; it could also be worn by aides to the sovereign (*see* Aide-de-camp).

In Denmark the officers of the Royal Life Guard wear the sovereign's cypher on the breast; there are several in existence, including the cyphers of King Christian X and of Frederick IX.

Many pre-1939 Polish regiments were named after famous generals, and their cyphers were worn on the shoulder straps. These cyphers were embroidered in silver wire on officers' and warrant officers' shoulder straps, but for field officers they were embroidered across their double bars. The cyphers worn by the other ranks were in white metal.

Two Italian cyphers follow, the floreal U of King Umberto I, which is perhaps not a

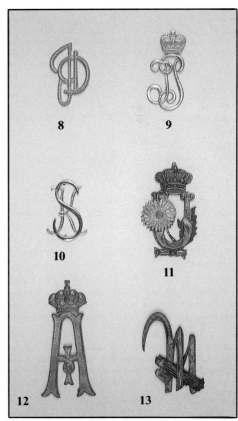

Danish Navy 'Søløjtnant' of the Fleet Air Arm.

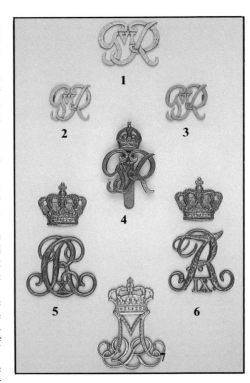

1, 2, 3. King George VI 4. King George VI crowned 5. King Christian X 6. King Frederick IX.

military insignia (*see* Epaulette), and that of Mussolini, which was taken from the initial of his signature.

The cypher of Alexander I of Yugoslavia was worn by his Royal Guards.

8. General J. Dwernicki 9. Prince Poniatowski 10. General K. Sosnkowski 11. King Umberto I 12. King Alexander I 13. Benito Mussolini.

D

DISTINCTION LACE Distinction lace is a texture woven in stripes of varying widths, which is now used primarily in the making of rank insignia. In the past it had many purposes, including being used to trim uniforms, to cover waist and shoulder belts, pouches and shabracks and in the making of sword knots. Lace is important as it could often be the only means of identification of an item of uniform or insignia.

The 1900 dress regulations for the British Army contain an eight-page appendix showing the various patterns of regimental lace used at that time (Bibl. 50).

All Austrian lace, except the very narrow examples, displays a zigzag pattern along its centre. Until 1918, the lace of the officers had a straight zigzag, while that of the administrative officials had a wavy zigzag.

Stripes of lace are now worn on the black band of the peaked cap. Officers have gold stripes: one wide stripe and one, two or three narrow stripes for generals; a medium stripe and one, two or three narrow stripes for field officers; and narrow stripes only for the others. The *Fähnrich* and the *Vizeleutnant* have special stripes: the three senior sergeants have stripes arranged like the field officers, but made of silver; junior sergeants have two wide stripes and one narrow silver stripe; and corporals wear one, two or three narrow grey stripes.

Until about 1948, Italian officers wore a similar type of insignia on their peaked caps, but generals had silver embroidery below the stripes. The same combination of stripes — wide and narrow stripes for field officers and narrow stripes only for company officers — was also worn on the sleeves below a **curl**. However, the stripes of the cap band were woven together in one piece while those for the sleeves were sewn separately on to a felt backing because the curl had to be made individually for each badge. This was the pattern of lace adopted in 1934 when gold was introduced for the insignia of all branches of service; a different type, consisting of longitudinal lines, had been used previously.

Warrant officers had a special pattern of distinction lace, and sergeants of the Fascist Militia wore their own pattern from 1931 to 1938.

The non-commissioned officers of the Polish Army wore lace 10mm (½in) and 4mm (¼in) wide, the former with red edging

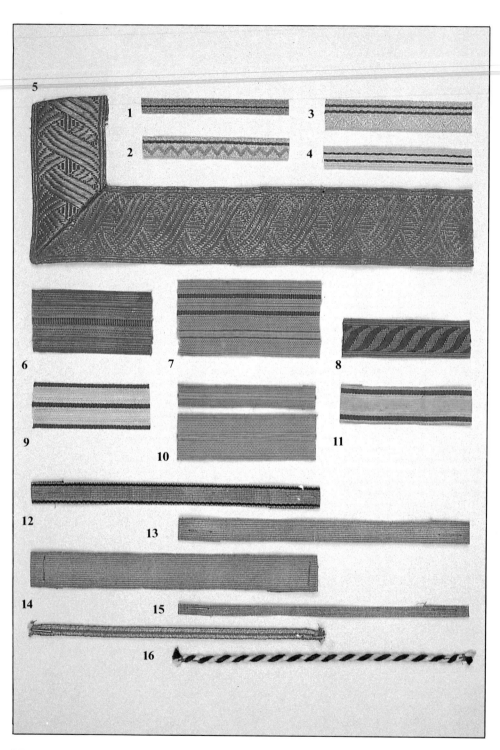

Modern Austrian lace: 1. 1st Lieutenant **2.** 'Fährich' **3.** 'Oberstabswachtmeister' **4.** 'Zugsführer' **5.** Pre-World War I collar lace of administrative offical, senior ranks **Italian lace: 6.** M.1934 peaked cap insignia of Lieutenant **7.** Lace for Sergeant Major's chevrons **8.** M.1915 cap stripe for warrant officers **9.** Lace for post-World War II rank insignia on chinstrap. **10.** Types of lace for M.1934 officers' sleeve insignia **11.** M.1931 lace for NCOs of the MVSN **Polish lace: 12.** NCOs **13, 14.** Officer Cadets **17.** Reserve Cadets.

stripes. The officer cadets used silver stripes of two sizes and a narrower pattern on the shoulder straps. The cadets of the reserve wore red and white twisted cords around their shoulder straps.

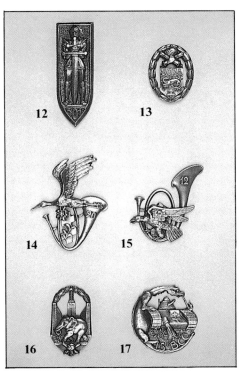

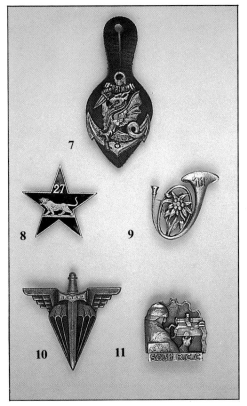

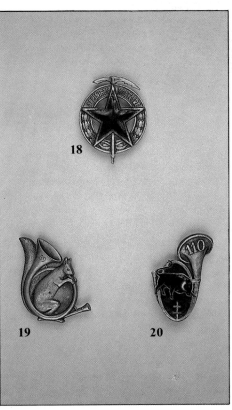

1, 4. 3rd and 10th Algerian 'Spahis' 2. Free France 3. French Fascists 5. 3rd Marine Infantry Parachute Regiment 6. 9th Parachute 'Chasseurs' Regiment 7. 8th Marine Infantry Parachute Regiment 8. 27th Battalion 'Chasseurs Alpins', Skiers 9, 14, 15. 11th, 20th and 12th 'Chasseurs Alpins' Regiment 10. Base School for Airborne Troops 11, 13, 16. 503rd, 507th and 511th Tank Regiment 12, 17. 501st, 15th Tank Battalion 18. Military Alpinists 19, 20. 89th and 110th 'Chasseurs a Pied'.

DISTINCTIVE INSIGNIA According to the terminology, distinctive insignia are solely US Army badges, which were worn until 1947 on the shoulder straps by officers and on the lapels of the jacket by enlisted men; later, they were worn on the shoulder straps by all ranks. They are now worn on the service hat and on shoulder straps.

France

French distinctive insignia originated in 1916, when the 3rd Aviation Squadron adopted its fuselage insignia, the stork, for wearing by all ranks on the left breast, above the ribbons. Other squadrons adopted badges to wear on their uniforms, and by the early 1920s many army regiments had their own distinctive insignia. As the choice of the insignia was left to the unit's commanding officer, who sometimes disagreed with the choice of his predecessor, several regiments and battalions had a number of badges, but, by the outbreak of World War II, most French units had their own distinctive insignia.

The Cross of Lorraine of the Free French had a counterpart in a badge displaying the French fasces, as badges continued to be made both in England and France during the war. Many post-war badges carried the Cross of Lorraine, but not necessarily all of them had a connection with the Free French. The 20th Battalion *Chasseurs à pied*, for instance, which had adopted its badge in 1920, became *Chasseurs Alpins* in 1927 when the edelweiss was added to the insignia.

Stars, crescents and Arabic inscriptions identify north African units, and wings and parachutes identify airborne units. The **foul anchor** of the marines and the griffon are depicted in the badge of the 8th Marine Infantry Parachute Regiment, and the badge of the 9th Parachute *Chasseurs* Regiment depicts St Michael, the patron saint of the parachutists.

Most of the 12 tank regiments in existence in 1940 displayed the knight's helmet on crossed guns upon their badges. Illustrated are the badges of the 503rd, 507th and 511th Tank Regiments.

The bugle has always been the emblem of the *Chasseurs*, and, with the addition of an edelweiss or eagle, the badges identify a battalion of *chasseurs alpins*. The blue star was worn by reconnaissance sections of skiers; in the version illustrated the battalion number and emblem, the tiger, are in the centre. The badges of the 89th and 110th battalions of *chasseurs à pied* were adopted in 1939.

In France these badges have always been worn on the pocket or suspended by a leather tongue, but, as they are badges of unit they may at any time be moved to the shoulder straps or anywhere else on the uniform.

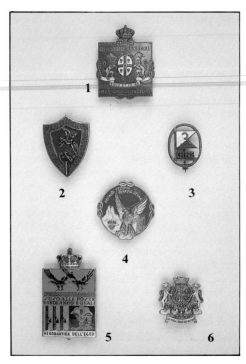

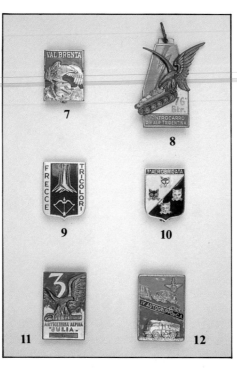

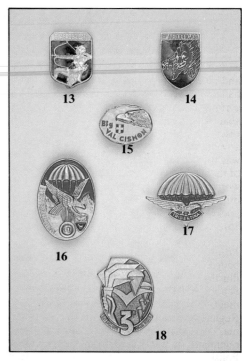

1. 'Sassari' Infantry Division. 2. 'Littorio' Armoured Division 3. 3rd 'Principe Amedeo di Aosta' Mechanised Division 4. Border Guards 6th Sector 5. Aegean Air Force 6. 151st 'Sassari' Regiment.

7. 'Val Brenta' Alpine Battalion 8. 76th Anti-Tank Battery 'Tridentina' Division 9. Air Force Acrobatic Team 'Frecce Tri-colori' 10. 3rd Air Brigade 11. 3rd Mountain Artillery Regiment 12. 4th Transport Group of Army Corps.

13. 5th Air Brigade 14. 6th Air Brigade 15. 'Val Cismon' Alpine Battalion 16, 17. Parachute units of 'Orobica' and 'Tridentina' Brigade 18. 3rd Parachute Battalion.

Italy
In Italy distinctive insignia are called *distintivi di reparto* (units' badges), and they were worn on the felt hat of the mountain troops until 1985. In 1985, however, new regulations ordered that unit badges had to be worn on the left breast pocket of the jacket (Bibl. 150), or attached by means of a leather suspender on the button of the left pocket of the summer shirt, as other Italian Army units had previously worn them.

The first Italian distinctive insignia appeared during World War I and proved very popular with the troops. After the war some veterans' associations distributed badges and medals, on a regimental basis, to their members, and manufacturers started to produce badges for the local Alpine battalions, which the soldiers pinned on their hats.

Under the Fascist regime, when the whole population was militarized and wore the uniform or at least the badge of some military, para-military or political organization, insignia proliferated. Metal and enamel distinctive insignia were made for army divisions and for smaller units. The air force formations started to wear special badges in the 1930s but the 'Alpine' badges were the more numerous. By the outbreak of World War II, when battalion badges already existed, every regiment had its own badge. More badges were made during

the war, and production continued after the war, reaching its apogee during the 1950s.

Some badges were modified during World War II. A gold medal for valour was awarded to the 3rd Mountain Artillery Regiment, and a new distinctive insignia was made with the decoration's ribbon on its base. Later, the same regiment was awarded another gold medal for valour, and another badge, with two stars on the ribbon, was made. Many badges were modified for the same reason, others were 'purged' after the advent of the republic: the shield of Savoy on the insignia of the *Val Cismon* Battalion, for instance, was retained, although the inscription *Savoia* in the centre of the cross was abolished.

In the 1950s some Alpine companies adopted their own distinctive insignia, and the various branches of service of each formation, at any level, had theirs.

Badges were often incorrectly enamelled. A batch of badges of the *Val Brenta* Battalion has a green sky, a detail that enhances the value of these badges.

The air force adopted many badges in the 1950s, one for each air brigade, for training schools and for the air acrobatic team.

A series of rather large badges is used by the personnel of the parachute battalions and services, all are self-explanatory.

Toward the end of the 1960s the quality of

19. 5th Parachute Battalion 20. Parachute Engineers 21. Parachute Signals.

distinctive insignia started to deteriorate as manufacturing firms began to use synthetic enamels, which allowed them to produce aluminium and plasticized badges.

After the reorganization of the army that took place in the 1970s, regiments have ceased to exist and most battalions have been re-titled. New distinctive insignia had to be made, therefore, in aluminium or plasticized patterns.

Poland

Polish distinctive insignia originated in the early 1920s (*see* Commemorative insignia), and by 1939 each unit had its own, in metal and enamel for officers and warrant officers, and in plain metal for the other ranks. These badges were awarded on the fulfilment of certain conditions: in peacetime, after one year of active service or, in the case of reservists, after having participated in two army manoeuvres. The Staff College badge was worn on the right pocket, and the badges of the armoured corps and of the signals were worn on the left breast above the ribbons; otherwise they were worn on the left breast pocket, 40mm (1½in) below the button (Bibl. 25).

The badge of the 1st (Legion) *Joseph Pilsudski* Brigade is the predecessor of the badge of the 1st infantry regiment. Also illustrated are the badge of the Officers' School and three examples of infantry regimental badges. The 8th (Legion) Infantry Regiment is an other ranks' distinctive insignia. As was the case with several other regiments, it was raised from the volunteer Polish legions of World War I and therefore retained the word 'legion' in its title. The badges of the 64th (Pomorski) Murmansk Rifle Regiment and of the 73rd Infantry Regiment are officers' and warrant officers' patterns, of metal and enamel. The tall *czapka* of the *ulans* (the Polish lancers) is depicted on the badge of the 2nd lancers.

In 1939 the Polish Army included 12 tank battalions, the badges of which depicted dragons, knights' helmets and other appropriate motifs; the enamelled colours were black and orange. The Armoured Corps and the Armoured Corps Training Centre had special badges, which are shown together with those of the 7th and 12th Armoured Battalions.

The badge of the Signal Corps was made by Collins, London, but most of the others, in the last two rows, were made in Italy. Divisional insignia made in Italy included the badges of the 3rd Carpathian Rifle Division, the 5th *Kresowa* Infantry Division and the 5th Division's Engineers.

As its background, the badge of the 663rd Bomber Squadron depicts the fuselage insignia of the Polish Air Force, the 303rd *T. Kosciuszkos* Fighter Squadron, which was formed at Northolt in August 1940. Its flying personnel wore a scarlet scarf.

Russia

Metal insignia were worn on the breast until 1917. Regimental and training schools' badges were worn on the left breast, while graduates of officers' schools and academies wore their badges on the right breast.

The badges of the 100th and 195th Infantry Regiments are illustrated.

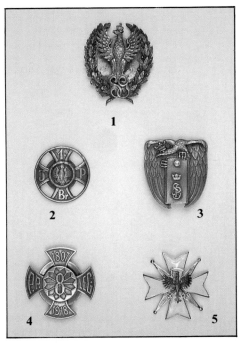

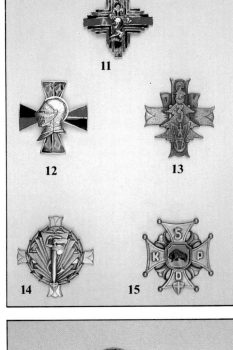

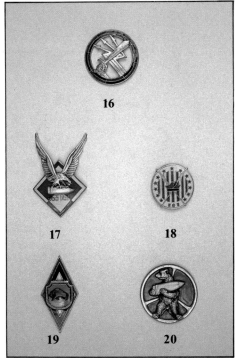

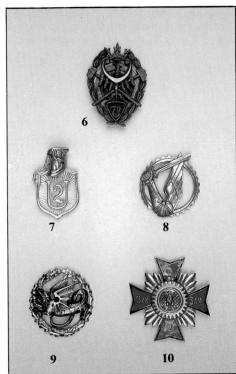

1. Staff College 2. 1st (Legion) 'Joseph Pilsudski' Brigade 3. Officers' School 4, 5, 6. 8th (Legion), 64th (Pomorski) Murmansk Rifle and 73rd Infantry Regiment 7. 2nd Lancers 8. Armoured Corps 9. Armoured Corps Training Centre 11, 12. 7th and 12th Armoured Battalion 13, 15 3rd Carpathian and 5th 'Kresowa' Infantry Division 16. Signal Corps 17. 663rd Bomber Squadron 18. 503rd 'T. Kosciuzko' Fighter Squadron.

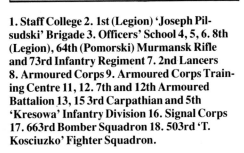

100th and 195th Infantry Regiment.

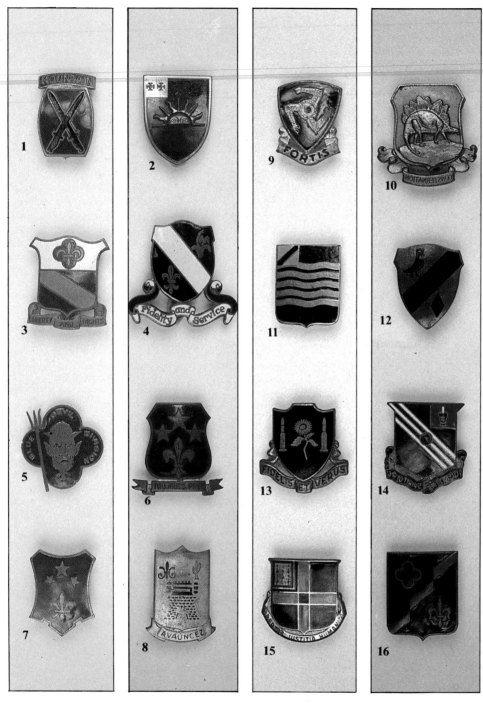

1. 10th Mountain Division 2. 63rd Infantry
Regiment 3. 349th Infantry Regiment 4. 350th
Infantry Regiment 5. 88th (Blue Devil) Infantry
Division 6. 351st Infantry Regiment 7. 351st
Infantry Regiment (variant) 8. 133rd Infantry
Regiment 9. 752nd Tank Battalion 10. 760th
Tank Battalion 11. 15th Armoured Artillery
12. 19th Field Artillery Battalion 13. 29th Field
Artillery Battalion 14. 76th Field Artillery
Battalion 15. 81st Field Artillery Battalion
16. 337th Field Artillery Battalion

United States of America

Each regiment and separate battalion (fixed type) of the US Army is authorized to display a coat of arms on its flag and to wear a distinctive insignia, the design of which is based on the coat of arms, on the uniform.

Distinctive insignia were authorized in 1902 for wearing on the cuffs or lapels of the newly adopted officers' mess jacket, but this authorization was withdrawn in 1911. Their use was approved again by the War Department in 1920, but for officers only, who could wear them on the collar of their white uniforms and on the lapels of their mess jackets. The authorization was confirmed in September 1921 when another circular order stated that only regiments could seek permission to wear distinctive insignia.

Initially, badges of metal and enamel were worn on the lapels of the mess jacket and bronze badges on the collar of the service dress. Bronze badges were abolished in 1922.

The use of distinctive insignia was extended to independent battalions in December 1926, and company-size organizations were included in March 1928 when army regulations were revised to substitute 'organizations' for 'regiments and independent battalions'. From 1941 onward, virtually any unit was eligible to wear a distinctive insignia. However, the United States was then at war, and 55½ tons of brass were needed each year to make insignia. On 2 January 1943, therefore, the War Department ordered that no more distinctive insignia would be approved or manufactured for the duration of the war.

Amercian units overseas continued to have distinctive insignia made by local firms in Britain, Italy or Germany, without asking for authorization from the War Department. This practice became widespread from the winter of 1944-5 until about 1947, and thousands of these insignia were made illegally all over the world.

The use of distinctive insignia was officially sanctioned again on 2 August 1947, and by 1951 units that did not have an officially approved insignia before the war also became eligible to apply for authorization. Only colour-bearing units were allowed to apply for authorization to adopt a distinctive insignia, however, which meant that many units that had worn 'illegal' insignia during the war were not entitled to wear them.

In 1965, during the Vietnam War, distinctive insignia started to be authorized to some non-colour-bearing units, and this concession was later extended to higher and logistical commands, groups and hospital staffs.

Distinctive insignia have been used at every level of the US Army organization from divisional headquarters to company size units. Many belonged to regiments, but the majority belonged to battalions, which were more numerous than regiments.

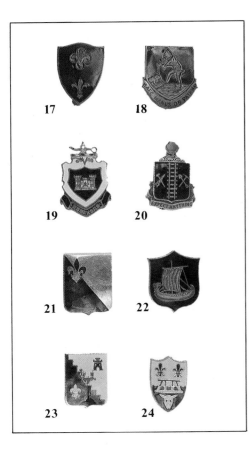

17
18
19
20
21
22
23
24

During World War II four field artillery battalions were attached to each infantry division, but only three to the armoured divisions and to the 10th Mountain Division. Illustrated are eight examples of artillery insignia, two of tank battalions, eight of engineers, two of medical battalions, and the distinctive insignia worn by 'short timers' who were due to go home.

The background colour of the badges usually indicates branch of service: blue, white or silver identified the infantry, red the artillery, red and white the engineers and maroon and white the medical corps. The symbols on the badges represent wars and campaigns in which the units participated or emblems connected with the state in which the unit was raised (Bibl. 168, 169, 170).

17, 18. 338th and 913th F. A. Regiment 19. Corps of Engineers 20. 21st Engineers Regiment 21, 22, 23, 24, 25, 26. 41st, 86th, 109th, 120th, 313th and 345th Engineers Battalion 27, 28. 109th and 313th Medical Battalion 29. 88th Signals 30. Short Timers.

25
26
27
28
29
30

E

EPAULETTE Derived from the French word *épaule* (shoulder), an epaulette is an old-fashioned decorative shoulder device consisting of a shield of gold or silver metal or lace, which is usually decorated with fringes on the outer end.

Epaulettes originate from the bundles of coloured cords that soldiers used to wear on the edge of their shoulders to stop their shoulder belts slipping off. When applied to a stiff shoulder piece, the cords developed into the epaulettes that became fashionable in the Napoleonic era and throughout the first half of the 19th century (Bibl. 6).

In Britain epaulettes were later worn only by naval officers, but in continental Europe they were worn in full dress by the army officers of several nations until the 1930s and, in simpler versions, by bandsmen. French *legionnaires* still wear the traditional epaulettes on parade dress.

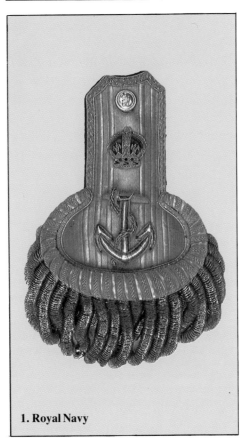

1. Royal Navy

2. Italian Army.

149

F

FACING Originally facing was the inner lining of 18th-century coats that was used as a means of distinguishing regiments.

The colour of the lining, which varied from regiment to regiment, was displayed when the end of the sleeves was turned up to make cuffs, and on the turn-backs of the skirt and the lapels.

Later the facing was applied directly on to the collars and cuffs of uniforms, thereby losing the original meaning of the word. The phrase the 'colour of the regimental facings' has become part of English military terminology, and it has the same meaning as **Waffenfarbe** in Germany — ie, branch-of-service colour.

FLASH In the armies of Britain and the Commonwealth countries, the flash serves the same purpose as the distinctive insignia used by other armies. It is basically a brightly coloured cloth badge, usually worn on the upper sleeve, but occasionally on the field hat, to identify branch of service or unit.

The flash and the **formation sign** have a great deal in common, but the formation sign identifies formations from the level of brigade upwards, while the flash identifies units up to regimental level. As a flash is essentially a plain coloured patch, it has a similar role to facing.

In reality, however, not all flashes are plain: the 4th/7th Royal Dragoon Guards adopted their embroidered blue, yellow and red arm flash in 1940 (Bibl. 75) and the 83rd (London) Signal Squadron has inherited the former World War I formation sign of the 47th (London) Division. Many authors would classify both these badges as regimental arm badges; others would consider the latter a formation sign. It is a controversial area.

The Royal Gloucestershire Hussars wear a yellow, maroon and royal blue flash, and the former Wiltshire Regiment wore a flash that had been worn in India before World War II as a **puggaree insignia.**

The units of the Parachute Regiment are distinguished by the smock flashes, which are rather large coloured patches made of felt. The 10th Parachute Battalion is identified by the Roman numeral in red on a black background, but most of the other units wear plain coloured patches.

Artillery units are identified by red and blue and engineers' units by blue and red,

colours they have worn in the form of various flashes in different shapes and sizes. The tunnelling speciality of the engineers was distinguished by a T of red felt.

All ranks of the 6th/7th Battalion, the Black Watch (Royal Highland Regiment), later 3rd (Territorial) Battalion, wore a patch of 42nd tartan cut in the shape of the cap badge on both upper sleeves and, below this patch, the ribbon of the French *Croix de Guerre*, which was awarded to the 6th battalion during World War I.

In the US Army the flash is worn by the

1. The Royal Gloucestershire Hussars 2. 10th Parachute Battalion 3. 16th Parachute Workshop REME 4. 4th/7th Royal Dragoon Guards 5. The Wiltshire Regiment (Duke of Edinburgh's) 6. Royal Regiment of Artillery 7. 83rd (London) Signal Squadron.

special forces on their green berets as a backing to the badge. The patterns vary according to the unit.

FORMATION SIGN Known in the United States as shoulder sleeve insignia or shoulder patch, a formation sign, which usually identifies a large formation from brigade upward, is worn on the upper sleeve or sleeves.

Formation signs are primarily an army insignia, although they could be used by other services. They were introduced in the trenches of the Western Front during World War I, and they took the form of coloured felt patches, which British soldiers initially had sewn on the back of their tunics, below the collar, later on the upper sleeves, to identify the formation to which they belonged.

Initially the coloured sign identified the battalion and brigade by means of geometrical patches, round, square, rectangular or triangular, which developed into the signs of higher formations.

John Player & Son issued two series of cigarette cards showing hundreds of these badges.

Belgium
The Belgian Army adopted formation signs during World War II in an effort to standardize its insignia with those of the British Army.

The first badge was adopted by the 1st Battalion Belgian Fusiliers in the United Kingdom, and it was followed in 1942 by the sign of Colonel Piron's Brigade, which depicted the head of the Belgian lion on a black triangle edged in scarlet.

From October 1944 several battalions of fusiliers were formed, and each wore a different formation sign made by local artisans from whatever materials were available. These were used until January 1945, when the battalions were grouped into five infantry brigades, each with its own badge (Bibl. 46).

Divisional signs adopted in 1948 all had a lion's head in gold on a different colour background. The formation sign of the 16th Armoured Brigade, which was adopted in 1950, is typical of the Belgian insignia of this type; it is made of woven silk, and either embroidered or printed.

The air force also adopted formation signs: the 1st, 7th, 9th and 13th Fighter Wing, for instance, wore the same badge but with different colour wings behind the wolf's head. The formation of the Air Force Base Command is embroidered on felt.

Britain
Although formation signs had been very popular among the troops and had proved useful during World War I, they were abolished in the early 1920s by the regular army, although they were still worn by the territorials. Many, therefore, remained in existence. The 47th (London) Division was disbanded in 1935, but its formation sign still managed to survive (*see* Flash).

Formation signs were reintroduced in 1940 for the use of command headquarters, armies, army corps, divisions, independent brigade groups and brigades. They were worn on both upper sleeves of the battledress blouse, below the **shoulder title** and above the **arm-of-service strip**; they were not worn on the greatcoat.

In hot climates they were worn on the shoulder straps of the shirt, usually by means of a **slip-on**, or, particularly in south-east Asia and India, one formation sign was displayed on the slouch hat or on the puggaree.

Two basic types of badges were used during World War II — the printed and the embroidered patterns — but others were made abroad by local artisans, in metal, plastic and in metal wire embroidery. Woven badges did not appear until after the war.

Embroidered formation signs should be divided into hand-embroidered and machine-embroidered patterns, and, although the skill of the embroiderer makes it difficult to tell them apart, hand-embroidered examples are made of thicker cotton or of thread.

Almost every British formation sign of the World War II era was made in an embroidered version. The highest type of formation sign illustrated is that of Headquarters 15th Army Group, which supervised the 5th US Army and the 8th British Army in Italy. It is a hand-embroidered badge.

The Garrison of Gibraltar had a special badge depicting a key, for Gibraltar was thought to be the key to the Mediterranean.

Two embroidered signs, with and without black trimmings, were used by the 1st Army, and the 8th Army had at least a dozen, the colour of the background varying from blue to black and different styles of embroidery used.

The 14th Army and the 3rd Indian Division (The Chindits) operated in south-east Asia; the Chindits' badge depicted the mythical Burmese beast Chinte, which gives its name to the force.

The 7th Armoured Division, the famous 'Desert Rats', wore three different formation signs. The first represented a realistic image of the jerboa, embroidered in pink silk on battledress cloth; a red rat within a red frame on a white background was used next; and finally, in France and Germany, the badge depicted a stylized red rat, picked out in white on a black background. The 4th Armoured Brigade was originally part of the 7th Armoured Division, and therefore, when it later became an independent brigade, it continued to wear the jerboa.

Dick Whittington's cat was the emblem of the 56th (London) Division, until it became an armoured division in 1947 and changed its badge to a motif that better suited its new role.

A macaw on a perch was the centrepiece of the 48th (South Midland) Division during

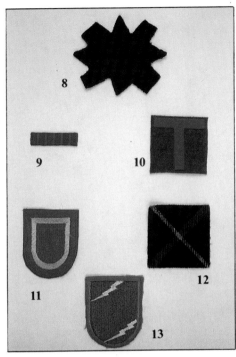

8, 9. Flash of the 6th/7th Battalion The Black Watch (Royal Highland Regiment) 10. Tunnelling Companies R. E. 12. Highland Light Infantry 11, 13. U.S. Special Forces.

1. HQ British Troops in Egypt and Mediterranean Command 2. 8th Army 3. 8th Corps 4. 43rd (Wessex) Division 5. 24th Independent Guards Brigade Group 6. 15th Army Group.

151

7. Garrison of Gibraltar 8. 1st Army 9, 10. 8th
Army 11. 14th Army 12. 7th Armoured
Division, 1st pattern.

13. As 12 but 3rd pattern 14. 56th (London)
Division 15. 3rd Indian Division (The Chindits)
16. 48th (South Midland) Division 17. 4th
Armoured Brigade 18. 40th Division.

World War II, while the cockerel was used by
the 40th Division, three battalions of which
formed the 27th British Commonwealth
Brigade that fought in Korea.

Every war-time formation had its own
printed sign, and printed formation signs
were, therefore, far more numerous than the
other patterns.

The 11th Corps, which was part of the
Home Forces, used a tower to symbolize its
defensive role in Britain. The 13th Corps,
which was formed in the Western Desert,
adopted an African motif, the gazelle, and,
just as appropriately, Roman ruins were the
motif used by the Cyrenaica District.

The formation sign of the Anti-Aircraft
Command was self-explanatory. The 4th Division adopted as its emblem a globe with its
fourth quadrant displaced, while the 46th
(North Midland) Division's badge depicted an
oak tree. The 53rd (Welsh) Division was
identified by a W in red on a khaki background; it should be noted that the badge
shown carries the **arm-of-service strip** printed
at its base.

The 52nd (Lowland) Division badge
showed the shield with St Andrew's cross set

above a scroll bearing the title 'Mountain',
which was the division's role. This insignia
was worn on the sleeves of an officer's service
dress, and it is printed on thick canvas instead
of the usual drill-like cloth

The three clover leaves were the emblem
of the 8th Indian Division, and also shown is

the Indian emblem of the 202nd Lines of
Communications Area in India.

The lion rampant of Scotland is depicted
on the badge of the West Scotland District,
which, after World War II, was redesignated
Lowland District, and on the badge of the
105th Coast Brigade RA (TA). Artillery signs

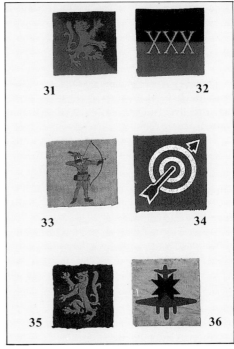

could usually be identified by the colour of the background — red and blue for the 30th Anti-Aircraft Brigade, for example, or red, although there are many exceptions to this rule.

Robin Hood was appropriately chosen to represent the North Midland District, whose headquarters was at Nottingham, and the last

19. 56th (London) Armoured Division **20.** 11th Corps **21.** Cyrenaica District **22.** 13th Corps **23.** 4th Division **24.** Anti-Aircraft Command. **25.** 46th (North Midland) Division **26.** 53rd (Welsh) Division **27.** 8th Indian Division **28.** 202nd Lines of Communication Area.

29. Lowland District **30.** 52nd (Lowland) Division. **31.** 105th Coast Brigade R.A. (T.A.). **32.** 30th Anti-Aircraft Brigade **33.** North Midland District **34.** 6th Anti-Aircraft Division **35.** Scottish Command **36.** 8th Anti-Aircraft Division.

shown is the wartime formation sign of the 6th Anti-Aircraft Division, which defended the Thames estuary.

Formation signs made of woven silk appeared during World War II, but although some very beautiful badges were produced in this style at that time, few units used them.

The personnel of Headquarters Scottish Command wore a woven sign, as did another Scottish formation, the 3rd Anti-Aircraft Division, which used as a motif the thistle of the World War I 9th Scottish Division. The 8th Anti-Aircraft Division was based in south Wales and western England, and the Eastern Command defended the eastern coastal area from The Wash to the Thames. Woven formation signs were, therefore, worn by units spread all over the country.

The use of formation signs continued after 1945, and recruits were issued with printed signs as before. Embroidered or other types of badges, strictly adhering to the design approved by the War Office, could be purchased privately. Woven badges came to compete with embroidered badges, which could be either hand- or machine-made, but woven versions were more accurately finished. Two types of weaving were prominent: the old silk method using synthetic silk, or cotton weaving, which developed in Germany.

Formation signs of woven silk could be found for every type of unit, from the British Commonwealth Forces, Korea and HQ Land Forces, Hong Kong, to divisions and brigades.

Some woven formation signs differ slightly from the original pattern; the background of that of the 6th Armoured Division, for instance, is dark blue instead of black, and the background colour of the two badges of the 6th Infantry Brigade varies, although both badges are woven.

Different types of formation signs were used during World War II in addition to those shown. They were worn for a number of reasons, but the two most probable explanations were the lack of any other badge or the temptation of wearing a more attractive badge than that on general issue.

Painted formation signs are not included in the latter category, although their quality may vary. It is not certain if formation signs were ever issued to minor African units, but the painted specimens illustrated for Sierra Leone and Nigerian units are the only examples known to the author. The painted sign of the 12th Corps was, on the other hand, as common as the other versions.

The 'felt on felt' method of manufacture was used for badges of simple design. The 3rd Division sign, for instance, was a simple design, but a printed version and one with the red triangle in embroidery also existed. The 1st Division was identified by a white triangle, and after 1945 the triangle of the infantry units was placed upon a larger triangle of scarlet

37

38

39

40

41

42

felt, with a yellow triangle for the armoured units. The 12th Division wore a white diamond, and the 42nd (East Lancashire) Division had the smallest badge in the British Army.

Some extraordinary embroidered badges were made in India, and the unusual style of

37. 3rd Anti-Aircraft Division 38. Eastern Command 39. British Commonwealth Forces Korea, 2nd pattern 40. 51st Independent Infantry Brigade 41. 6th Armoured Division 42. 56th (London) Armoured Division, 3rd pattern.

43

44

45

46

47

48

49

50

51

52

53

54

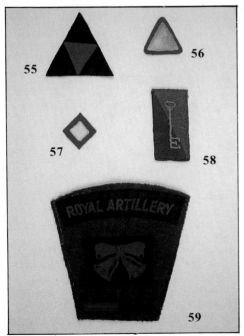

55

56

57

58

ROYAL ARTILLERY

59

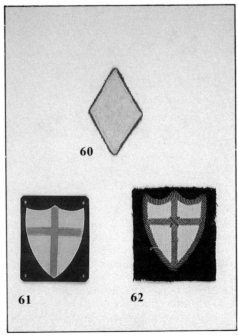

60

61

62

63

45. 7th Armoured Division 44. Hamburg District (BAOR) 45. HQ Land Forces Hong Kong, 2nd pattern 46. Hanover District (BAOR) 47. 6th Infantry Brigade 48. 31st Independent Infantry Brigade.

49. 6th Infantry Brigade 50, 52 Sierra Leone and Nigeria units 51. 12th Corps 53. Kohat District 54. The War Office.

55. 3rd Division 56. 1st Division 57. 42nd (East Lancashire) Division 58. Gibraltar Royal Artillery 59. 57th (London) Division, Royal Artillery 60. 12th Division 61, 62, 63. 8th Army.

1. 2nd Army 2. 2nd Division 3. 4th Division 4. 8th Division 5. 13th Division

6. 25th Airborne Division 7. 25th Parachute Division 8. 29th Division 9. Troops in the Southern Territories.

their embroidery identifies them immediately as Indian-made insignia. American-made badges, even though machine embroidered, are also easily identifiable.

Gold and silver embroidered formation signs were privately purchased by British soldiers in Italy, and as this trade proved profitable for the Italians, firms started to make formation signs in plastic and in metal. The metal shield illustrated was supposed to be mounted on a black felt backing.

On the second pattern of patch worn by the 47th (London) Division, Royal Artillery, are placed the **shoulder title**, the formation sign and the **arm-of-service strip** in order as worn on the sleeves of the battledress. The Bow Bells are embroidered on a twill backing instead of on felt.

France
The French Army introduced formation signs for wearing on the right upper sleeves after World War II.

By 1945 France had two armies, the 1st Army, which was identified by the *Rhin et Danube* insignia, and the 2nd, with the American-made cockerel badge in woven texture.

The patches of the 2nd Division of the 25th Airborne Division, first pattern, and the badge worn by Troops in Southern Territories are machine embroidered on a felt background, but all the other badges illustrated are of woven silk, sewn on a black felt backing.

The 4th Division used two formation signs. The first pattern depicted a pine tree, but the second pattern was changed to display the divisional number on a yellow and green background.

The badges of both the 8th and 13th Divisions display heraldic lions, but the 8th Division has two versions — with and without the yellow edging to the lion, crown and lettering.

The 25th Airborne Division was formed in February 1946 by the conversion of the 25th Infantry Division but was disbanded in 1948. The 25th Parachute Division was formed in Algeria in June 1956 and disbanded in April 1961 (Bibl. 94). The red eagle was worn by the 29th Division (Bibl. 23).

Germany, Federal Republic of
The *Bundeswehr* adopted formation signs in December 1962 for wearing on the left upper

1. Ministry of Defence 2. Central Military Stations 3, 4. 6th Armoured Division 5. 12th Armoured Division, 2nd Brigade.

sleeve of the service dress jacket. The eagle identifies headquarters organizations, and crossed swords identify schools and depots. Divisional badges display different emblems.

Military personnel serving at the Ministry of Defence wear a badge with a yellow and black border. The same badge, but with a silver and black border, would be used by personnel of the Territorial Defence Command, with a red border by personnel of the

Bundeswehr Central Military Stations and with a blue border by the personnel of the Central Medical Stations.

Each of the army's 12 divisions (1975) has its own emblem in the centre of the shield. The badge of the personnel of divisional headquarters is distinguished by a silver and black border, while the 1st, 2nd and 3rd brigades of each division have, respectively, white, red and yellow borders on their shield.

There are two basic types of badge: padded and hand finished and with an edging of twisted cords and machine made.

Ireland, Republic of

Formation signs were adopted in 1943 for Army Headquarters, Army Troops, for the two divisions and four commands, or districts, then in existence. The badges of the commands depicted a yellow star on different colour backgrounds (Bibl. 125).

These badges were changed in the 1960s when Army Headquarters adopted a gold sword hilt as its emblem, and the Air Corps adopted a winged Celtic boss in the national colours. New formation signs were adopted for the commands and for the Curragh Training Camp, which was formerly a command. The badge of the Eastern Command depicts a dark red spearhead on a yellow shield.

Later many badges were introduced for the branches of services of the higher formations. These attractive badges are all machine embroidered on coloured felt.

Italy

Divisional badges were adopted in September 1934 in the form of shields made of brass and enamel for officers and warrant officers, and painted on brass for the other ranks.

The basic design of the shield, which was the same for all divisions, was the Roman

sword on oak leaves at the top, but with different divisional numbers below the sword. The divisional title and the specification of the type of division were embossed on the sides.

The background of the shields of infantry divisions was blue; it was dark blue or black for other ranks. The badges of the Alpine division had a green background and the shield used by personnel of motorized divisions had a red background.

In 1938, for reasons of economy, cloth badges were adopted. They were in gold embroidery on coloured felt for officers and warrant officers and woven in rayon for other ranks.

The infantry divisions in North Africa, such as the 63rd, although not motorized were classed as motorized, and their shields had the red background.

The 31 infantry divisions were reorganized in 1939-40. One infantry regiment was taken

1. Army Headquarters 2. Air Corps 3. Army Headquarters Signals 4. Western Command 5. Southern Command 6. Curragh Training Camp 7, 8, 9. Western Command Artillery, Signals and Motor Transport.

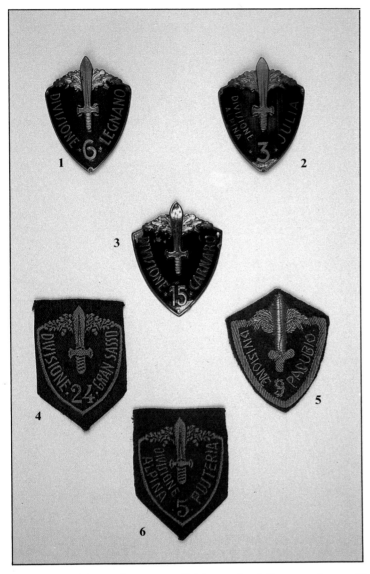

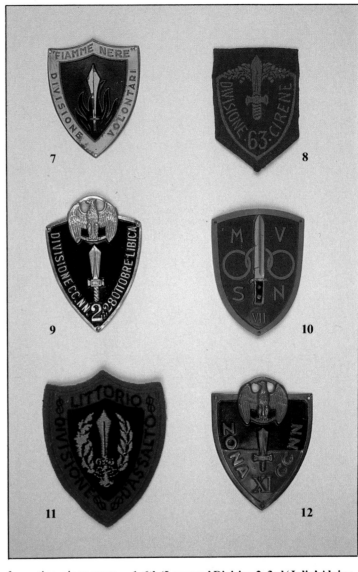

from each division to form a new division, and all were re-numbered and most re-titled.

The Fascist Militia organized its own independent formations during the Ethiopian campaign and the Spanish Civil War, and four MVSN divisions were permanently stationed in Libya by the late 1930s.

At home, the militia was divided into 14 territorial administrative zones, the personnel of which wore coloured arm shields with the zone's number. Two types of shields were used, the first made of bakelite and the second of painted metal. There were five versions of the painted metal type, which had the fasces in the centre for headquarters staff, the Roman sword with crossed rifles for fusiliers, and a machine gun for machine gunners with a burst of flames for support units.

After the Armistice of September 1943, the Black Brigades operating in the north of Italy adopted several unofficial formation signs, which they wore on the breast or on the

left upper sleeve. No formation signs were adopted by the regular army.

In the south the royal government formed five 'combat groups', some of which took part in the operations that led to the breaking of the Gothic Line. The formation signs of the combat groups depicted the group's emblem on a tri-coloured flash. There were several variants of these badges, made in metal or plastic, and printed or embroidered on felt or silk.

Shields were re-adopted in 1948 after the formation of divisions and brigades. The combat groups that were converted into divisions retained their emblems, and these were set in the centre of the new shields, new emblems being adopted for the new formations.

Most infantry formations had red shields; armoured formations had blue and red shields. Officers, warrant officers and sergeants wore embroidered shields, while the

1. 6th 'Legnano' Division **2.** 3rd 'Julia' Alpine Division **3.** 15th 'Carnaro' Division **4.** 24th 'Gran Sasso' Division **5.** 9th 'Pasubio' Division **6.** 5th 'Pusteria' Alpine Division **7.** Volunteers 'Fiamme Nere' Division (Spain) **8.** 63rd Motorized 'Cirene' Division **9.** 2nd Libyan Division '28 Ottobre' **10, 12.** 7th and 11th Zone, different patterns **11.** 'Littorio' Assault Division (Spain).

other ranks had woven badges, which, in the 1950s, were replaced by plastic shields stamped on khaki felt. Alpine formations wore green and parachutists light blue shields.

Light blue was also the branch-of-service colour of the veterinaries, and light blue was, therefore, the background colour of the badge of their training schools, while red was the colour for the school of infantry.

Because veterinaries were all officer cadets, they wore embroidered badges.

19

20

21

22

23

13. 'Aldo Resega' Black Brigade 14. Black
Brigade of Bologna 15. 'Cremona' Combat
Group 16. 'Cremona' Division 17. 'Ariete'
Armoured Division 18. 'Pinerolo' Brigade.

19. 'Granatieri di Sardegna' Division
20. 'Taurinense' Alpine Brigade
21. Parachute Brigade
22. Veterinary Training School
23. Infantry Training School

**1. The King's Guards 2. North Norway Brigade
3. 6th Combined Regiment 4. Varanger
Battalion.**

**1, 2. 4th Infantry Division 3. 1st Armoured
Division 4, 5, 6, 7. 2nd Corps.**

Norway
The combat formations and units of the Royal
Norwegian Army wear diamond-shaped
woven patches. Other units, the King's
Guards for instance, have different types of
badges. The army is formed by two brigades,
the South and the North Norway Brigades,
two divisions, nine combined regiments and
two independent battalions.

Poland
The Polish Army adopted formation signs in
the early 1940s when it was reorganized in the
West, its personnel wearing British battledress.

The divisions that belonged to the 1st
Polish Corps in Britain wore Polish formation
signs manufactured in the usual British patterns. The formations of the 2nd Polish Corps
were in Italy, where they used both British
issued and locally made badges.

The formation signs of the 2nd Corps

include examples of printed, machine-
embroidered and hand-embroidered badges
in thread and in silver wire. There are also
versions in plastic and in metal (*see* Slip-on).

The badge depicting the Mermaid of
Warsaw had a red background for corps
headquarters and a blue background for corps
supplies.

Spain

Since the end of the Civil War, the Spanish Army has used a vast array of badges, which have been embroidered, made of metal or plastic, and woven or printed.

Hand-embroidered or metal badges, also made in metal and enamel, were used during the Civil War. The formation sign of the 1st Independent Brigade is an example of an embroidered badge of that period. The sign of the 41st Infantry Division is woven in silk and sewn on khaki felt, and that of the 42nd Infantry Division is made of painted brass.

The emblem on the shield of the 31st Infantry Division of Maestrazgo is printed on white felt sewn on a blue backing. There is also a plastic version of this badge, with the divisional title shown around the edges.

United States of America

In the summer of 1918, when the 81st Division was at Hoboken, New Jersey, waiting to embark for France, its men wore the silhouette of a cat on the left shoulder as an identification mark; the division had come from the Carolinas where wild cats were common on the mountains.

It was the first patch to be worn on US Army uniform. Its use was officially authorized, and the other formations of the American Expeditionary Force were advised to adopt similar insignia, which were already used in France by the British Army.

These badges, called corps or divisional insignia, are still commonly known as shoulder patches, but their official designation is **shoulder sleeve insignia.**

The badges used in 1918 and in the early post-war years differed in many respects from the well known shoulder patches of World War II. The first patches were usually made of felt or hand embroidered, and the colour of some divisional insignia identified the branch of service of the wearer. The wild cat of the 81st Division and the frame around the patch were blue to indicate infantry and red for artillery. A coloured patch was placed be-

1. 41st Infantry Division 2. Ist Independent Brigade 3. 42nd Infantry Division 4. 31st Infantry Division.

1. 81st 'Wild Cat' Division, World War II pattern 2. 92nd Division, World War II pattern 3. 92nd 'Buffalo' Division, World War II pattern 4. 88th Division, World War I pattern 5. 88th 'Blue Devil' Division, World War II pattern 6. 6th Division.

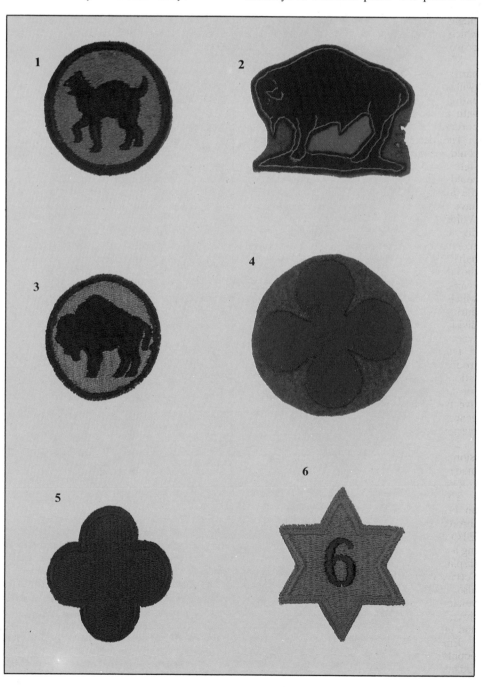

tween the legs of the buffalo of the 92nd Division and the clover leaf of the 88th Division was blue for the infantry, red for the artillery and black for the other branches. The insignia of the 88th depicts two crossed figure 8s, hence the clover leaf.

When divisions were reactivated for service in World War II, the design of many shoulder sleeve insignia was modified, and the new patches were machine-made in woven textile. Some World War I patches were also made for collectors in woven textile, including that of the 6th Division with its blue number.

The old Army Air Force patch, which symbolized a propeller in motion, was changed in March 1942 to the winged star, which was either machine embroidered on felt or woven.

Many other shoulder sleeve insignia were partly machine embroidered on felt or on twill, but the majority were in woven textile, entirely embroidered by machine, and often with an additional olive drab (khaki) outer border.

The design of shoulder sleeve insignia could refer to the formation's number, its state of origin or former battle deeds, or it could refer to some obscure event, related to the formation's history. Some divisions also have nicknames. The 81st is known as the 'Wildcat' division, and the 92nd, the 'Buffalo' division, was formed by Negroes whom the Indians called buffaloes, because of their curly hair. The 3rd Division's title was 'Marne', and the three white stripes on its blue patch symbolize the three major engagements in which it participated on the Marne front during World War I. At least four of this division's badges exist, including the woven type, and made by different manufacturers.

During World War II, when American troops were posted overseas, local populations provided for officers' use, particularly for those of the US Army Air Force, alternative types of insignia, smarter than those of general issue. Some of these badges are masterpieces of embroidery.

The patches of the 70th 'Trailblazer' Division and of the 75th Division were probably made in Europe. The latter is partly made in coloured cottons and partly in silver wire.

The European Theater of Operations was an organization that was based in Europe throughout the war years. The insignia of ETO depicted two flashes of lightning breaking a chain, while that of ETO Advance Base displayed in addition the emblem of the Army Service Forces at the top. Both insignia were also made in Britain, the latter in three versions: hand embroidered in coloured thread, of gold, silver and coloured thread, and printed.

Embroidered shoulder sleeve insignia were popular, especially among air force personnel, judging by the great quantities that have been

7. Army Air Force, 1st pattern 8. As 7, 2nd pattern 9. 3rd Cavalry Division 10. London Base Command 11. Aleutian Islands Base 12. 3rd 'Marne' Division.

13, 14, 3rd 'Marne' Division 15. 70th 'Trailbrazers' Division 16. 75th Division 17. European Theatre of Operations Advance Base 18. 8th Army Air Force

made in different patterns.

Shoulder patches of the 8th Air Force were made in Britain in at least three unofficial versions, and there is a printed version of the 9th's badge as well as embroidered types.

The shoulder sleeve insignia of the US Air Force Europe is of woven silk, made in Germany.

In 1946-7 the US 88th 'Blue Devil' Division and units of the British 13th Corps were stationed in the north-east of Italy as occupation troops. The Italians, realizing that the British soldiers had shoulder titles and that the Americans did not, endeavoured to fill this gap by producing hand-embroidered titles combined with matching clover leaf for every unit of the 88th.

These are examples of 'combined' insignia: the tab identifies the division's title and number and often the battalion's number and role, and it is worn with the shoulder sleeve insignia. These tabs cannot, therefore, be classified as either shoulder titles or shoulder tabs.

As these badges were unofficial and were privately purchased by 'short timers' due to go home (most GIs were waiting for discharge at the time), they were made in great numbers

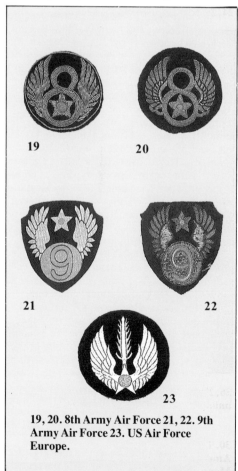

19, 20. 8th Army Air Force 21, 22. 9th Army Air Force 23. US Air Force Europe.

24, 25. 88th 'Blue Devil' Division.

26, 27, 28, 29. Examples of unofficial tabs of units of the 88th 'Blue Devil' Division.

30. Trieste, US Troops 31. 82nd 'All Americans' Airborne Division 32. 10th Mountain Division 33. US Forces in Berlin.

and variety, embroidered in silver, gold or in coloured thread. Badges embroidered in silver or gold were duplicated by badges in white of yellow thread. There were special gold or yellow tabs for cavalry reconnaissance, but always with the matching clover leaf below. Some clover leaves had the devil's head embroidered in the centre, as may be seen in the distinctive insignia of the divisional headquarters (*see* Distinctive insignia).

The clover leaf insignia of the 337th Field Artillery Battalion was edged in red thread and that of the 338th in white thread, to match the coloured edging of their titles.

Not surprisingly, when the time came to choose a special insignia for the US Army contingent in the Free Territory of Trieste (1947-54), a tab was selected, set above the

34. Korea Military Advisory Group **35.** 1st 'Spearhead' Armoured Division **36.** 1st Army, 1st pattern **37.** US Army Europe.

38. 1st Army, 2nd pattern **40, 39, 41.** 6th Army **42, 43.** 4th 'Ivy' Division.

clover leaf, with the city's coat of arms in the centre.

Since the early 1940s many shoulder sleeve insignia have been worn in combination with tabs, and the most common is 'Airborne', worn on the top of the formation patch. Some insignia, for instance that of the Airborne Command, had the tab woven in one piece with the formation emblem. The tab 'Mountain' could be worn only with the insignia of the 10th Mountain Division, the only US Army division trained in this role. The patch of the US Forces in Berlin had an integral tab, with 'Berlin' woven on the top.

Some tabs could be worn at the bottom of the main insignia; the personnel of the Korea Military Advisory Group had the initials KMAG below the insignia of the Military Government in Korea, and the armoured divisions had their own individual titles on straight tabs sewn below the triangular patches.

The design of several shoulder sleeve insignia was changed during or after World War II: for example, the background colour of the 1st Army patch was changed after the war from olive drab (khaki) to white and red. The shoulder patch of the Supreme Headquarters Allied Expeditionary Force, which was worn by General Eisenhower's staff during the campaign in north-west Europe, was re-

44, 45. 7th Army 46, 47. Combat Development 48. 40th Armored Brigade 49. 20th Engineers Brigade.

deployed after the war as the insignia of US Army Europe, but with a blue instead of a black background.

The insignia of the 6th Army was changed altogether during the war, and in 1957 the colour of its background changed from olive drab (khaki) to army green.

On 1 July 1957 the army green uniform replaced the olive drab (khaki) uniform, and the olive drab background of several shoulder sleeve insignia was changed to army green at the same time. Some insignia had an olive drab outer border, which also had to be changed to army green to match the colour of the new uniform.

The background colour of some patches, whether olive drab or army green, is supposed to match the colour of the uniform, but, as army green did not match the tan colour of the summer shirt, new badges with tan backgrounds were adopted.

All modern shoulder sleeve insignia have a woven border to prevent the badge from unthreading at the edges. This border represents the latest stage in the progress that distinguishes new badges from older ones. The difference may be seen between the old and new shoulder patches of the 7th Army and of the Combat Development.

Subdued shoulder sleeve insignia are worn on field uniform and different types are used.

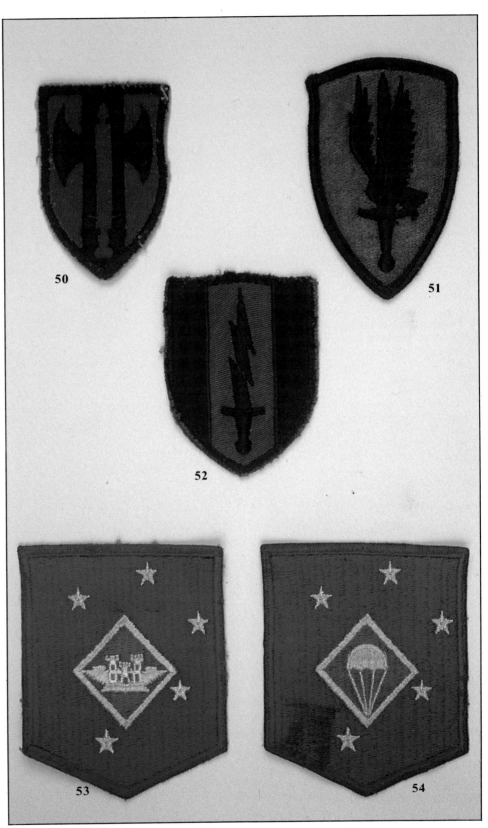

50. 18th Military Police Brigade 51. 1st Aviation Brigade 52. 1st Signals Brigade 53, 54. USMC Aviation Engineers and Parachutists.

A woven pattern, black on olive drab with woven border, is worn by the 40th Armoured Brigade and 1st Aviation Brigade, while another pattern depicts the main insignia in black machine embroidery on various shades of olive green twill.

The commandant of the US Marine Corps (USMC) authorized the wearing of shoulder sleeve insignia in 1943, and several were adopted before the end of the war.

The personnel of the 1st Marine Amphibious Corps used seven patches, which had a blank red centre of a speciality emblem. The nine types of shoulder patches of the Fleet Marine Forces—Pacific identified the assignment of the wearer.

Six divisions and three corps, numbered the 1st, 3rd and 5th, were formed during World War II. The 'Guadalcanal Blaze' of the 1st Marine Division was the first divisional insignia adopted in March 1943. It was followed by the 2nd and then by the others.

Aviation personnel adopted patches based on the design of the aircraft fuselage insignia, which were replaced by a winged USMC emblem above the wing's number.

The wearing of shoulder sleeve insignia by personnel of the USMC was forbidden in September 1947.

The patch worn by the Amphibious Forces, US Navy depicted the inter-allied emblem of combined operations in gold on a red background. A similar patch but on blue background was used by the army.

55, 57. USMC Aviation, 3rd and 1st Wing, different patterns 56. Fleet Marine Forces – Pacific, Artillery Battalions 58. 2nd Marine Division, 2nd pattern 59. 5th Marine Division 60. Amphibious Forces US Navy.

Vietnam, Republic of

Many different formation signs were used by the army of the Vietnamese Republic, and, although its allies changed in time, the badges maintained their Vietnamese character. Many depict eagles and tigers or mythical animals in printed, woven or embroidered versions.

The formation signs of the corps depicted Roman numerals in a ring, in red. Divisional patches displayed various emblems, usually on a blue background for infantry divisions. The patches of the marine battalions displayed animals.

The ARVN Rangers, formed in 1960, were in separate companies that were deployed in anti-guerilla warfare. Innumerable shoulder and pocket patches of rangers' units, identified by tabs within the shoulder insignia, were worn together or separately. Until 1973 the colour of the tab identified the corps of which the ranger unit was part — green, red, maroon and yellow for the 1st, 2nd, 3rd and 4th Corps, respectively — but after 1973 the tabs of all ranger units had a blue background.

The Vietnamese special forces had many different patches, and, following the American custom, several Vietnamese formations raised their own independent reconaissance units, which adopted their own insignia. Most of these badges were worn on the left upper sleeve, but some may have been worn on the breast.

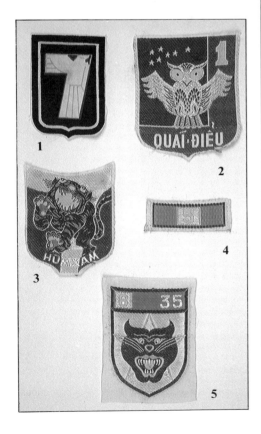

1. 7th Infantry Division 2, 3. 1st and 7th Marines Battalion 4. ARVN Rangers 5th Group 5. 3rd Corps, 6th Group, 35th Battalion 6. VNSF Mobile Strike Force 7. 3/573rd Provincial Reconnaissance Group 8. 3rd Infantry Regiment, Reconnaissance Company, 2nd pattern 9. 6th Group, 35th Battalion (Mobile Assault).

FOUL ANCHOR In nautical terms, the word 'foul' means 'entangled'. An anchor consists of a vertical iron shank that ends in curved arms, terminating in triangular points called flukes, and is usually provided with a transverse bar at the top, called a stock. It is the implement used to hold a vessel at rest in shallow waters.

A foul anchor is an anchor that has a rope twisted around it; it is the emblem of most of the world's naval organizations.

FOURRAGÈRE A French decoration for bravery instituted by Napoleon I, a *fourragère* is conferred upon units that have fought with distinction. Since World War I the *fourragère* has been conferred on recipients of more than one citation in the orders of the army. It may also be worn as a personal decoration.

It consists of a braided cord, in the colours of the ribbon of the *Croix de Guerre*, worn around the left shoulder.

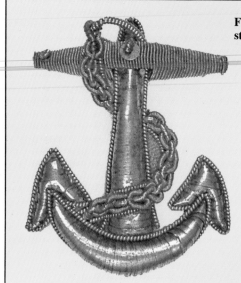

Foul anchor, Royal Navy pattern, for shoulder straps of Commodore 1st Class.

G

GIMP A twisted, plaited or woven cord made of silk or other material is known as a gimp. It is, for example, the cord that decorates the **gorget** patches of British brigadiers and substantive colonels.

GORGET Originally the part of a suit of armour worn to protect the throat, a gorget developed into an ornamental, crescent-shaped device, engraved or embossed with a coat of arms, that was worn by officers around the neck as a rank distinction. Neglected for about a century, the gorget re-appeared in Germany in the 1930s, when it was worn by standard bearers and military policemen.

Gorget patches were adopted by the British Army at the end of the 19th century for wearing at the front of the stand collar by staff and departmental corps officers, and, from 1921 onwards, by colonels and higher ranks only.

Field marshals and generals wear scarlet gorget patches with an embroidered ornament of gold oak leaves and acorns, brigadiers and substantive colonels wear patches with a **gimp**. The length of the patches varies according to the order of dress. The colour of the patch and of the gimp of brigadiers and substantive colonels corresponds to the colour of the branch of service (Bibl. 59).

The button of the gorget patch indicates class of rank or branch of service.

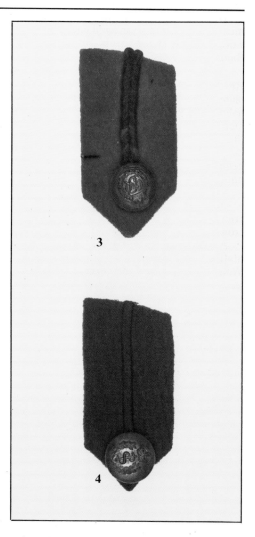

1. Generals' gorget patch 2. Brigadier's and substantive colonel's gorget patch 3. As 2 but small size 4. As 3 but of the Royal Army Medical Corps.

HI

HACKLE A bundle of feathers worn on the head-dress in combination with, or in place of, the cap badge, the hackle is the device peculiar to the British fusiliers. The Lancashire Fusiliers wore a primrose yellow hackle, the Royal Irish a green one, the Royal Inniskilling a grey one and the Royal Northumberland Fusiliers a red and white one. The other fusiliers regiments wore the white hackle.

All the battalions of the Royal Regiment of Fusiliers, which embodies all the former regiments, now use the red and white hackle,

The Black Watch (Royal Highland Regiment) is entitled to wear a red hackle which is worn in place of the cap badge on the blue Balmoral.

HELMET PLATE In general terms a helmet plate could be any badge that is worn on a helmet, although the word 'plate' describes a metal device. In British military terminology, the phrase refers to the large star-shaped badge worn by all ranks on the blue cloth helmet adopted in 1878 and used in full dress until the outbreak of World War I.

Helmet plates, in officers' and other ranks' versions, were ensigned by the Victorian **crown** until 1902 and then by the Imperial crown.

An officers' helmet plate of the North Staffordshire Regiment (The Prince of Wales's) is shown on the cover.

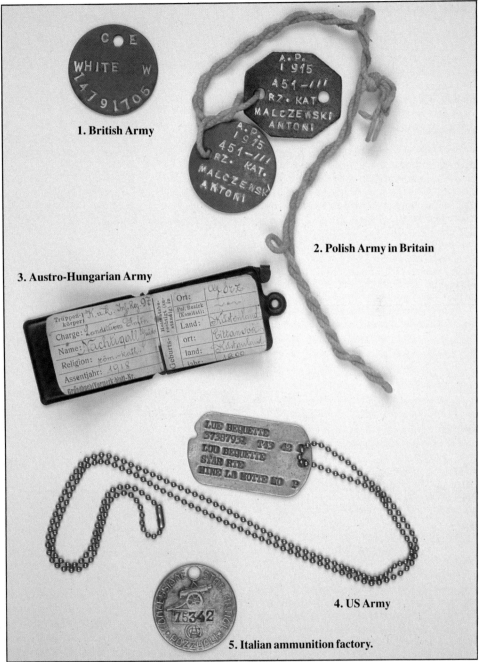

1. British Army

2. Polish Army in Britain

3. Austro-Hungarian Army

4. US Army

5. Italian ammunition factory.

Hackle of the Black Watch (The Royal Highland Regt).

IDENTIFICATION TAG Known also as a 'dog tag' and worn by soldiers in two world wars, identification tags are suspended around the neck.

During the 19th century the first identification tags were usually sewn into the field jacket. Later two tags were worn around the neck, suspended by means of a string or a chain, the idea being that one was taken to account for the casualty while the other remained with the body.

Identification tags were made in bakelite, plastic and metal, and the information they carry varies from the succinct, used by the British Army, to the type used by the Austro-Hungarian Army during World War I, which consisted of a flat metal box containing four pages listing the number of the regiment, branch of service, the soldier's name, religion, the year and precise locality of his birth, the address of next of kin and dates of smallpox, typhus and cholera inoculations.

American tags also displayed the address of the next of kin, and they were attached to an attractive and functional chain.

Workers in ammunition factories were often issued with identification tags, as their jobs had obvious risks.

L

LANYARD Derived from the Latin *lana* (wool), a lanyard was originally a woollen cord, straight or plaited, that could be worn in a variety of ways, but usually from the outer end of the shoulder strap, under the sleeve to the breast pocket button.

Lanyards have been made of wool, silk, rayon and other materials, and they are often composed of single and plaited strands of cord, some almost graduating to the status of **aiguillette**. Some bear a whistle, which is kept in the breast pocket.

They are worn for many purposes, according to national custom, including the identification of appointments or units. Instructors are often identified by a lanyard, and in Britain for instance, the 1st, 2nd, 3rd and 4th battalions of the Parachute Regiment are identified by green, yellow, red and black lanyards, respectively.

LAPEL The part at the front of a coat or jacket that is folded back is known as a lapel (*see* Facing).

LONG-SERVICE INSIGNIA Although in most countries long service and good conduct are rewarded by medals, insignia are also used.

British soldiers, up to the rank of corporal, serving in the regular army wear 'service stripes' on the left forearm to identify periods of long service. These stripes are actually chevrons; the first is awarded after two years, the second after six, the third after twelve years and another chevron is granted after each subsequent period of six years. Territorials, however, wear stars, one for each period of four years' service.

Members of the Danish Home Guard are awarded long-service badges; the green badge is granted after 10 years and the silver badge after 20 years of continuous service.

The US Army grants one service stripe for each three years of honourable service. The stripes are worn on the left forearm of the jacket and were olive drab (khaki) on a dark blue background for federal service and on buff for National Guards (Bibl. 164). Since 1957 the stripes are golden yellow on an army green background.

Enlisted men in the US Navy obtain one stripe for each period of four years' service. The stripes are worn on the left forearm and

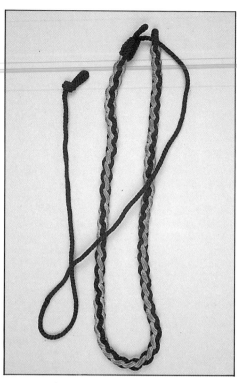

Examples of lanyards: the average pattern and the 'double' pattern with twisted and plaited cords.

are red for the blue uniform and blue for the white uniform. Three consecutive stripes with good conduct entitle the holder to wear gold stripes on the blue uniform.

1. Danish Home Guard 10 years service 2. As 1 but 20 years service 3. US Army 4. US Navy.

N

NATIONALITY INSIGNIA Included in the category of nationality insignia are all badges that identify the nationality of the wearer — coloured cockades and shoulder titles and some cap badges depicting a national coat of arms (the American eagle, the Polish eagle and the Nazi eagle, for example). The Nazi eagle was worn as a **cap badge** and above the right breast pocket by *Wehrmacht* personnel and on the left upper sleeve by the SS.

All ranks of the Dutch Army and Air Force display on the left upper sleeve the Nassau lion holding a sheaf of seven arrows, representing the seven provinces of the old republic of the United Netherlands. The motto traces its origins to 1544, when William of Orange inherited the principality of Orange from his cousin René de Châlons.

This badge was adopted during World War II, by the Netherlands armed forces in Britain, as a nationality title, and it displayed the wording 'Nederland' or 'Netherlands' in place of the motto at that time.

During World War II many volunteers joined the Polish armed forces in Britain. They were given special badges, which, by means of flags, identified their country of

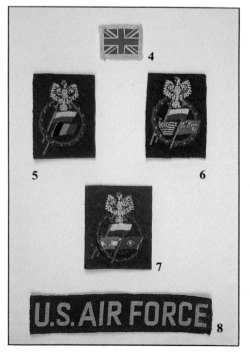

1. 'Wehrmacht' breast badge, army officers
2. Waffen SS sleeve badge, other ranks, as issued. 3. Netherlands Army sleeve badge, post-World War II.

4. British badge 5, 6, 7. Polish Volunteers from Belgium, North America and South America
8. US Air Force breast insignia.

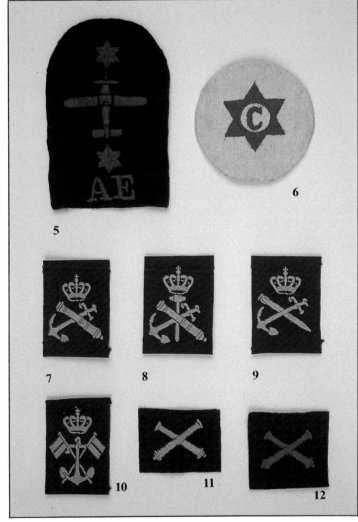

A selection of British non-substantive insignia including: Grossed Cannons 1. Torpedoes 2. Signallers' Flags 3. Signallers' Initials 4. Writer.

Royal Danish Navy: 7. Gunner 8. Gunner Mechanic 9. Torpedoman 10. Signaller Finnish Navy Gunners 11. Petty Officers 12. Seamen.

origin: Belgium, North or South America, for example. The badge of the volunteers from France displayed the French tri-colour only.

At the same time the Norwegian armed forces in Britain started to wear their national flag on the left upper sleeve, a custom that has been adopted by the *Bundeswehr* and other armies, for field uniform.

All ranks of the US Army wear the 'US Army' tab above the left breast pocket; air force personnel wear 'US Air Force'.

NON-SUBSTANTIVE INSIGNIA In British naval terminology non-substantive insignia are the badges worn by seamen on the upper right sleeve. They consist of a special device combined with the crown, six-pointed stars or letters of the alphabet. In most other navies they are called trade badges, and in the US Navy they are known as speciality and distinguishing marks.

Britain
The first non-substantive badge, for gunners, was adopted by the Royal Navy in 1860. It took the form of an old cannon barrel, which was modified to the current pattern in 1903. The torpedo was adopted in 1903 and crossed flags in 1890. The six-pointed star with initials in the centre — W for writer, C for cook and others — was introduced in 1932 and the aviation badges in 1935. The aeroplane depicted in the first badges had straight wings, but these were changed to swept wings from 1939 onward.

Red non-substantive badges are worn on blue uniforms, and blue on white uniforms; badges embroidered in gold are for the No. 1 uniform. Chief petty officers wear non-substantive badges on the collar of their blue jackets and on the right forearm of white jackets (Bibl. 60).

Badges with the crown and two stars are not used any more, and many others have

been changed since their adoption because of constant technological developments.

Denmark
The Royal Danish Navy used trade badges embroidered on black felt, but without the crown, until 1951.

Yellow badges woven on black silk backgrounds were adopted in 1951, all depicting the crown and the anchor combined with another device: the gun for gunners, gun and hammer for gunner mechanics, torpedo for torpedomen, crossed flags for signallers and others. The crossed flags were introduced in 1955.

Finland
Only two examples of trade badges of the Finnish navy have been included as most are self-explanatory; petty officers wear yellow badges, and conscripted seamen have red badges.

175

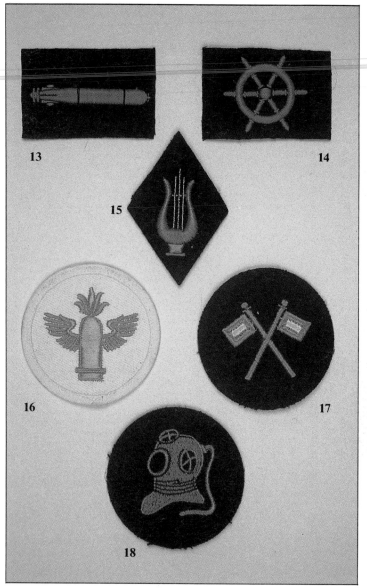

13. Torpedoman 14. Helmsman 15. Musician of the French Navy. 16. Gunner 17. Signaller 18. Diver of the German Democratic Navy.

19. Radar Specialist 20. Radio Signaller 21. Gunner 22. Helmsman 23. Artificer and Fireman of the Italian Navy.

France

The badges worn by French seamen on the left sleeve are called 'speciality insignia'.

Until 1940 there was a great variety of badges, in gold, silver and red embroidery, and cut out from red felt. Modern trade badges have assumed a more conventional appearance. Examples are shown of those of a torpedo specialist, musician and helmsman, which are machine embroidered on black felt.

Germany

The naval tradesmen of the German Democratic Republic wear machine-embroidered badges on round, dark blue backing for wear-ing on blue uniforms, and on white backing for white uniforms. They are worn on the left upper sleeve.

Although other naval insignia have been kept in the traditional German shape, size and appearance, the trade badges have changed in shape (from oval to round), while the majority of trade emblems have been modernized. The emblems of gunner, mine specialist, of engine and of electro-technician and of diver have been retained, but all the others have been updated, and most are now self-explanatory.

Italy

In the Italian Navy petty officers use gold trade badges to match the colour of their chevrons: red badges on blue or black are worn on blue uniforms and on white on the white summer uniform. Hand-embroidered badges on medium blue twill background were used on the fatigue jacket; badges on a dark blue or black background were worn on both sleeves of the walking out uniform.

In the 1960s hand-embroidered red badges were replaced by machine-embroidered badges, and plastic badges eventually appeared.

Italian trade badges, as those of other nations, have been modified several times during the present century as new specialities have developed.

O P

OVERSEAS SERVICE INSIGNIA The British Army adopted chevrons for overseas service during World War I. Each arm of the chevron was 20mm (¾in) long and was worn on the right forearm; one red chevron was awarded for service in 1914 and a blue one for each subsequent year. Similar chevrons were used during World War II, but not strictly on the basis of overseas service.

The US Army adopted overseas service chevrons during World War I. These were inverted gold chevrons, which were worn on the left forearm above the **long service stripes**, one for each six months of overseas service. The same insignia on the right forearm identified war wounds.

Yellow bars were granted during World War II and during the Korean War; each indicated six months' service in an operational area.

British and US Army overseas service insignia.

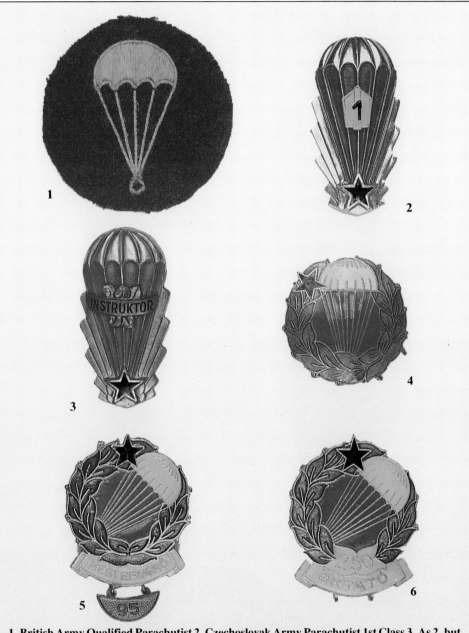

1. British Army Qualified Parachutist 2. Czechoslovak Army Parachutist 1st Class 3. As 2, but Instructor 4. Hungarian Army Parachutist 5. Master Parachutist, 95 jumps 6. Instructor, 250 jumps.

PARACHUTE INSIGNIA Not all nations adopted **wings** as the emblem for their paratroopers, as the parachute, which is the principal item of equipment, makes a decorative emblem in its own right.

The parachute on its own is worn in Britain on the left forearm by qualified parachutists who do not belong to an airborne unit.

The Czechoslovak badges illustrated were adopted in 1965; they are made in three classes, plus master, instructor and the badge of the basic brevet, which has the silhouette of a plane in its centre.

The previous badges had different wings on the sides of the parachute, and from 1951 to 1962 a miniature replica of the Czechoslovak Army cap badge was displayed in place of the proficiency number.

Several different types of Hungarian postwar parachutists badges can be found: the first badges were made of metal and enamel; later they were coloured with synthetic enamel; and finally plasticized badges appeared.

All the badges illustrated have two small hooks at the bottom, on which are hung the shields indicating the number of jumps made.

Some badges, however, display the number within the badge or they have a brass number stuck on the centre. The latest pattern for master parachutists displays the airplane and the number of jumps in the centre, but a separate brass plane and a tablet with a higher number of jumps are often stuck above the original ones.

Italian paratroopers initially wore wings with a white parachute in the centre, below the crown, but about 1940 the parachute insignia was adopted, first embroidered and later in metal. The men of *Folgore* and

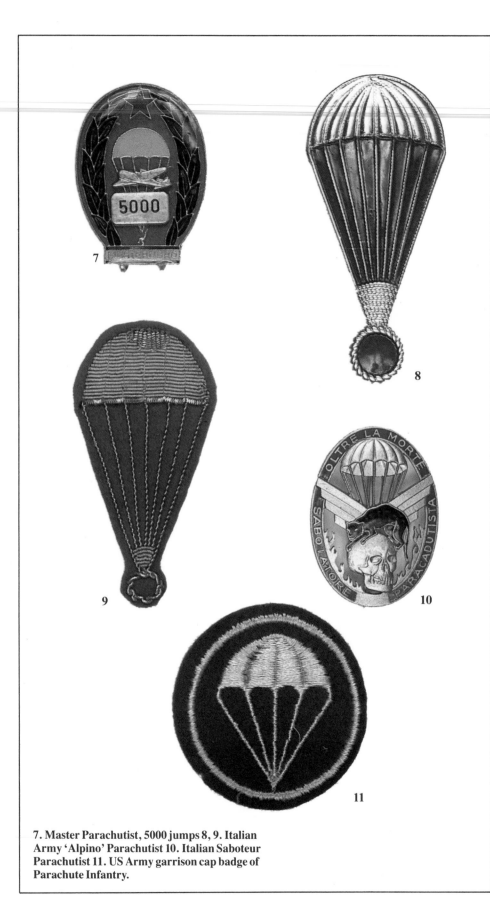

7. Master Parachutist, 5000 jumps 8, 9. Italian Army 'Alpino' Parachutist 10. Italian Saboteur Parachutist 11. US Army garrison cap badge of Parachute Infantry.

Nembo divisions had a gold badge on grey-green felt, while a silver embroidered badge was used by the *Carabinieri* Battalion. Coloured backgrounds were added under the parachute after the war: green for the Alpine parachute platoons, black for *Carabinieri* and blue for all ranks of the parachute brigade. Special airborne units wear additional badges on the left breast pocket.

The last insignia shown is the US Army patch, which is worn on the right side of the garrison cap, the parachute on a blue background identifying airborne infantry.

PIP Pip is the nickname given to the British Army officers' rank stars. *See* Rank insignia and Star.

PIPING Coloured felt stripes, which identify branch of service or regiment, are known as piping. They are usually worn along the outer edges of the shoulder straps, on the collar or elsewhere on the uniform. Gold or silver piping may identify class of rank.

Piping is applied in the following manner: the piping felt is placed on top of the cloth so that the edges of both are aligned; the two are sewn together in a straight line as near as possible to the edge; and the felt is then turned behind the cloth. The result is an even stripe of piping along the edge of the cloth. Modern piping is ready-made to be sewn where required.

POCKET INSIGNIA Pocket insignia are divided into two groups: pocket badges, which are usually made of metal, and pocket patches, which are of cloth and worn mainly by the personnel of the US armed forces.

Unit badges worn on the pocket have been dealt with under **distinctive insignia.**

Pocket badges A number of metal badges were adopted in Germany during World War II as combat awards for the personnel of the army, navy and air force. Two army badges are shown as examples.

The tank battle badge was instituted in December 1939. It was awarded for participation in three actions against the enemy on three different days. In June 1943 two new badges were instituted, which displayed at the bottom the number of engagements (25 or 50 and 75 or 100) in which the recipient participated.

The general assault badge was instituted in June 1940, originally only for the personnel of assault engineers units, but later it was made available to all combatants not entitled to other similar awards. In June 1943 two new badges, as in the case of the tank battle badges, were adopted. These badges have a pin at the back and were worn on the left breast pocket.

The pilots of the Italian Air Force were awarded gold, silver and bronze badges according to the number of combat actions. The gold badges had the central device in gold only, and by 1942 the badges of the first two classes were made of aluminium while the central devices of first-class badges were painted yellow.

There were 10 different badges, one for each flying speciality.

Many NATO insignia are worn on the breast pocket: the Ace Mobile Force (Land) (AMF) was formed in 1960. FOURATAF (Fourth Allied Tactical Air Force) was formed earlier in Germany; the badge is worn by a recruiter of the US Army Reserve.

Pocket patches : In the US armed forces formations from the level of brigade upward are authorized to wear shoulder sleeve insignia. Ranger battalions, for instance, were granted shoulder tabs only. Regiments and other units that do not qualify for a shoulder insignia wear the unit patch on the pocket of the field dress. Before the introduction of subdued insignia, coloured patches were used; those of the 3rd 'Brave Rifles' Armoured Cavalry Regiment and of the 14th Armoured Cavalry Regiment are examples of pocket patches used in the 1950s.

All the others are self-explanatory. The 501st Tactical Missile Wing is a unit of the US Air Force, which is in charge of 'Cruise' missiles, and the last illustrated example is the pocket insignia of the Special Forces.

POMPON See Tuft.

1. 3rd 'Brave Rifles' Armored Cavalry
Regiment 2. 14th Armored Cavalry Regiment
3. 1st Battalion 13th Infantry Regiment,
Reconnaissance 4. 501st Tactical Missile Wing
5. Special Forces.

1. World War II German Tank Battle badge 2. General Assault badge 3, 4, 5. Italian Air Force Reconnaissance at Sea, Assault-Combat and Interceptors badges 6. Ace Mobile Force (Land) AMF 7. 4th Allied Tactical Air Force 8. US Army Reserve Recruiter.

Czechoslovak proficiency insignia: 1. Exemplary Soldier 2. 'Vzorny Posluchac' 3. Specialist 1st Class 4. Rifle Shooting Award 3rd Class 5. Military Innovator.

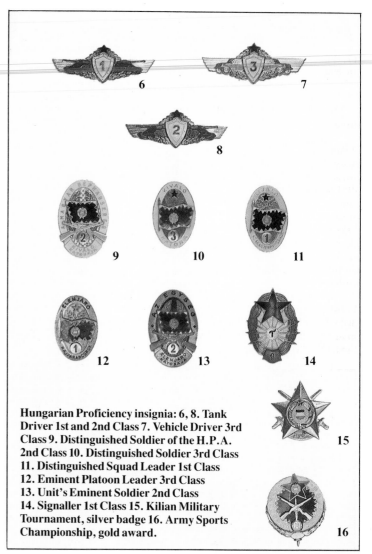

Hungarian Proficiency insignia: 6, 8. Tank Driver 1st and 2nd Class 7. Vehicle Driver 3rd Class 9. Distinguished Soldier of the H.P.A. 2nd Class 10. Distinguished Soldier 3rd Class 11. Distinguished Squad Leader 1st Class 12. Eminent Platoon Leader 3rd Class 13. Unit's Eminent Soldier 2nd Class 14. Signaller 1st Class 15. Kilian Military Tournament, silver badge 16. Army Sports Championship, gold award.

PROFICIENCY INSIGNIA Badges of the Warsaw Pact armies that are awarded to individuals or to units to encourage and reward personal skills and general efficiency are known as proficiency insignia.

The badges cover all fields of activity, military and sporting in particular, and some nations have introduced branch-of-service insignia that display a proficiency class number (*see* Parachute, Trade insignia and Wings) to further stimulate the pride of the soldiers.

These badges are usually made of metal, and they are worn on the right breast of the service dress jacket.

Czechoslovakia
In Czechoslovakia special badges are granted to exemplary soldiers and exemplary students frequenting military schools. Two of the latter type bear the lettering *Vzorny Zák*, for students at basic schools, and *Vzorny Posluchac*, for students at colleges and at the academy. Specialists may be eligible for wings of 3rd,

2nd, 1st class or with an M in the centre for master specialist.

Proficiency in rifle shooting is rewarded by a star, and any individual, of any rank, who puts forwards any viable suggestion or invention that would improve the efficiency of the establishment, is eligible to the badge of 'Military Innovator'.

Hungary
Some remarkable badges made of metal and enamel reward individual proficiency in the Hungarian Army. Most are made in separate parts, meticulously joined together. Numbered interchangeable shields are set on the base of the badge by means of a screw and small nut. Even a football is fixed in this manner.

Tank drivers and vehicle drivers wear winged badges numbered 3, 2 or 1, with the letter M for masters.

The badges for distinguished performance were adopted in 1967 for soldiers, squad and

platoon leaders, company and battalion commanders. All are numbered from 3 to 1.

Proficiency badges are awarded to individuals or to individuals within units and, each year, at top level to the best servicemen within the army.

Self-explanatory badges are awarded to individuals for distinguished performance in their duties or for advanced performance. Such badges are also awarded to an individual within the unit.

A special proficiency badge, in three classes, is worn by signallers, and badges in gold, silver, bronze and iron were given to participants to the Kilian Military Tournament. A similar badge carries the letters KTP under the star.

Badges for sporting achievement include the Army Championship Award, in gold, silver and bronze, and the championship badges of the military academy and of other establishments and units, which are made in gold, silver and bronze.

17. 'For Our Socialist Country', gold award
18. Sports badge, gold.

The star 'For Our Socialist Country' is in three classes (Bibl. 122, 123).

Poland
A set of 20 branch-of-service badges, made in brass and enamel, was adopted in Poland in 1951 for wearing on the breast. They were the same for all ranks and displayed the branch-of-service badge, set in relief, in the centre. In 1958 the driver trade was divided into three classes, and a new, slightly smaller, badge was made, with a flat branch-of-service emblem set in the enamel and the class number at the bottom.

Polish insignia: 19. Driver 3rd Class 20. Sailor 3rd Class 21. Tankman 2nd Class 22. Infantryman 3rd Class. 23, 24, 25, 26. Examples of Soviet Proficiency badges.

Proficiency badges for soldiers (*Solnierz*) and sailors (*Marynarz*) in gold or silver were introduced in 1958 and later divided into three classes. Wings for tank crews were adopted in the same year, with number 3, 2, 1, or the letter M for masters (Bibl. 156, 157).

Shoulder patches displaying the branch-of-service badge and proficiency number are now used by army and navy personnel.

Soviet Union
In the Soviet Union proficiency badges rewarded sport and industrial achievements long before the war. The well known Guards' badge was adopted in May 1942 for the personnel of units that had gained particular distinction on the battlefield. In the same year a series of 25 metal and enamel badges, one for each branch of service, was introduced to reward individual proficiency. The pattern of these badges was changed in 1955, when several branch-of-service badges were modified. The centre of the previous badge displayed the hammer and sickle only, on a round red background. New badges are worn now, which display class of proficiency.

PUGGAREE INSIGNIA Puggaree insignia is a stripe of cloth, originally muslin, wound around the base of the colonial helmet but above the brim. The British foreign-service, or Wolseley pattern helmet, adopted in 1934, was available in white and khaki versions, or with a white cover, and a white puggareee could be fitted on the khaki helmet.

The puggaree was usually the same colour as the helmet, although some regiments used coloured puggarees on the white helmet: The Buffs (The East Kent Regiment) wore a buff puggaree, the Northumberland Fusiliers had a red and white puggaree, and the Duke of Cornwall Light Infantry a red one.

Generals and staff officers and others holding special appointments wore the **aigrette** on a white helmet, in dress order, but usually the cap badge was worn at the front in the centre of the puggaree, or a **flash** on one side.

Many of these flashes were very simple: square- or diamond-shaped, they depicted the regimental or branch-of-service colours. Others were in the form of a **shoulder title** and bore the regimental title and often also the number of the battalion.

Puggaree insignia of the King's Regiment (Liverpool) and of the 6th Battalion of The Royal Sussex Regiment.

R

RANK INSIGNIA All the devices and badges displayed on the uniform to identify the position of the wearer in a specific hierarchy of command are rank insignia.

Any conventional army is composed of officers and other ranks (in the United States, officers and enlisted men), but, technically, there are three classes of rank — officers, non-commissioned officers and rank and file — and often there are four — officers, warrant officers, non-commissioned officers and rank and file. The rank and file includes corporals and privates (enlisted men in the US Army).

The officers' class of rank is sub-divided according to the type of formation or unit they command, a rule that varies from nation to nation according to the nature of the army establishment. General officers command higher formations — ie, armies, army corps divisions and brigades, although often the rank of brigadier may be a temporary appointment rather than a general officer's rank. The other officers' ranks could be sub-divided into field officers, captains and subalterns — ie, company officers — or into senior officers (down to major) and junior officers (from captain to second lieutenant) according to national custom.

Apart from rank insignia, officers and other ranks wear badges that differ in quality, and non-commissioned officers often also wear different badges, which could be considered as a class of rank distinction. General officers, flag officers and officers of air rank, who are at the top of their services' hierarchy, usually wear their own distinguishing cap badges; these cap badges identify class of rank, and, in the case of British field-marshals, the badge identifies one rank.

Chinstraps, cap bands or other head-dress or tunic devices were and are used to display rank, in combination with, or in lieu of, the main rank insignia. The other means of rank identification are dealt with in the appropriate sections of this book.

At the beginning of the 20th century the rank within the armies of the major powers established four different systems or fashions, which were copied by other nations and still survive:

1. Austria: all ranks' insignia were worn on the collar of the tunic on branch-of-service colour.

2. Britain: officers' rank insignia were worn on the shoulder straps; other ranks' insignia on the sleeves.

3. France: all ranks' insignia were worn on the sleeves.

4. Russia: all ranks' insignia were worn on the shoulder boards together with branch-of-service colour (*see* Shoulder strap).

The German system deviates from the Russian, with shoulder cords replacing shoulder boards.

Army establishments that used one or the other system of rank identification did not necessarily adopt the whole system. In Belgium, for example, army officers have Austrian-style badges, while non-commissioned officers wear **bars**.

Fashion — and often political reasons — also caused some nations to change their army ranking from one system to another.

Austria-Hungary
All ranks' insignia were displayed on the collar of the tunic, which was faced in branch-of-service or regimental colour; later it was worn on coloured patches, and, from 1917, rank insignia could be worn directly on the collar. Field officers, however, usually retained the badges on the collar patches.

Marshals were identified by special gold embroidery on a scarlet collar.

Generals wore a 33mm (1⅓in) stripe of gold lace sewn along the front and bottom edges of their scarlet collar, with three silver stars joined by a wreath for the *General-Oberst* and three, two or one stars for the other generals.

Field officers wore gold or silver lace stripes, according to the colour of the buttons, and from one to three stars in opposite colour — gold stars on silver lace and *vice versa*. Company officers wore from one to three gold or silver stars according to the colour of their buttons.

The embroidered six-pointed stars were, and are still, made in a manner that recalls the shape of the edelweiss. The junior ranks wore a combination of narrow stripes and stars, and the last three ranks wore on their collar patches celluloid stars, which were later sewn directly on the collar.

The administrative officials of the armed forces had different rank titles, used different pattern of lace and wore rosettes instead of stars on the collar (*see* Distinction lace).

Austria
1933-8 : The same type of rank insignia that had been worn in the Imperial Army — stars and lace in opposing colours — was adopted by the Republic of Austria for wearing on collar patches that identified the branch of service.

Austro-Hungarian rank insignia of corporal.

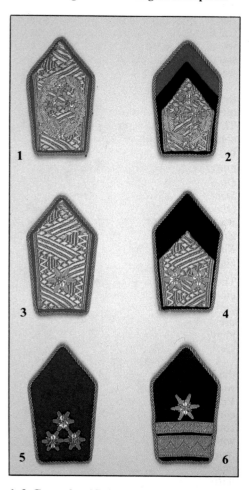

1, 3. General and Brigadier 2, 4. Field officers 5. Captain 6. Fährich'

1955-86 : Austria regained independence by the Four Powers Agreement on May 1955, when the armies of occupation were withdrawn and the new Federal Republic of Austria began to rebuild a new army. Rank insignia are worn on the head-dress (*see* Distinction lace) and on the collar of the jacket or on the shoulder straps of the combat and fatigue uniforms (*see* Slip-on).

The collar patches of the grey jacket display rank insignia on branch-of-service colours (*see* Collar insignia), and, according to tradition, the stars still recall the image of the edelweiss. The patches are pentagonal in shape and fit the collar. Those of the officers and of the non-commissioned officers are edged with gold or silver twisted cords, respectively. The *Vizeleutnant* wears special gold and silver edging. Gold or silver, gold and silver (*Vizeleutnant*) or no edging at all is used to identify class of rank on the spearhead-shaped collar patches of the greatcoat, which are always worn with a button.

The patches worn by generals and field officers on their jackets have silver embroidered stars on gold lace in a traditional Austrian zigzag pattern. The General and the Chief of Staff wear three stars and a silver oak wreath; the *Korps-kommandant* wears three stars, and divisional generals and brigadiers wear two and one stars, respectively.

The company officers have gold stars, and the *Fähnrich* (Ensign), the lowest of the officers' class, wears a special collar patch. The *Vizeleutnant* is classed as the first non-commissioned officers' rank and is followed by:

Offizierstellvertreter	silver stars on
Oberstabswachtmeister	large and narrow
Stabswachtmeister	silver lace
Oberwachtmeister	silver stars on
Wachtmeister	large lace
Zugsführer	grey stars without
Korporal	lace
Gefreiter	

The non-commissioned officers' stars could be embroidered in silver or in grey cotton.

Rank insignia are displayed on the headdress in the form of lace stripes, and they identify each individual rank from general to *Gefreiter*.

Rank stripes are worn on the black band of the peaked cap, in gold for officers, in silver with a gold zigzag design for *Fähnrich* and *Vizeleutnant*, in silver lace for the non-commissioned officers and in grey lace for the corporals. Generals wear one large gold stripe with narrow stripes above, according to the number of stars on the collar patch, and the field officers have a medium gold stripe with narrow ones above it. Company officers wear the narrow stripes only. When more than one stripe identifies a specific rank, the stripes are woven in one piece.

A similar system of rank identification is used on forage caps: the stripes are placed below the cockade in an inverted V-shape, with a large stripe above narrow ones.

Belgium

The officers and warrant officers of the Belgian Army wear rank insignia on the collar patches of their dress and service dress uniforms.

Generals have two gold bars surmounted by one, two or three six-pointed stars and by

the *foudre* or, in the case of 'technical' generals, by the corps badge. Field officers wear one bar surmounted by stars, and the *Capitaine-commandant* wears three stars surmounted by a narrow bar (*see* Collar insignia). Company officers have the stars only, in silver for cavalry officers and in gold for all the other branches.

Warrant officers wear silver rank badges:

7. 'Vizeleutnant' 8, 9. Senior NCOs 10. Junior NCO 11, 12. NCOs for greatcoat.

one star for the *Adjutant* and one star above a silver wreath for the *Adjutant-chef*, who replaced the warrant officer 1st class who used to wear one star below a small silver bar.

The type of insignia displayed on the peaked cap and the chinstrap identify class of rank (*see* Cap badge). In barracks dress and shirt sleeve order or in combat and fatigue uniforms, rank insignia are worn on the shoulder straps; ranks below warrant officer use plastic **slip-ons** with white chevrons.

There are now four services in Belgium — the army, navy, air force and medical service. The medical service was formed by the amalgamation of the medical branches that had previously belonged to the other three services.

Naval personnel wear conventional navy rank insignia. The air force adopted British-style rank stripes during World War II, when Belgian airmen wore British uniforms. Rank insignia were previously displayed on the collar. Officers and warrant officers of the medical service wear rank stripes as the air force, but made of gold.

Sergeants and corporals of the four services wear bars on the forearms of the jacket.

Belgian Colonel of infantry.

Britain

The modern rank insignia of the three services of Britain are the result of a constant process of developement that, in the case of the Royal Navy, started in 1783 when **distinction lace** was introduced for flag officers. Distinguishing marks of rank for the **epaulettes** of army field officers, in the form of crowns and stars, were adopted in 1810. In 1855 rank insignia were moved to the collar, and two or one stars were granted to captains and lieutenants, respectively. The 2nd lieutenants did not get the **pip** until 1902, and lieutenants then obtained two stars and captains three.

In 1880 rank insignia were again transferred to the shoulders, on shoulder cords or **shoulder straps** according to the type of uniform, but other trimmings were used to identify rank or class of rank, including embroideries, stripes of lace or Austrian knots.

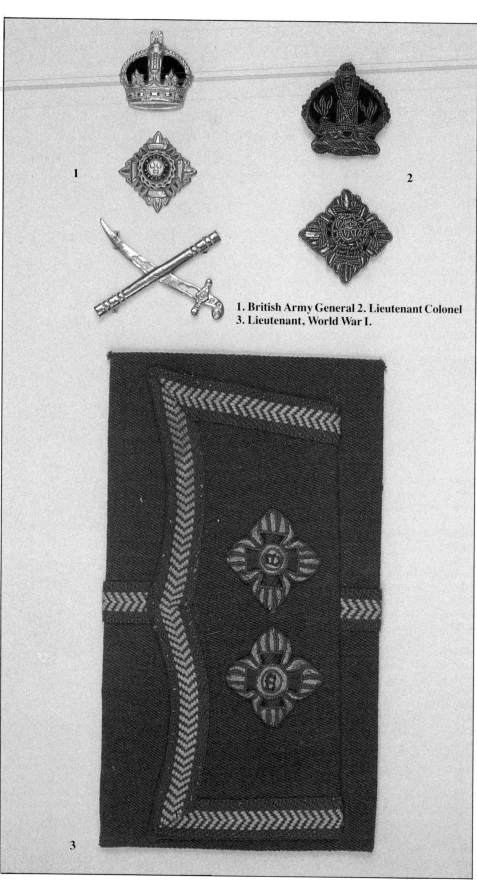

1. British Army General 2. Lieutenant Colonel 3. Lieutenant, World War I.

The army rank insignia displayed on the shoulders are formed by a combination of devices: the **crown**, the **star**, the crossed baton and sword for generals, and the crossed batons set on a laurel wreath, below the crown for the Field-Marshal. These devices were made in metal, often with enamelled details, or in metal wire embroidery.

The officers' khaki service dress was adopted in 1902, and in November 1902 a new definitive system of officers' rank insignia was adopted for all except Scottish service dress.

The badges were displayed on the cuffs in the form of thread-embroidered crowns and stars stitched on a false flap decorated by a stripe of chevron lace. Additional stripes were sewn around the cuff; one stripe for sub-alterns, two for captains, three for majors (with stripes of gold braid in between), three khaki stripes and four gold stripes for lieutenant-colonels, and four khaki and five gold stripes for colonels. The officers of the Scottish regiments did not wear the flap, and had the stripes set in a different manner (Bibl. 60).

Badges of rank made of bronze were introduced during World War I for wearing on the shoulder straps of the service dress, and in 1920, after the abolition of insignia on the cuffs, they became standard rank badges for all officers.

Plastic badges were introduced during World War II as an economy measure, and thread-embroidered badges on coloured **backing** were adopted in 1940 for the shoulder straps of the battledress. Plastic badges were also worn on battledress, but with coloured backing underneath.

After 1945 crowns and stars were worn without any coloured backing, embroidered on khaki felt or on **slip-ons** (*see* Aide-de-camp).

The **crown** was changed in 1953 to the St Edward's pattern, and at about the same time the generals' device, the crown and the star appeared in their latest versions, made of anodized aluminium.

The cuff stripes of the Royal Air Force officers were introduced in 1919; they are still used today.

Finland
Except in wartime, when officers pinned their rank devices directly onto the collar and sergeants wore their stripes on shoulder straps, insignia of rank have always been worn on the collar of the tunic, on embroidered patches identifying the army branch of service.

Air force personnel wear the same rank insignia as the army, but on blue and black collar patches.

The branch of service is identified by the colour of the patch and by the colour of its embroidered frame, but the colour of the frame also identifies class of rank. All officers

and officer cadets are distinguished by two fir twigs embroidered in the corners at the front of the patch within the frame. The general officers' frame has one large and one narrow embroidered stripe; field officers have two narrow stripes; and company officers one stripe only, as do the other ranks.

Generals' collar patches display one, two

or three gilded Finnish lions, set upright in relation to the wearer on the stand-and-fall collar, or one above the other on the patch used on an open collar, which is worn vertically. The Finns follow the Russian tradition of appointing generals of the branches of service, instead of keeping the general officers as a separate class.

4. Captain, bronze 5. Colonel, plastic 6. Major, Corps of Royal Engineers 7. 2nd Lieutenant, Infantry and a selection of modern rank insignia.

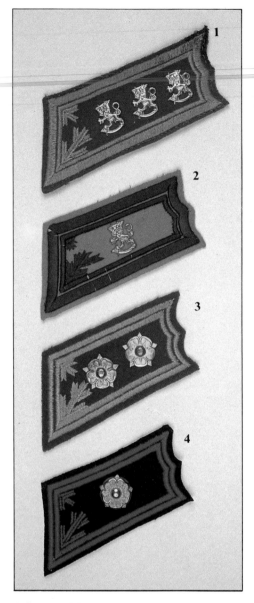

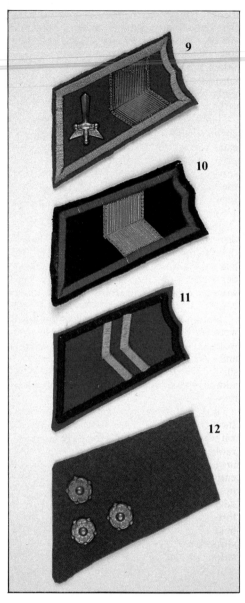

1. General GS 2. Major General, Cavalry 3. Lieutenant Colonel, Engineers 4. Major, Coast Artillery 5. Captain, Artillery 6. 2nd Lieutenant, Reserve 7. Officer Cadets

8. Military Specialist 9. Warrant Officer, Specialist Service Corps 10. Sergeant Major, Coast Artillery 11. Junior Sergeant, Air Force 12. Captain, World War II field uniform.

Field officers wear from one, two or three gilt or brass roses, 16mm (¾in) in diameter; captains and subalterns have from one to three smaller roses, 13mm (½in) in diameter, in the following order: *Kapteeni* (three roses), *Yliluutnannti* (two roses and gold bar in between), *Luutnantti* (two roses) and *Vänrikki* (one rose). Until 1941 the officers of the Reserve wore silver collar devices.

Technical officers wear the normal rank devices preceded by the technical branch badge, which replaces the fir twigs. The collar patches of the Military Specialists have no fir twigs; they wear six-pointed gilt stars instead of roses and the specialist's branch badge.

Chaplains wear the Latin cross surrounded by a laurel wreath on a black patch. The 1st-class chaplain is comparable with the general's rank and has one large and one narrow yellow stripe around the collar patches, while the other two classes wear two or one narrow crimson stripes.

Officer cadets wear company officers' type patches, dark blue with a yellow frame, and the Cadets School badge. They have chevrons on the shoulder straps.

Until 1952 there were four ranks for non-commissioned officers, in addition to that of corporal, which is classed as rank and file. The junior sergeant, sergeant and senior sergeant

wore two, three or four yellow chevrons, and the sergeant major wore a large gold chevron, 20mm (¾in) wide. The collar patch illustrated belongs to a specialist warrant officer of the Service Corps. Two other ranks were added later: those of senior sergeant and the warrant officer, who wear a large chevron in front of one or two narrow chevrons, respectively.

Senior non-commissioned officers down to the rank of senior sergeant were also granted the fir twigs on the collar patches.

Rank insignia are placed on the cuffs of the greatcoat and raincoat in the form of stripes or chevrons, sewn on to hexagonal patches for the cuffs of raincoats (Bibl. 90, 91, 92).

Italy

The Italian Army adopted officers' rank insignia on shoulder straps in 1902. Previously the generals had worn embroidered cuffs, and the other officers had gold or silver chevrons surmounted by Austrian knots above the cuffs. **Epaulettes** were also used until the 1930s

In 1902 generals obtained shoulder straps covered with silver lace displaying gold rank stars; field officers had silver stars and a stripe of gold or silver lace, according to branch of service, along the sides and the inner end of the straps; the other officers' ranks were identified by stars only, in gold or silver (Bibl. 131).

In 1907 warrant officers were granted their distinguishing lace (**see** Distintion lace), which they displayed on the head-dress and in one, two and three narrower stripes on the shoulder straps until the 1970s. The other ranks wore gold or silver chevrons, with red for the corporals, above the cuffs.

During World War I the officers' rank stars were moved to the cuffs, where they were worn on a silver rectangular patch for generals and within a rectangular frame of gold or silver for field officers. Black chevrons, adopted for sergeants and corporals, were retained by corporals until 1939.

In 1926 rank insignia were restored on the shoulder straps, but in 1934 new uniforms, with an open collar, were adopted for all ranks, and new officers' rank badges were introduced for use on the forearms above the cuffs. These consisted of stripes, embroidered in silver above the *greca* (the traditional device of Italian generals), with one, two or three gold lace stripes above a larger one for field officers and one, two or three narrow stripes only for company officers. The upper stripes of each rank badge and the single stripe of the 2nd lieutenant had an oval **curl**.

New **shoulder straps**, adopted in 1934, were worn with or without rank stars, according to the type of uniform on which they were worn.

Naval officers had the same type of badges, in gold for flag officers and with a round curl on the first stripe. The officers of the air force and of the MVSN had the same type of stripes, but with a diamond-shaped ornament instead of the curl, in gold for generals and with a different embroidered ornament below the stripes for the generals of the militia.

Inverted **chevrons** on both upper sleeves were adopted for sergeants and corporals in 1939, initially in red for corporals, but later in black rayon.

In 1940 the officers' rank badges were reduced in size, and a new pattern of badges, made in yellow lace and with smaller curl, was adopted for wearing on the cuffs of the jacket and greatcoat.

Rank insignia on the shoulder straps, re-introduced after World War II, are still in use today. However, in 1973 new metal badges were adopted for officers and warrant officers. The five-pointed **star** remained as basic insignia of rank, but the gold stripe around the shoulder straps of the field officers was replaced by a mural **crown**. The silver lace of the generals' straps was replaced by a small silver *greca* which, like the mural crown, is worn on the outer ends of the shoulder straps.

The longitudinal stripes of lace worn by warrant officers were replaced by metal bars, which were worn at the outer end of the shoulder straps, with one, two and three stripes on black background for the three basic ranks. One new rank was added, and the top rank obtained three stripes on red background surmounted by a gold star with red edges.

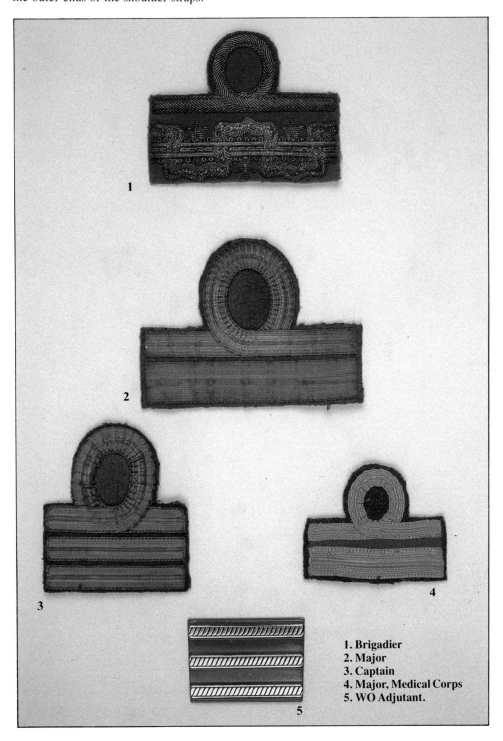

1. Brigadier
2. Major
3. Captain
4. Major, Medical Corps
5. WO Adjutant.

Japan

The rank insignia of the Imperial Japanese Army were displayed in the form of five-pointed stars and bars, which were worn on red shoulder tabs until 1938 and on red collar patches from 1938 to 1945. The air force was a branch of the army, and its personnel therefore used army rank insignia.

The average shoulder tab was 90 × 25mm (3½ × 1in) in size, with a button and two short tongues on the back, which kept the tab slightly curved. The shoulder tabs of the generals were covered by a stripe of gold lace 15mm (⅔in) wide and edged by gold embroidery, showing a narrow line of red backing on both sides between the lace and the embroidery. The other officers' and the warrant officer's tabs had gold embroidery along the outer edges, with two gold lace stripes for field officers and one stripe for company officers and for the warrant officer. The sergeants' tabs had the stripe of lace without embroidery. The stripe of gold lace was 6mm (¼in) wide.

One, two or three small, gilded metal stars were pinned on the shoulder tabs for each class of rank except warrant officers. Leading privates had one, two or three yellow stars, made of cloth or embroidery, on plain red tabs.

The M.98 uniform was adopted in 1938. In fact the uniform itself did not change, but all the insignia were modified. Rank badges were moved to the collar and worn in the form of patches. They were similar to the shoulder tabs but considerably smaller in size — 40 × 18mm (1½ × ¾in) — and all the metal stars were made of white metal, although those of the leading privates were machine woven in yellow silk.

As before, the officers and the warrant officer had gold embroidery along the longer sides of the patches; during the war the

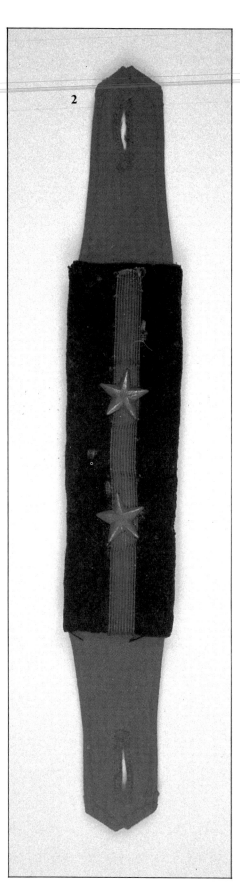

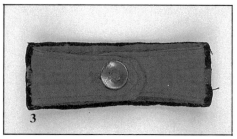

1, 2, 3 — Shoulder tab of the M.90 (1930) uniform, Private 1st Class
Collar patches of the M.98 (1938) uniform:
4 — Lieutenant Colonel
5 — Major
6 — Captain
7 — Lieutenant
8 — 2nd Lieutenant
9 — Warrant Officer
10 — Sergeant Major
11 — Sergeant
12 — Leading Private
13 — Private 2nd Class
14 — Private 1st Class, for field dress
15 — Private 1st Class.

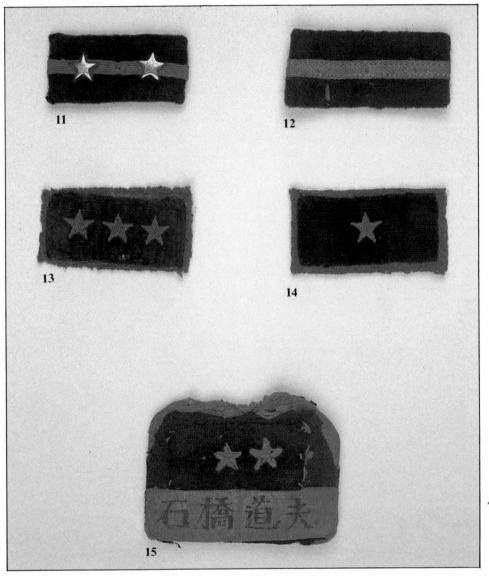

embroidery was yellow. A new rank, officer candidate, was added at this time, which wore red patches edged by gold embroidery.

The hierarchy of the rank and file was modified by the addition of a new rank of leading private, which was identified by a gold or yellow stripe.

These patches were worn on the collar of the tunic, greatcoat and cape, and on the collar of the shirt when in shirt sleeve order. In field dress only one badge could be used, and it was worn attached above the left breast pocket of the shirt.

Stripes of brown lace were worn around the cuffs of the greatcoat to identify class of rank, and during World War II the same stripes were worn in combination with stars on the tunic of the service dress to identify individual rank. The generals had three stripes, field officers two, company officers one; warrant officers had one narrow stripe

(Bibl. 26, 152, 153, 154).

The naval officers had the same rank titles as the officers of the army preceded by the word *Kaigun*, which means navy.

Rank distinction was displayed on the cuffs of the dress tunic and of the overcoat in the form of the conventional naval gold lace with curl, and in black lace stripes with curl on the service dress tunic. Shoulder boards, worn on the white and khaki tunics, displayed class of rank in form of longitudinal gold lace stripes on which small silver cherry blossoms were pinned to identify individual ranks.

Collar patches were worn on the blue service tunic, khaki tunic and on the summer shirt. They were made of blue cloth and identified rank, from admiral to warrant officers, in the same way as the collar patches of the army, by means of silver cherry blossoms and gold stripes, but without any additional embroidery (Bibl. 29).

United States of America

The same type of officers' rank insignia is used in all the services, although naval officers wear also **distinction lace** on the cuffs of the blue uniform and on the shoulder boards.

The badges of rank are unique as they depict eagles, leaves and bars instead of the **star** that is used by most other nations. Only the generals and officers of corresponding ranks in the other services wear five-pointed stars in white metal. In the case of the top rank — General of the Army, General of the Air Force, Fleet Admiral — five stars are worn together in a pentagonal shape.

Before 1851 infantry colonels wore gold eagles, while colonels of other corps had silver eagles. From 1851, however, the silver eagle has been the rank insignia of colonels. The insignia of lieutenant colonels and majors depicts a leaf, in silver for lieutenant colonels and in gold for the majors.

Captains and lieutenants wore gold bars until 1872, later silver bars, and the 2nd lieutenant's rank was instituted in 1917, identified by one gold bar.

American rank badges were made in Britain during World War II, and they differ considerably from the American patterns.

The bars for chief warrant officer and warrant officer junior grade were adopted in January 1942, in metal and brown enamel, since brown is the distinction colour of the warrant officers.

The ranks of warrant officers were modified in 1956, when two new ranks were added and new rectangular badges were adopted. The first two ranks had silver badges and the other two gold badges, with three or two blocks of brown enamel according to rank. The warrant officer 1 (WO1), which was the lowest rank, wore two brown enamel blocks on a gold badge; the chief warrant officer 2 (CWO2) had three brown blocks on a gold badge; and the two ranks above, CWO3 and CWO4, had similar badges but made of silver. As these badges caused a great deal of confusion new ones were adopted in December 1972, which are all made of silver with from one to four black enamel blocks, according to rank.

These badges are worn on the shoulder straps, on the right side of the collar of the summer shirt and on the left side of the garrison cap (Bibl. 164).

Subdued rank badges are worn on field uniform: black embroidery refers to silver and yellow embroidery to gold metal.

Non-commissioned officers of the army and of the air force wear **chevrons**.

Crossed **foul anchors** is the insignia of the warrant officers of the US Navy, and they are worn on the cap, on the shoulder boards and on the sleeves of the blue uniform, above warrant officers' lace and in miniature metal versions on the shirt collar.

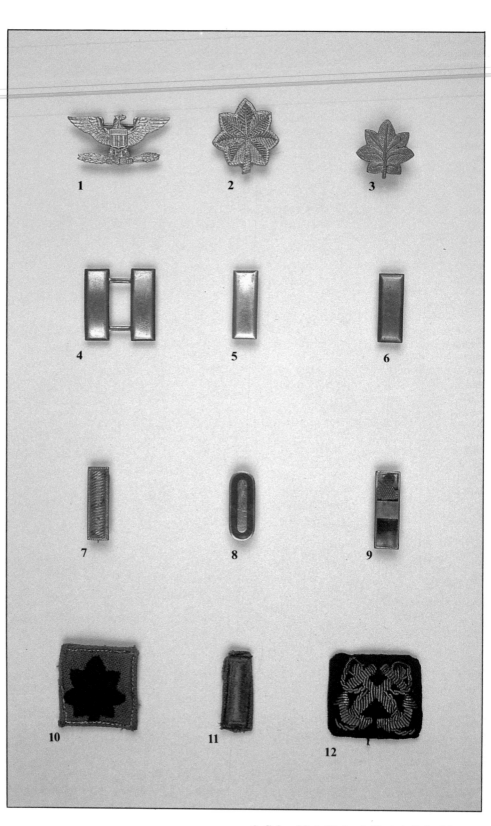

1. Colonel 2, 3. Major 4. Captain 5. 1st Lieutenant 6, 7. 2nd Lieutenant 8. Chief Warrant Officer 9. Warrant Officer 1 10, 11. Lieutenant Colonel and 2nd Lieutenant for field uniform 12. US Navy Warrant Officer.

Yugoslavia

All the officers of the Royal Yugoslav Army, except generals, had four-pointed silver stars on gold lace or metal shoulder boards. Generals wore six-pointed gold stars above the cuffs and gold shoulder cords.

Field officers used plain shoulder boards edged in branch-of-service colours, while company officers wore narrower shoulder boards and carried a longitudinal coloured stripe along the centre as well as the outer piping; they wore from one to four stars.

The ranks of senior and junior non-commissioned officers were also identified by stars, but they were smaller and made of brass. One, two or three stars were used for the lower ranks, and four stars below gold stripes were worn by the three sergeant majors classes.

After World War II the socialist government adopted shoulder boards again for the officers, but with the five-pointed stars of Soviet pattern. These were later changed to shoulder straps with five-pointed stars of a special Yugoslav pattern (*see* Slip-on). Metal bars are worn on the shoulder straps of the field uniform.

The most important developments happened during World War II, however, when the whole conception of rank insignia was changed. The Partisans Army abolished conventional insignia of rank and adopted 'appointments of command', and, as in the Soviet Union of the 1930s the field commander shared his position with a political commissar.

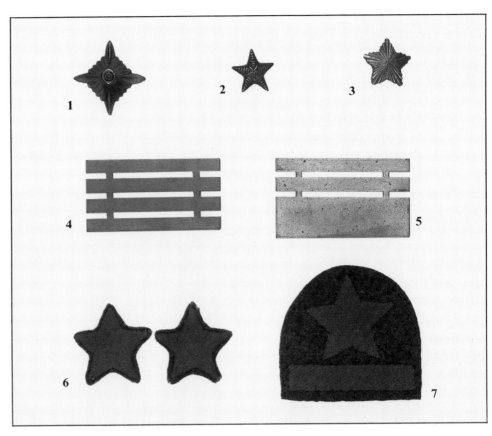

1, 2, 3. Pre- and post-World War II rank 'stars' and modern star 4, 5. Modern field uniform rank insignia, 1st Captain and Lieutenant Colonel 6. Sergeant 7. Commander of Company 8. Commissar of Company 9. Commissar of Brigade.

The corporal wore one red star on the left upper sleeve, the sergeant had two and the commanders of company, battalion and regiment wore one, two or three red bars ensigned by the red star. The brigade was the highest formation and its commander wore the star below a chevron. The commissars wore the same badges, but their red star displayed the hammer and sickle.

Toward the end of 1942, the structure of command was modified: the commissars' titles and badges were abolished as they became 'assistant commanders' of units and adopted the badges previously used by the commanders. Commanders obtained vertical red bars ensigned by the red star. Field commanders were granted one bar more than their assistants. The commander of brigade therefore obtained a new badge, which depicted the red star within a red triangle.

The appointment of chief of staff was created also, represented by the initial N (*Načelnik Staba*), worn above the command badge.

The brigades operating in a specific area were put under the control of the commander of operative zone, who wore two red diamonds surmounted by the red star. His assistant had one diamond, and the chief of the general staff wore three diamonds and the star.

In the meantime the Partisans' Army was redesignated Volunteer Army and Partisan Detachments, and the Liberation Army in the spring of 1942.

On 1 May 1943 the command titles and insignia were abolished in favour of military titles and new badges were worn on the forearms.

The non-commissioned officers obtained six-pointed silver stars, the sergeant major, for instance, wearing three stars above a silver stripe. The officers had gold stars above gold stripes — which were mainly of Italian origin — thin stripes for company officers, two large stripes for field officers and three large stripes for the generals.

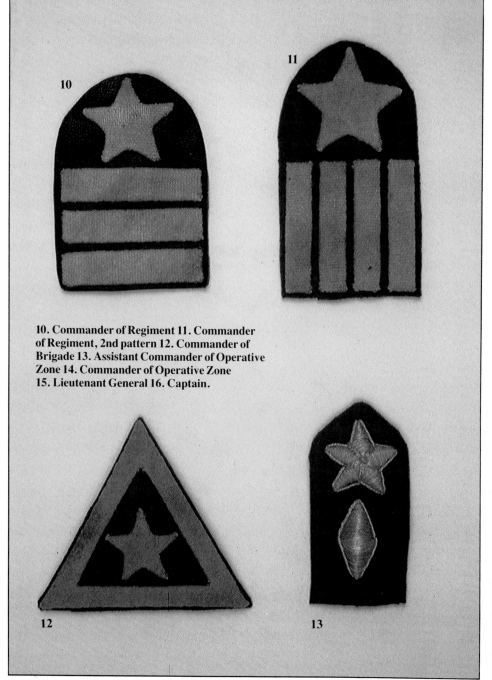

10. Commander of Regiment 11. Commander of Regiment, 2nd pattern 12. Commander of Brigade 13. Assistant Commander of Operative Zone 14. Commander of Operative Zone 15. Lieutenant General 16. Captain.

1. Royal Navy Petty Officer 2. Leading Seaman
3. US Navy Chief Petty Officer, Electrician

4. 3rd Class Petty Officer, Special Artificier
5. Seaman, Seaman Branch.

RATING The classification and insignia of the lower ranks of most naval organizations follow the army pattern, but in some nations the navy developed as an entirely separate organization with its own ranks, called ratings, and different badges.

Petty officers wear the officers' type of uniform, with the peaked cap and distinguishing cap badges. In the British Royal Navy chief petty officers are identified by three buttons on both lower sleeve petty officers wear a crown and crossed anchors on the left upper sleeve; and leading seamen wear the anchor. These badges are in red on blue or in blue on white, according to the type of uniforms, and in gold embroidery for the No. 1 dress.

The rating badges of the US Navy are worn on the right upper sleeve by personnel of the seaman branch and on the left upper sleeve by other branches. The insignia consists of the eagle, one **arc**, chevrons and a speciality mark in the centre. The senior and the master chief petty officer have additional stars above the eagle.

The colour of the background, blue or white, matches the colour of the uniform, the arc and chevrons are red and the eagle and speciality mark are white for the blue uniform.

Chief petty officers and petty officers are eligible to wear gold chevrons and arc, with a silver embroidered eagle and speciality mark, after 12 years' service and three good conduct awards.

The silver-embroidered eagle and speciality mark, combined with a red arc and chevron, is an optional badge (Bibl. 164, 167).

Rate marks in the form of one, two or three diagonal bars are worn on the left upper sleeve by enlisted men. The bars are white for the blue uniform and blue for the white uniforms; personnel of the other branches have red bars for both uniforms.

ROSETTE Although rosette generally has the same meaning as **cockade**, it may also refer to a small rose, which is, for instance, the rank insignia of Finnish officers.

S

SHOULDER PAD A shoulder pad is the padded cloth device that is sewn at the outer end of the shoulder, on the seam that joins the shoulder to the sleeve, to prevent shoulder belts or leather straps from slipping off.

One of the first British experimental field uniforms was fitted with shoulder pads instead of shoulder straps. Other ranks of the Italian Army wore tunics with shoulder pads displaying the company number until 1923.

SHOULDER SLEEVE INSIGNIA The American term shoulder sleeve insignia, which describes cloth badges worn on the upper sleeves, is discussed under Formation sign.

SHOULDER STRAP A shoulder strap is worn on the shoulder of the uniform and displays rank insignia and/or branch-of-service insignia according to national custom and service.

There are two types of shoulder straps — the fixed type, which is sewn in the outer ends of the shoulder seam, and the detachable type, which is usually stiffened by the addition of a cardboard frame inside and is technically known as shoulder board.

Shoulder cords, which consist of gold, silver or braid cords, are different but are dealt with here because they originated from the **epaulette**, and, regardless of appearance, they are used for the same purpose. In any case, it is impossible to divide the 'shoulder devices' into separate categories. German field officers, for example, wear twisted shoulder cords, while company officers have their cords set flat, which may, perhaps, more properly be called shoulder boards.

When the use of epaulettes was discontinued, some nations opted for shoulder boards, others for shoulder cords. Shoulder boards are retained by naval organizations and by most of the Warsaw Pact armies; shoulder cords are still used on full dress uniforms and by the *Volksarmee* of the German Democratic Republic.

Britain
The officers and the warrant officer of the Royal Navy use shoulder boards, faced with gold lace for flag officers and gold stripes and the curl for other officers. The **foul anchor** in silver embroidery below two stars and the

1. Royal Navy Vice-Admiral 2. 'Foul anchor' 3. Lieutenant.

crown is worn by the Commodore 1st Class.

Officers of all British naval organizations wear shoulder boards, but with different rank insignia and buttons.

In 1881 the rank insignia of army officers were moved from the collar to the shoulder cords of the tunic. Embroidered rank insignia were also worn on the shoulder straps of the patrol tunic, frock coat and mess jacket.

Crowns varied according to the monarch, while stars of the same pattern, although in different sizes and different types (*see* Rank insignia), were used by all army officers except foot guards.

The service dress jacket of the officers of the Royal Air Force has no shoulder straps, but they are worn on the full dress and mess dress jackets.

4, 5. British 'crowns'
6. Territorial Lieutenant
7. Generals' insignia
8. Rank 'star'
9. Irish Guards 'star'.

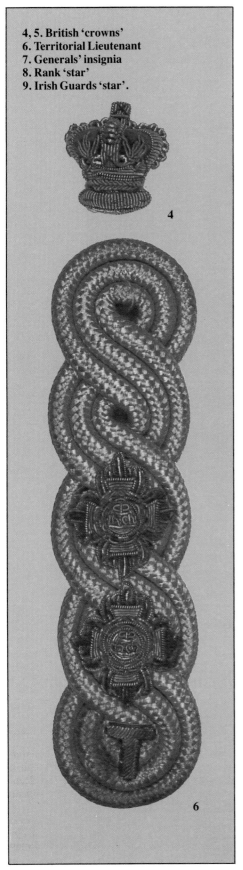

4

6

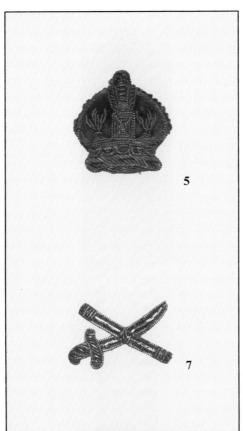

5

7

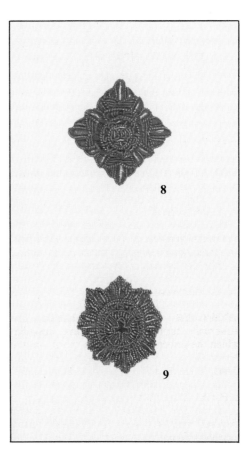

8

9

10. Merchant Navy 2nd Officer
11. Royal Air Force Flight Lieutenant.

10

11

Italy

Italian army officers wore shoulder boards on dress and service dress jackets and fixed shoulder straps on their field uniforms.

Generals had shoulder boards covered with silver lace displaying the Savoy eagle — or, in the case of generals of the commissariat and medical corps, branch insignia — and also rank insignia, according to order of uniform.

In 1934 metal shoulder boards were adopted for the officers' grey-green full dress, field officers had a thick ornamental edging, and a thinner stripe was worn by the others. The metal plate was mounted on a backing in branch-of-service colour, and the branch-of-service badge was detachable. Sergeants and the rank and file wore a pentagonal brass plate on the shoulder straps of the dress jacket.

The cloth shoulder boards of officers' white summer uniform displayed rank insignia, while those worn on the grey-green service dress indicated branch of service in the form of piping and the embroidered badge, and field officers' class of rank was shown by means of a stripe of gold lace.

Black shoulder boards were used on the black full dress and on the khaki uniform used in the colonies, with branch-of-service badges and rank stars embroidered on black felt.

Navy flag officers had shoulder boards covered with gold lace. The shoulder boards of the other officers were dark blue, with a gold embroidered edging stripe for senior officers. All wore the crown and rank stars.

Air force personnel, who had grey-blue uniforms, used grey-blue shoulder boards, covered with gold lace for the officers of air rank and with the additional gold embroidered edging stripe for senior officers. Officers' shoulder boards had additional twisted cords around the edges.

The crown, branch insignia and rank stars were worn by all officers, and the shoulder boards of non-flying officers carried piping in branch-of-service colours. Airmen in full dress wore the air force emblem in brass on the centre of the shoulder straps, and below it, on the outer ends, the branch of service disc.

Germany

1939-45 During World War II German officers displayed rank insignia on the shoulder cords, and the coloured base on which the cords were placed identified branch of service. The type of shoulder cords identified class of rank: generals, officers of air rank and navy flag officers wore three interlaced cords, two of gold and one of silver. Field officers and senior officers of the other two services had two silver double cords interlaced, and the other officers had their cords set straight on the coloured backing.

On dress and service dress uniforms the cords were of bright gold or silver, while those used on the field uniforms were dull.

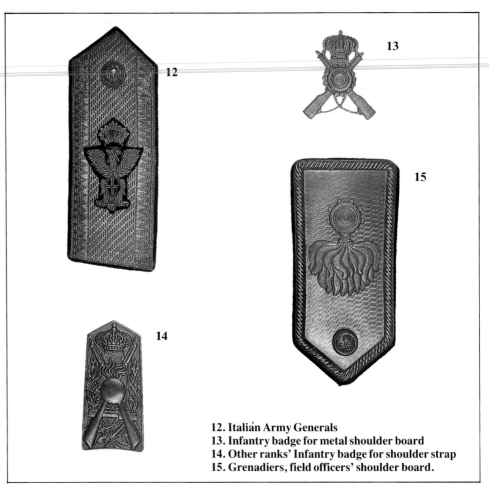

12. Italian Army Generals
13. Infantry badge for metal shoulder board
14. Other ranks' Infantry badge for shoulder strap
15. Grenadiers, field officers' shoulder board.

16. Colonial Rifles 17. Air Force other ranks
18. Colonel Medical Corps 19. Italian Navy
'Tenente di Vascello'.

20. Italian Air Force 2nd Lieutenant, Engineers
21, 22. Branch of service discs for Fitter and Electrician.

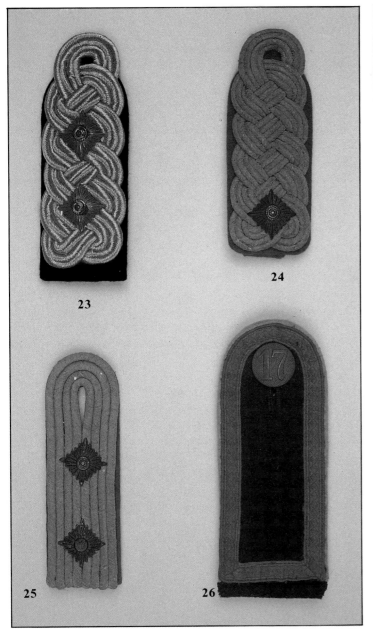

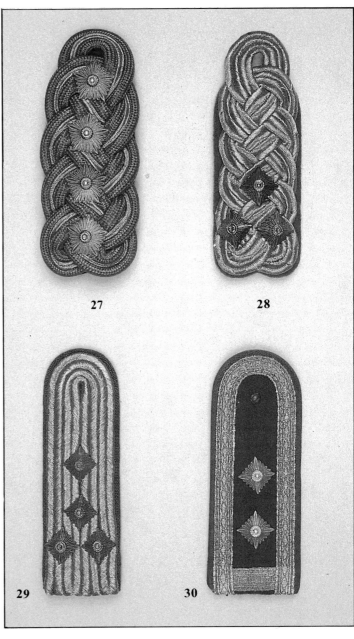

23. Lieutenant Colonel, Artillery 24. Major, Cavalry or Flying Personnel 25. 1st Lieutenant, Mountain Troops 26. 'Feldwebel', Infantry

27. 'Armeegeneral' 28. Colonel, Air Force 29. Captain, Armour 30. 'Oberfeldweben', Signals.

The officers of all three services used the same type of shoulder cords and rank stars. Those of the army and of the air force were placed on coloured backing according to their branches of service (*see* Collar insignia), while navy officers had a dark blue backing.

Musicians had silver and red cords, and administrative officials wore a dark green backing under the shoulder cords.

The other ranks wore detachable shoulder straps. Initially they were made of dark bluish-green cloth, but later during the war they were made of field grey uniform cloth. These shoulder straps displayed rank insignia in the form of bright or dull silver stripes and white metal stars and piping in branch of service colours. Dress shoulder straps could also show the number of the unit or bear a special badge in metal or embroidery, according to rank.

Tankmen wore black uniforms and black shoulder straps, airmen had grey-blue shoulder straps and naval personnel wore shoulder straps with pointed ends made of dark blue cloth with gold accessories.

German Democratic Republic : Traditional German rank insignia were adopted for the armed forces of the German Democratic Republic. Officers' shoulder cords and non-commissioned officers' lace stripes were identical to those used before 1945, but rank stars differed. Five-pointed silver stars were adopted for army generals and equivalent ranks of the other services, and smaller, four-pointed stars of gold and silver were worn by the other officers and non-commissioned officers.

Underlays to the cords in branch-of-service colours were re-introduced (*see* Collar insignia) for the army. Bluish-green was adopted for the whole air force.

Soviet Union

The shoulder boards were the most important item of the Imperial Russian Army uniform as they displayed rank, branch of service and regimental insignia. Many types were used, in coloured cloth or khaki, with or without piping and with metal or embroidered cyphers and regimental numbers. All were abolished in 1917.

They were re-adopted, however, in January 1943. Officers of combatant branches had gold or yellow silk lace shoulder boards, and non-combatants in dress order wore silver boards. Marshals and generals had gold lace and silver stars on their shoulder boards, and field officers had two stripes of branch-of-service colours woven in the lace and large stars. Company officers' boards bore one stripe and smaller stars. The other ranks wore shoulder boards in branch-of-service colours, with lace stripes for non-commissioned officers.

The following were the colours of the piping of the officers' shoulder boards:

Infantry and Commissariat	raspberry red
Artillery, Armour, and Medical Veterinary and Legal Services	red
Cavalry	blue
Engineers and Technical Staff	black

The colours of the other ranks shoulder boards and piping were:

	Shoulder board	Piping
Infantry	raspberry red	black
Armour	black	red
Cavalry	blue	black
Engineers and Technical Troops	black	black
Medical and Veterinary Service	dark green	red

The shoulder boards of the field uniform were khaki with red stripes for officers, and an outer piping in the colours of the branch of service. Other ranks wore coloured piping and coloured rank stripes according to branch of service.

The personnel of the air force used shoulder boards with light blue piping, and naval personnel had dark blue piping for the line branch with other colours for the service branches.

The branch-of-service badges were modified in 1955. All were reduced in size, some were changed — for example the badge of the armour, the tank, was modernized — and others were abolished.

Bulgarians wear shoulder boards similar in size and appearance to those of the Russians,

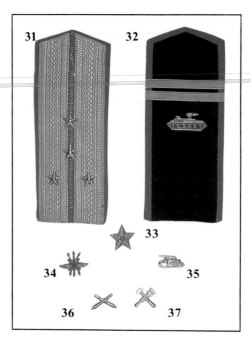

31. Captain, Infantry 32. Junior Sergeant, Armour 33. Field officers' 'star' 34, 35, 36, 37. Modern branch of service badges for Soviet shoulder boards.

38. Rumanian Colonel, Border Guards
39. Rumanian Sergeant, Infantry
40. Hungarian Lieutenant Colonel, Border Guards 41. 'Star' of rank, company officers.

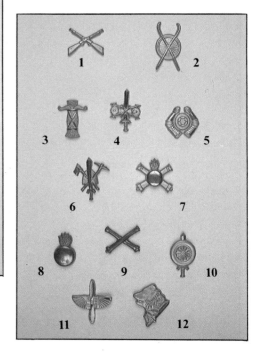

1. Infantry 2. 'Jäger' 3. Guards 4. Signals
5. Armour 6. Engineers 7. Anti-Aircraft
8. Field Artillery 9. Coast Artillery 10. Service Corps 11. Air Force 12. Frontier Guards.

while the Hungarians and Rumanians have narrower boards.

Those of the army officers of the Rumanian Socialist Republic display longitudinal coloured stripes according to class of rank and piping as on the shoulder boards of the Soviet Army. Warrant officers are identified by silver chevrons and small bars, and non-commissioned officers wear gold stripes.

In the 1920s the Hungarian Army adopted collar patches that identified rank and branch of service, while the air force had shoulder straps instead. Stiff, detachable shoulder straps were introduced for army personnel after World War II, but they were later modified to fit into the seam of the shoulder. The positioning of the rank stars was changed so that they faced inward.

Generals wear gold lace shoulder straps. Field officers have a stripe of gold lace in the centre of the shoulder straps on which one, two or three large silver stars are pinned. Company officers have smaller brass stars pinned directly on to the shoulder straps.

Those of the officers and warrant officers have twisted gold cords around the edges, while senior sergeants have silver cords. A combination of silver stripes and gold or silver stars identify warrant and non-commissioned officers.

SHOULDER STRAP BADGE

Finland

Branch-of-service badges were worn by non-commissioned officers and privates on the shoulder straps of the service dress (on parade and walking-out order) and of the greatcoat until 1967. The badges could be worn in combination with letters of the alphabet or numbers identifying a specific unit or organization, a custom that was abandoned during World War II.

The crossed rifles of the infantry could be worn above: P (Pori Regiment); U (Uusimaa Regiment); T (Tampere Regiment); V (Viipuri Regiment); KS (Central Finland Regiment) or PS (North Savo Regiment).

The *Jägers* badge, which depicted crossed skiis above a bicycle wheel, was worn above the battalion number, 1, 2 or 3. The wheatsheaf, which was taken from the coat of arms of Vaasa, was the emblem of the Guards because Vaasa was the headquarters of the Finnish White Guards during the Civil War. The badges of the signals and of the engineers are easily identifiable, and both were also worn with an E underneath by personnel of independent companies. The 'iron clutch' was, and still is, the emblem of the armoured corps.

The badge of the field artillery was a flaming grenade, which could be worn above regimental numbers or above another badge, the Finnish lion on top of a tower, which identified the *Jäger* Artillery Regiment. The personnel of the anti-aircraft batteries wore the anti-aircraft artillery badge above a swastika. The swastika was a traditional Finnish and Estonian emblem, unrelated to the swastika adopted in the Third Reich. The badge of the coast artillery was two crossed gun barrels, and it was worn by the personnel of the headquarters coast artillery and coast defence staff, above the numbers 1, 2 or 3 by personnel of the regiments and above number 4 by the 4th Indpendent Coast Artillery Battery. The crossed cannons above the initial K

(Kuolo) were used at the Naval School, as the coast artillery organization was dependent on the navy.

Numbers were also worn below the badge of the service corps to identify the battalions. The air force had a winged propeller with a swastika in its centre. A bear and two fir twigs over a sword were depicted in the badge of the frontier guards and symbolized their task in the northern forests.

Many other badges were worn, including the bugle of the *Jägers* and the crossed swords of the cavalry. In addition, letters of the alphabet were combined to display the initials

of various military organizations.

Embroidered branch-of-service badges were worn by soldiers on the M.1936 great-

13. Helsinki Headquarters Company 14. Horse Artillery Battery of the Cavalry Brigade. 15. Regular Army officers 16. Artillery School 17, 18, 19. 'Pohjanmaan', 'Karjalan' and 'Satakunnan' Field Artillery Regiment 20, 21. 'Jäger' and 'Pohjois-Karjalan' Independent F. A. Battery 22, 23. 'Suomenlinnan' and 'Turun' Coast Artillery Regiment 24. 'Helsingin' Anti-Aircraft Regiment 25, 26. 'Tampareen' and 'Pohjanmaan' A.A. Battery.

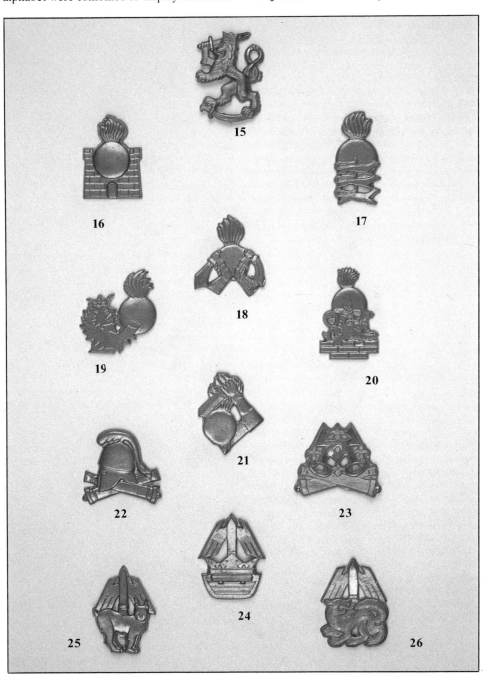

coat, on the summer blouse and on the field tunic. Illustrated are those of the Helsinki Headquarters Company and of the Horse Artillery Battery of the pre-war Cavalry Brigade.

Regular army officers wear the Finnish lion on their shoulder straps.

In 1967 new metal badges were adopted for the individual units of the various branches of service. The examples shown are all artillery badges.

The first is the badge of the school, followed by three regimental badges of the field artillery and by the badges of two independent batteries. The coast artillery is composed of two regiments and three batteries. The anti-aircraft artillery has one regiment and four batteries, of which two badges are shown.

Holland
After World War II regimental and branch-of-service badges were adopted by the Netherlands Army for wearing on other ranks' shoulder straps. Initially these badges were made of brass; later they were of anodized metal.

The Fusilier Guards *Prinses Irene* Regiment traces its origins to the Royal Netherlands Brigade, which was formed in Britain in January 1941. It was redesignated *Prinses Irene* Brigade on 27 August 1941 and became a regiment in 1946, a guards regiment in 1948 and a fusilier guards regiment in March 1952.

The *Garderegiment Jägers* traces its origins to a regiment formed in 1665, and it became *jäger* in 1939. Re-formed in 1947, it assumed the present title the following year.

The *Stoottroepen* Regiment derives from the Netherlands Interior Forces of wartime and was formed in September 1944. Regiments that were formed in the 1940s but did not possess a traditional emblem were granted the infantry badge, although some were entitled to wear special badges, such as the Infantry Regiment *Johan Willem Friso* and the Infantry Regiment *Menno van Coehoorn*, which obtained their regimental titles and special badges in 1950 and 1953, respectively (Bibl. 120, 121).

Other badges were used by the personnel of the artillery, engineers, medical corps and quartermaster staff.

These badges were abolished in 1963 when the regimental and branch-of-service insignia were transferred to the collar (*see* Collar insignia). Some were re-adopted in smaller size, but the patterns of others were changed.

SHOULDER TAB   A shoulder tab is a rectangular device, worn on the outer end of the shoulder in lieu of a shoulder strap. They were and still are worn by US Army officers, although now on dress uniform only, to display rank insignia and branch-of-service colour.

1. Fusilier Guards 'Princes Irene' 2. 'Garderegiment Jagers' 3. 'Stoottroepen' Regiment
4. Infantry 5, 6. 'Johan Willem Friso' and 'Menno van Coehoorn' Infantry Regiment 7. Artillery
8. Engineers 9. Medical Corps 10. Quarter-master Staff.

SHOULDER TITLE An insignia worn on the shoulder to identify the regiment or corps of the wearer is known as a shoulder title. The term generally refers to badges that are worn on the shoulder straps and on the top of the sleeve, provided that the badge spells out the title or name of the regiment or corps.

Britain
Shoulder titles were adopted in 1881 as a complementary device of regimental or corps identification, and they were initially embroidered on the outer ends of the other ranks' shoulder straps of the tunic. Later, metal titles were adopted, and, because they were cheaper and detachable, they slowly replaced the embroidered versions. The metal titles were made of brass or white metal, and they were fastened on to the shoulder straps by means of a split pin.

Shoulder titles are worn in pairs, but, as

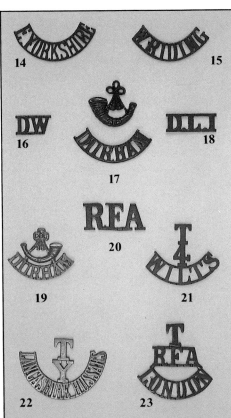

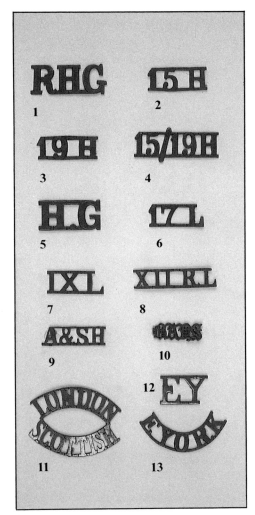

A selection of British shoulder titles made of brass, white metal (22. The Lancashire Hussars), gilt and silver (28. The Royal Northumberland Fusiliers), anodised metal

(31. The Royal Anglian Regiment) and the black titles (4th Battalion The Wiltshire Regiment (The Duke of Edinburgh's)) of the rifle battalions.

both are equal, they are collected singly. They have been used for more than a century, and the scope is vast. Often a regiment's basic history may be traced by its shoulder titles: 15th (The King's) Hussars and 19th (Queen Alexandra's Own Royal) Hussars merged to form 15th/19th The King's Royal Hussars. Large shoulder titles were eventually replaced by smaller versions or changed to different versions, or even abolished altogether.

Many were changed, often several times. The East Yorkshire Regiment, for example, changed the spelling of its title in 1921, and the first version of the title of The Duke of Wellington's Regiment (West Riding) spelled WEST RIDING until 1915, followed by DUKE OF WELLINGTON'S or DUKE OF WELLINGTON, both on three lines, the last version being curved upwards and followed by the initials DW in 1931, and, in 1970, by DWR in anodized metal. The Durham Light Infantry, in common with all light infantry regiments, wore its title in combination with a bugle: DURHAM and DLI below the bugle; the bugle and DURHAM in brass as a one-piece badge; and the same but in white metal, later anodized aluminium.

Four variants of the Royal Artillery shoulder titles existed: the obvious RA, RFA (Royal Field Artillery), RHA (Royal Horse Artillery) and RGA (Royal Garrison Artillery). There were others for volunteer and territorial brigades.

Territorial infantry battalions were usually identified by a T above the battalion's number or above the battalion's title; rifle battalions used blackened shoulder titles. The initial Y below the T was worn by yeomanry regiments, and volunteer battalions wore V in white metal below a number. Several others were also available (Bibl. 68). The number, the T or V and the title were often worn separately, or they were roughly soldered together. Some were made by local firms; for instance, the T over 5/6 of the North Staffords, which was made in 1961.

Regiments of foot guards had special shoulder titles, and fusiliers also wore the grenade, a blank grenade or the regimental grenade.

Officers' training schools had innumerable shoulder titles, and the latest restructuring has led inevitably to the formation of new regiments and new shoulder titles, some of which are made of brass, some of anodised aluminium and some of black metal.

The coloured cloth shoulder title was worn on battledress until the battledress was abolished. It had been invented and worn before then, however, even by some volunteer battalions from about 1900 (Bibl. 72).

The Army Council Instructions of 18 September 1940 specified that 'all ranks [of the Foot Guards] will wear the authorized regimental designation in worsted at the top of each sleeve of the blouse, ie, above the corps or divisional sign', and that 'warrant officers, non-commissioned officers and men will wear on the shoulder strap of the battledress blouse the authorized worsted titles, except as ordered otherwise by the local military authority during active operations'. It is clear that the Guards, although prevented by the same instruction from wearing arm-of-service strips (*see* Arm-of-service strips), were the first regiments to be given shoulder titles, while the other regiments and corps obtained the official permission to wear slip-on cloth titles instead.

The guards wore shoulder titles that were embroidered on felt, the letters with serifs. The Grenadier Guards wore white on red and the Welsh Guards wore white on black, with square ends. The other three regiments wore titles with rounded ends.

The colours of the shoulder titles of the branches of service were based on those of the arm-of-service strips, with an extra colour when necessary. Except the rifle regiments all the infantry had white lettering on scarlet, the KRRC and the Rifle Brigade had rifle-green badges with red and black lettering, respectively, in accordance with the regimental piping. The Royal Ulster Rifles, the Gurkhas and other regiments adopted black on green titles, others red on green, like the KRRC.

The regiments of light infantry wore shoulder titles with white lettering on scarlet; The Duke of Cornwall Light Infantry had CORNWALL and DCLI titles, in white on a scarlet background. The Durham Light Infantry wore initials on the metal title only, and DURHAM LI on the cloth shoulder titles. Later, all the light infantry regiments changed to yellow lettering on a light infantry-green background.

Some Scottish regiments adopted shoulder titles, but others chose to display the regimental flash (*see* Shoulder flash) as their only identifying device.

The first pattern of shoulder titles issued during the war were made in two versions: embroidered on felt or printed on cloth.

The shoulder titles of the Royal Artillery had red letters on blue, while the Royal Engineers had blue letters on a red background. Many among the other branches and the full corps title on the badge as well as a shoulder title bearing the initials only; for example ROYAL ARMY SERVICE CORPS and RASC.

After the war, the prefix 'Royal' was granted to many regiments and corps, and thereafter their shoulder titles were changed: the CMP (Corps of Military Police) became RMP (Royal Military Police), and the AD

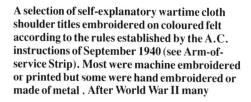

A selection of self-explanatory wartime cloth shoulder titles embroidered on coloured felt according to the rules established by the A.C. instructions of September 1940 (see Arm-of-service Strip). Most were machine embroidered or printed but some were hand embroidered or made of metal. After World War II many

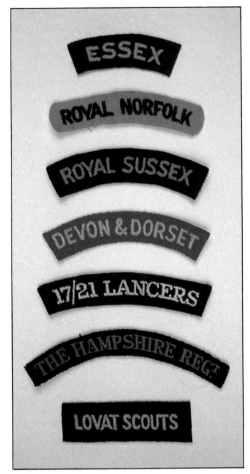

CORPS (Army Dental Corps) became the RADC (Royal Army Dental Corps) in 1946.

Personnel of the Army Air Corps, of the Parachute Regiment and of the Glider Pilot Regiment initially wore light blue titles with dark blue lettering. The Parachute Regiment later adopted maroon titles to match the colour of their berets.

After World War II many regiments adopted new shoulder titles in regimental colours. These were based on the colours of the facings of their predecessors. The Essex Regiment had inherited the yellow from the 44th and the purple red from the 56th Foot, the former East and West Essex regiments that amalgamated in 1881.

Some extraordinary titles appeared as a result. The hand-embroidered title of The Hampshire Regiment is a beautiful example. In the post-war years The Durham Light Infantry had three shoulder titles, DURHAM LI was used by other ranks, the full regimental title in yellow on green was used by officers and the same, but with red letters, belonged to the 6th territorial battalion.

As regiments were amalgamated, new titles had to be made for the new unit, which usually bore the name of both its predecessors. Some very large shoulder titles appeared, including that of The North Somerset Yeomanry & 44th RTR.

The Royal Air Force Regiment, which was raised in 1942, was formed by ground personnel employed primarily in the defence of RAF installations. Another well known RAF shoulder title is that of the Air Training Corps, which is in light blue capital letters on a grey-blue background.

The shoulder title was also used as a device to identify nationality. During World War II many volunteers from other nations joined the armed forces in Britain and elsewhere, and they wore special 'nationality' shoulder titles, which were more numerous in the air force than in the other services. The white on red POLAND titles, used by the Polish Army in Italy, were made in Italy; the badge at the bottom is made of metal. Officers in the RAF wore curved nationality titles embroidered in light blue thread on a grey-blue background, while the other ranks had titles in light blue on a dark blue or black background, which was usually rectangular in shape. However, all ranks wore red lettering and badges on khaki on their tropical uniforms.

Other RAF nationality titles include Norway, Belgium, Mexico (Bibl. 166), Australia, Canada, Channel Islands, Newfoundland, Rhodesia and South Africa.

The Canadians retained the shoulder title as a national insignia, and, according to an identification booklet published by NATO in the 1950s, the Norwegian Air Force still wore the NORWAY title on the left sleeve, while army personnel had NORGE in white letters

infantry regiments adopted shoulder titles which displayed regimental colours and often individual battalions wore different titles (see Durham Light Infantry). Nationality titles were worn by Commonwealth and foreign contingents attached to the British armed forces (see next page).

on a khaki background.

The personnel of the Home Guard wore shoulder titles with yellow or black letters on khaki; below the title were two badges, one above the other, displaying the county or town initials and the unit's number. The yellow letters were embroidered or painted, but the initials and numbers of the badges were printed.

Canada

The Canadian Army used large and very colourful cloth shoulder titles during World War II.

The 7th/11th Hussars was a regiment formed in 1937 by the amalgamation of the 7th and of the 11th Hussars. The 8th Hussars was redesignated 8th Princess Louise's New Brunswick Hussars in 1922. The Cameron Highlanders of Ottawa (*see* Cap badge) became a machine gun unit in 1939, and the Three Rivers Regiment was deployed as a tank unit during World War II.

United States of America

Shoulder titles are called 'shoulder tabs' in America, and they have never been used as widely as in Britain.

The Rangers wore shoulder tabs on the left upper sleeve during World War II, and seven of their battalion tabs exist. Other tabs appeared after the war (*see* Formation sign) and in the 1950s. Location tabs — Panama, Okinawa and so on — were also used (Bibl. 166).

The raising of special forces started an urge for individuality among US Army units, and in Vietnam especially many tabs were adopted, although most were unofficial. Divisional and regimental airborne-ranger detachments adopted their own in colour or subdued, which were worn on field dress above the shoulder sleeve insignia.

The US Navy uses shoulder tabs to identify the name of ships in the same way that other navies use the **tally**.

SLIP-ON Derived from the verb to slip, ie, to move smoothly along a surface, a slip-on refers to a piece of cloth, doubled up and sewn at the back, which is worn slipped on the shoulder strap. It is usually worn on the shoulder straps of the summer shirt, shirt sleeve order, field uniform, or any other uniform that requires frequent washing.

Depending on national custom, a slip-on could carry any type of insignia — regimental, divisional, branch-of-service or rank insignia or other. In the US Army, for instance, the **Combat leader insignia** is worn on a green slip-on.

The Austrian Army uses the slip-on as rank insignia for the field uniform.

In the British Army the slip-on had different roles. It was used to display regimental

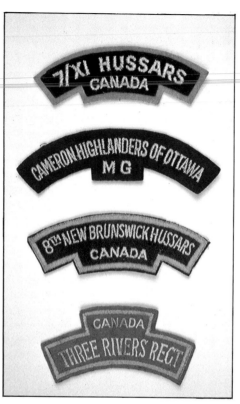

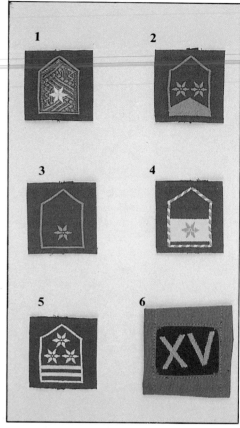

Slip-ons used by the Austrian Army: 1. Brigadier 2. Lieutenant Colonel 3. Lieutenant 4. 'Vizeleutnant' 5. 'Offizierstellvertreter'. The slip-on could display a regimental designation (6. The East Yorkshire Regiment (The Duke of York's Own) 8. The Devon and Dorset Regiment), a 'formation sign' (7. Australian Army Headquarters) or 'rank insignia' (8. 2nd Lieutenant 9. Polish Army Lieutenant Colonel). 10. Polish Army slip-on with plastic shoulder title and metal formation sign. 11. Italian slip-on which displays title, formation sign and rank insignia 12, 13. Swiss Army slip-ons with unit number on branch of service colour and also rank insignia 14. Jordanian Army General 15. Yugoslav Army First Captain.

devices, or a formation sign could be worn on a slip-on on shirt sleeve order. From the 1960s, the slip-on incorporated the rank insignia and the regimental title.

During World War II the Polish 2nd corps adopted removable rank insignia for wearing on the summer shirt, and a special slip-on, or flap, was worn, which fitted under the outer end of the shoulder strap and on which were displayed the **shoulder title** and **formation sign**. The Polish 2nd corps was in Italy at that time, and after the war the Italian Army adopted the same type of slip-ons, further developing the Polish patterns until the integral slip-on and flap appeared, which carried all the insignia.

The Swiss Army uses slip-on tabs with the number of unit on branch-of-service colour for the rank and file, with numerals and stripes for officers.

The slip-on rank insignia of a general of the Jordanian Army as worn on battledress is illustrated.

The Yugoslav Army has perfected a style of slip-on shoulder strap, in which can be inserted the shoulder strap of the shirt, both fastening with the same button.

SPECIALITY INSIGNIA A speciality is an activity or job at which the person who carries it out is particularly proficient. In the context of this book it refers to individuals, known as specialists, who have attended a special course or school.

All tradesmen are classed as specialists in some armies. In the British Army the skill-at-arms badges are speciality insignia, and these include the **wings** of the parachutists and of the glider pilots.

Before an independent signal corps was instituted, the signallers of most armies were classed as a speciality of the engineers. And further back in time, the grenadiers, light infantry, rifle and mountain troops were specialists of the infantry.

SQUADRON INSIGNIA The badges of air force squadrons are known as squadron insignia; they are worn by air crews on the breast of their flying jackets or overalls.

Squadron insignia were initially painted on the fuselage of aircraft, but during World War I some were reproduced in cloth or metal versions (*see* Distinctive insignia and Sweetheart badge) and worn on the uniform by members of the squadrons.

The custom of wearing these badges spread during World War II, and groups, commands and other air force organizations later adopted the practice.

The badge used in the 1950s by the Italian acrobatic team, 'Red Devils', which won the international aerobatic competition at Soesterberg, Holland, is painted on leather. The US Air Force badge of the 366th Fighter Bomber Group is woven.

STAR The knowledge of small items such as stars to indicate rank is invaluable for the positive identification of insignia and uniforms.

All armies use different types of rank insignia, and many may be seen under various entries in this book, particularly under Rank insignia and Shoulder strap. However, most armies use stars in one way or another.

The Austrian star (*see* Rank insignia) depicts an edelweiss. The gold or silver stars worn by Belgian Army officers may be found in either metal or embroidered versions, the latter being embroidered directly on to the collar patch.

The British star illustrated is that of the military division of the Order of the Bath. In its centre are depicted the crowns of England, Scotland and Ireland and the motto *Tria Juncta in Uno,* which refers to the United Kingdom.

Before World War II the Czechoslovak Army used five-pointed stars and three-pointed stars in gold for officers, and three-pointed stars in silver for senior non-commissioned officers. Now only five-pointed stars are used; they are in gold for officers; smaller, silver stars are worn by non-commissioned officers.

The officers of the Danish Army use three types of stars according to class of rank. The large star identifies a major general, the medium star a major and the smallest would be used by a 2nd lieutenant.

Two examples of Air Force Squadron badges. The first painted on leather belonged to the Italian Acrobatic team, Red Devil. The second, woven, was the insignia of the 366 Fighter Bomber Group, USAF, stationed at Aviano, based in the 1950s.

German officers have always worn four-pointed stars with the exception of the generals of the *Volksarmee*, who now use five-pointed stars. In Ireland, the Irish officers' badges are called diamonds, as they are square and display only an interlaced Celtic design on the four sides. Embroidered diamonds, worn from 1942 to 1944, were replaced by the bronze pattern.

Gold or silver six-pointed stars were worn by Dutch officers on the collar patches until 1963; two types may be found — those with a smooth or a lined surface. Officers' rank insignia and the other ranks' badges and chevrons are now worn on the shoulder straps.

The Italian Army adopted metal stars for the officers' shoulder straps in 1973. They had previously been embroidered in gold wire or made of brass, finished to imitate embroidery. The Norwegians use five-pointed stars of an unmistakable pattern to identify officers' ranks.

Field officers of the Spanish Army wear eight-pointed stars, and company officers wear six-pointed stars. The two badges illustrated belong to the Civil War period.

SUBMARINE INSIGNIA Patches worn by the crews of US Navy nuclear submarines are known as submarine insignia. USS *Nautilus*, the first nuclear submarine, famous for its voyage across the North Pole, did not have a badge.

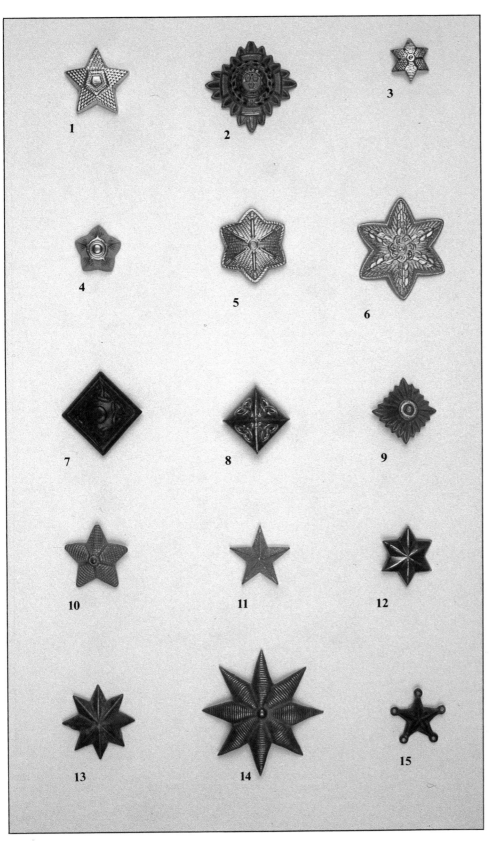

1. Belgium 2. Britain 3. Czechoslovakia 4, 5, 6. Denmark, for generals, field officers and company officers 7. Germany 8, 9. Ireland 10. Holland 11, 12. Italy 13. Norway 14, 15. Spain.

Two woven badges of the US Navy of the nuclear submarine USS 'Swordfish' and of the USS 'George Washington' respectively.

SWAGGER STICK The stick carried by British officers and warrant officers on duty as an insignia of command is called a swagger stick.

Some swagger sticks are made of polished wood, others are covered with leather; all display the regimental badge embossed on the silver knob.

SWALLOW'S NEST Also known as **wings**, the swallow's nest are the flaps worn by bandsmen on the outer ends of the shoulders.

SWEETHEART BADGE Badges of military type were bought by soldiers for their sweethearts, who wore them as brooches. They became very popular during World War I, when all kind of miniature replicas of regimental badges were made on enamel or other decorative backgrounds for this purpose. There are at least two sweetheart badges of the Cheshire Regiment, which depict the regimental badges used before and after 1922. An enamelled brooch commemorates the battle of Ypres, and a set of French-made badges displays the coats of arms of towns that became well known during that war: Vimy, Bapaume, Combles, Peronne and so forth.

Beautifully executed in metal and coloured enamels, Royal Air Force squadron badges have always been very popular in miniature replicas, and they are still made with the St Edward's crown.

American distinctive insignia were also reproduced in small replicas as sweetheart

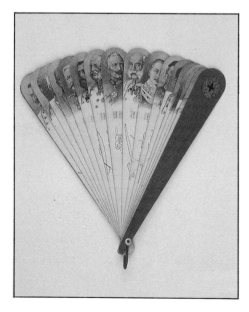

The British sweetheart badges shown here are made of metal and enamel while the Soviet 'souvenir' badges are made in anodised metal, painted.

The 50th anniversary of the foundation of the Soviet Union was commemorated by badges as well as battles, famous leaders and military formations.

badges or souvenirs; for example, the pine tree of the 92nd Division or the badge of the 349th Infantry Regiment (*see* Distinctive insignia).

It is difficult to establish the difference between a sweetheart badge and a souvenir badge. During World War I the Austrian Red Cross produced a fan depicting portraits of all the major Austrian and German generals and bearing their signatures. These fans were used by ladies.

In the Soviet Union souvenir badges related to military and other events are worn by men and women. An aluminium badge depicting the ship *Aurora* could be purchased in Leningrad, and a number of badges were made in 1967 to celebrate the fiftieth anniversary of the October Revolution.

SWORD KNOT A strap with a tassel would be worn wound around the hilt of swords, bayonets and daggers, or around the bayonet's frog, in a manner precisely described by dress regulations.

The knot was originally used to prevent the sword being lost in action, for the strap was twisted around the wrist.

In Germany coloured side-arm knots had the precise function of identifying units down to company level, and in Italy gold knots, the pattern varying according to class of rank, were worn with the dagger by MVSN officers.

Non-commissioned officers of the Imperial Austrian Army displayed the national colours, yellow and black, on the side-arm knot.

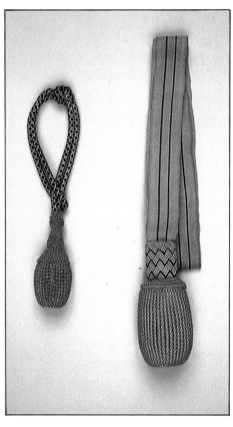

The sword knot used by company officers of the Italian MVSN is shown on the left, followed by that worn by the NCOs of the Austro-Hungarian Army.

T

TALLY Worn on sailors' hats, a tally is a black ribbon used to identify the ship, naval establishment or nationality of the wearer.

The seamen of the *Volksmarine* of the German Democratic Republic do not wear tallies bearing the name of their ships, and Americans wear the US Navy tally, and the name of the ship as a **shoulder title.**

The name of the ship is not usually displayed in wartime for security reasons. In Britain the initials HMS — His (or Her) Majesty's Ship — are used. The initials ORP stand for *Okret Rzeczypospolitej Polskiej* (Ship of the Polish Republic).

TIE See Arc.

The pre-World War II British tallies displayed gold woven lettering which have now been replaced by yellow silk.

TRADE INSIGNIA The distinguishing marks identifying a man's specific job within an organization are called trade insignia.

Trades have developed in different manners in the armed forces of different nations; therefore what constitutes a 'trade' in one nation may be considered a speciality, a proficiency or a skill at arms in another.

Britain

In the British Army, trade badges are worn on the right upper sleeve by the rank and file only, and they relate to jobs similar to civilian crafts.

The crossed axes are one of the best known of the sappers' insignia, used in Britain by assault pioneers and in France by regimental sappers of infantry.

British trade badges are made of brass or embroidered thread. French badges were cut out from felt and partly or fully embroidered in thread or metal wire.

Other old British trade badges are the horse bit and the cart wheel. Blacksmiths, fitters, welders and all trades related to mechanical engineering are identified by the hammer and tongs. Drivers' badges were all replaced in 1950 by a star.

Letters of the alphabet within a wreath are used to identify groups of tradesmen; the letter A, for instance, includes almost fifty trades, and these badges may be found with letters in capital, script or old English characters.

Instructors' badges are worn on the left forearm: the QI badge below a grenade, for instance, was used by qualified instructors in field engineering, and the crossed signal flags, worn by instructors in signalling, was also worn by signallers as a skill-at-arms badge. This badge could be found in both small and large versions, the small pattern as illustrated or in brass or brass and enamel; while the large size was embroidered in coloured thread on khaki, embroidered in gold wire and coloured thread on a black background or printed. These are the modern variants, and doubtless there are many others as the badge was adopted in 1881.

MM and R are skill-at-arms badges for motor mechanics and range takers, 1st class, Royal Artillery.

In the British Army musicians wear badges of appointment on the upper right sleeve or above chevrons, which could be worn on the forearms. The drummer badge shown is worn on full dress; brass or worsted drums are worn on other types of uniform.

Germany

During World War II the personnel of the German Army wore trade badges on the right forearm, except for signallers and helmsmen of engineers assault boats, who wore their badges on the upper left sleeve. Airforce personnel wore trade badges on the left forearm.

Similar circular badges were adopted by the *Bundeswehr* in the 1950s for wearing on the left forearm by specialists, including officers. These badges were embroidered in grey cotton for specialists and in silver for officers. The speciality badges of medical officers, veterinaries, dentists and pharmacists were transferred to the shoulder straps in 1972, and later, new specialists' badges in the form of wings, in gold, silver and bronze metal, were adopted for wearing on the breast.

The *Volksarmee* of the German Democratic Republic adopted oval badges, with the emblem initially embroidered in yellow. From 1957 to 1966 it was embroidered in branch-of-service colours, and later machine embroidered in silver grey cotton.

In both German organizations these badges are called specialists' insignia, but they have the same function as the trade badges used in other countries.

Hungary

Metal and enamel badges are worn on the breast in Hungary to identify the specific trade

British Army trade badges are worn by qualified tradesmen below the rank of sergeant on the upper right sleeve. Some of the badges shown above are not technically 'trade', as for instance the 'QI' worn by qualified instructors below the rank of warrant officer on the left forearm, and the drum which is a badge of appointment.

of the wearer and his degree of proficiency (*see* Proficiency insigna), from 3rd to 1st class. The shield below the flags is removable, fastening on the badge by means of a screw and a nut so that the wearer may change his class number if required.

Badges are available for tank drivers, armoured car and vehicle drivers, for tank, armoured cars and vehicle fitters, for signallers and signals technicians, for armament technicians and for any other trade of the army and air force.

Italy
Until 1934 the Italian army used gold or silver embroidered trade badges, according to

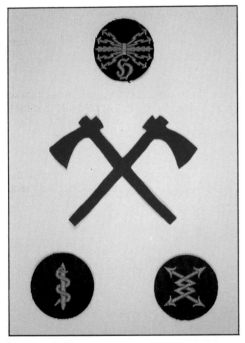

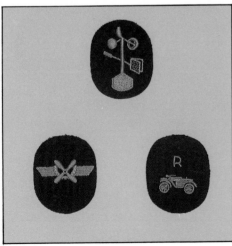

Pre-1945 German Army trade badges were embroidered on dark green background, air force badges on grey background. Grey oval badges are used by the 'Volksarmee', army. **Metal trade badges which include a proficiency number are generally used by the Warsaw Pact** armies and five Hungarian badges have been included.

branch of service for warrant and non-commissioned officers. After 1934 only gold badges were worn. Badges embroidered in black thread on uniform cloth were used in wartime, and embroidered in red thread on black in the years between the world wars. Trade badges made of brass were made in 1946–7 for drivers and motorcyclists.

Before 1915 trade badges were embroidered in branch-of-service colours, they then changed to black for reasons of camouflage. It is interesting to note that the badges of the machine gunners depicted the silhouette of a particular type of machine gun; Fiat, St Etienne and Maxim gunners wore slightly different trade badges. The badge of a driver depicted the motor car in use at the time, from the veteran cars of 1915 to the rounded *Aprilia* of the late 1940s.

Trade badges on a khaki background appeared after World War II, in coloured embroidery or in plastic, and trade badges set on an embroidered shield became a fashionable alternative in the 1950s.

Plastic shields were adopted in due course, and small metal and enamel shields were worn pinned on the left breast pocket of the summer shirt.

Dress regulations published in 1971 listed, described and illustrated the 32 insignia to be worn on uniform; all others were abolished.

Spain
Various types of trade badges have been worn in Spain since the Civil War; all are self-explanatory, as the badges were made of metal and depict the weapon or vehicle handled by the tradesmen.

The half-track *automitrailleuse de combat Schneider P16 (M29)* and an Hispano Suiza may easily be identified among these badges.

TUFT Also known as a pompon, a tuft is the woollen ball, of varying sizes and shapes, worn on the head-dress either as a plume holder or as an ornament.

Coloured tufts used to be worn on the front of kepis and shakos, above the cap badge, to identify regiment or branch of service.

French sailors wear a red tuft on the centre top of their hats, and Italian Alpine troops wear an oval tuft in branch-of-service or battalion colour on the left side of the hat as a feather holder.

Tuft of Italian Alpine Engineers, other ranks.

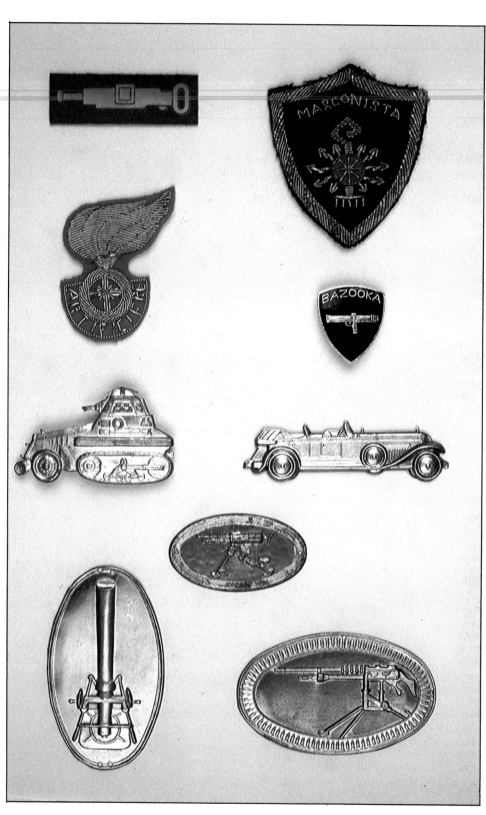

The Italian Army trade badges are self-explanatory, Spanish badges depict in detail the vehicle or weapon that the tradesman is qualified to handle.

W

WAFFENFARBE This German term means colour of arm or branch-of-service colour.

WINGS Three categories of badges are in the form of wings: those used by aviators, those worn by airborne troops and the **proficiency insignia** worn by the Warsaw Pact armies.

Not all parachute brevets are displayed on the uniform as wings as the parachute is the principal symbolic emblem of this speciality, and some other parachutists' badges are discussed under **parachute insignia**.

Aviation wings
Military aviation commenced during the first decade of this century with the sole purpose of observing the movements of the enemy; the task of the observer was therefore as important as that of the pilot.

As independent air forces did not yet exist, 'flyers' were distinguished from the rest of the military or naval personnel by special badges, and, appropriately, most nations chose wings or eagles in flight.

Some countries opted for metal badges. The Austro-Hungarian pilots, for instance, had a golden eagle in flight set on an enamelled wreath of oak leaves, ensigned by the crowns of the dual monarchy. The Austrian wings illustrated were adopted in 1956.

Britain : In Britain the first wings were granted to qualified pilots in 1913, and when the Royal Air Force was formed five years later the initials in the centre of the wings were changed from RFC (Royal Flying Corps) to RAF. Badges were embroidered on khaki, dark blue or black backgrounds. The observer's badge was adopted in September 1915 and existed until 1942, when it was replaced by the navigator's wing. Air gunners wore a metal badge depicting a winged bullet from 1923 to 1939, when it was replaced by the single wing with the initials AG. As a rule, the pilot was and is still distinguished by the double-winged badge, while the air crew wear the single wing, a custom that was adopted throughout the Commonwealth.

The wing of the observer had at least 14 feathers, while those of the other air crew badges had only 12. All these embroidered wings, of both pilots and air crew, exist in padded and in flat versions.

There are a dozen single wings with differ-ent initials within the wreath or the parachute.

Smaller wings, embroidered in metal wire on grey-blue cloth, are worn on the mess dress.

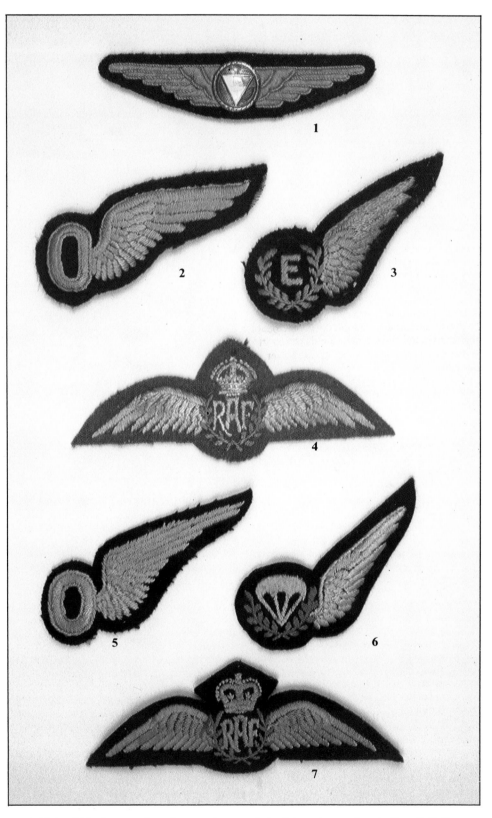

1. Austrian wings and a selection of pilot's wings (4.7) and air crew single wings of the Royal Air Force.

Germany : During World War II German and Rumanian airmen wore metal breast pocket badges. The German qualification badges were adopted in March 1936, for pilot, observer, pilot/observer and for the wireless operator/air gunner. The air gunner/flight engineer's badge was instituted in 1942. Unqualified air gunners who had participated in at least 10 operations in that role were granted a badge made of reversed metals in 1944, ie, a silver eagle on a darkened wreath.

The Rumanian air force had three badges, for pilot, pilot-bomber and for observer.

Denmark : In Denmark, as in Britain, the air force is divided into two separate branches and the helicopter pilots of Danish Fleet Air Arm (*see* Curl) wear their wings on the lower sleeve.

France : The French aviators obtained special insignia in 1913, which were worn on the collar and on the right upper sleeve, later on the left sleeve.

The collar badges depicted a five-pointed star and a wing, in different colours according to class of rank. The sleeve badge was a winged propeller, embroidered in metal wire for officers, a white propeller and red wings with gold feathers for non-commissioned officers, and a white propeller with red wings for the rank and file.

After World War I the sleeve badges were replaced by qualification wings, with a star in the centre for aviation personnel and a cogwheel for aerodrome specialists. The wings were and are still worn above the right breast pocket of the tunic. Other ranks with flying qualifications wore metal badges on the right breast of the tunic (Bibl. 28).

Hungary : The Hungarian badges illustrated were adopted in 1975. Before 1931 metal and enamel badges of Austrian style had been used. These were followed by gold or silver embroidered badges depicting an eagle in flight for the observer, and the same eagle, ensigned by the Hungarian crown, for pilots. After the war three types of badges, each in three classes, were granted to aviators. The pilots had a winged badge, similar to the one illustrated but with a red, white and blue enamelled shield, according to class. Navigators had a bomb in place of the shield, and engineers were distinguished by a shield above a crossed hammer and spanner.

The wings with a wreath of a modern pilot 1st class have an 18-carat gold finish; the wings of the pilot 1st, 2nd and 3rd class without the wreath are made of polished brass. The navigators' wings have a slightly different design (Bibl. 122, 123, 124).

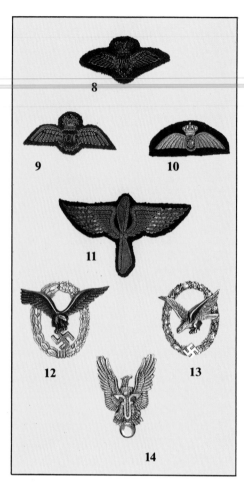

10. **Danish Fleet Air Arm Pilot 11. French pre-World War I Pilot 12. 'Luftwaffe' Pilot 13. Air Gunner/Flight Engineer 14. Rumanian Pilot/Bomber.**
The picture on the right shows a selection of Hungarian and Italian wings.

Italy : During World War I Italian aviators wore embroidered qualification insignia on the left upper arm; pilots had an eagle in flight surmounted by the crown. About 1919 their badge was changed to a winged propeller, and gold metal badges were introduced after 1923, when the *Regia Aeronatica* became an independent service. The fasces were added to the pilot's badge in 1935, while the observer's insignia depicted a winged sceptre surmounted by the crown.

The royal **crown** was replaced for pilot officers only by the mural crown in 1948. Air crew specialists had a series of white metal wings, with the speciality insignia in the centre, which were re-adopted in the 1950s. Warrant and non-commissioned officers of air crews used a variety of unofficial badges, privately purchased. The pilots of the army light aviation wear a torch combined with the eagle.

Japan : The Japanese pilots' badge was made of silver and yellow silk with a gold metal star in the centre. It was worn above the right breast pocket.

Poland : The Polish flying eagle was adopted in 1919 for pilots and with additional flashes of lightning for observers. The pilot's badge was made of white metal, the observer's in brass, but in 1928 a two-metal badge was instituted for the dual qualification of pilot/observer, which had a silver eagle and gold wreath and lightning.

Some eagles carried the 'combat wreath', which was made of green enamel, in their beaks, and in 1933 qualifications of first and second class were introduced; the eagle of the latter did not carry the gold wreath.

These badges were re-adopted in Britain in 1942 with a number of modifications, and they

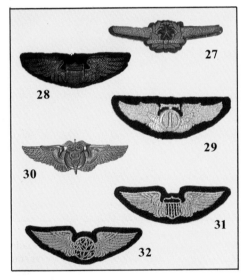

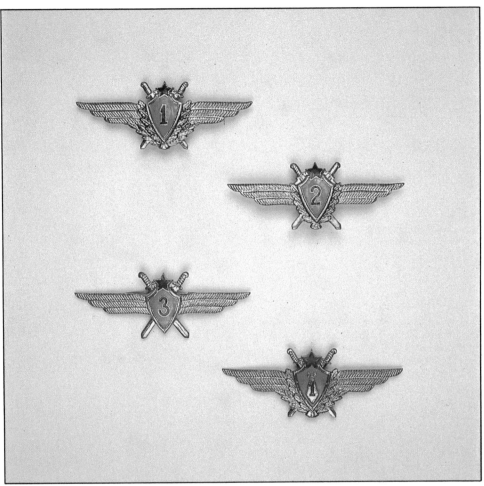

The Polish wings were worn on the left breast and the hook of the small chain was pinned under the lapel of the jacket.
27. Japanese Pilot wings, followed by a selection of different USAAF and USAF wings in embroidery and in metal: 28. Pilot 29. Technical Observer 30. Flight Surgeon (made by Gaunt, London) 31. Pilot 32. Navigator.
The last picture shows four Soviet Air Force wings with proficiency numbers.

were modified again in 1944 when initials were placed in the wreath to identify air crew qualifications: S (Air Gunner); R (Radio Operator/Air Gunner); B (Bomb Aimer); H (Flight Engineer).

Soviet Union : The Soviet aviators used to wear two crossed swords and a propeller, sided by wings, with the red star in the centre, and the design of the modern badges is still based on these motifs. The propeller has been replaced by a shield, which displays the class number; as well as the class, there are three categories of wings, with a large wreath, a small wreath and with no wreath.

United States of America : The first American pilots' badges were awarded in 1913 to 14 officers of the Signal Corps. Conventional wings, of the type still worn today, were adopted in 1917 in embroidery and in oxidized metal from December 1918. The winged shield of the airplane pilot was adopted in a metal version in 1921, and the badges of the senior pilot and command pilot were introduced in 1941.

By 1947, when the US Air Force became an independent service, 21 different wings existed, and several others were added later. Although the average pattern was made of oxidized metal, the wings of the flight surgeon were of gilded brass. Others were embroidered in silver or in white silk on an olive drab

or a blue background.

Different qualification wings were used by the US Navy and by the US Marine Corps.

Parachute wings
Although experimental training in parachuting and gliding started in the 1920s, the first qualification badges of these new specialities did not appear until the late 1930s.

German parachutists obtained their badge in November 1936, and the French *brevet de l'infanterie de l'air* was adopted in 1937.

The British parachute wings were adopted in 1940, and they are still in use although many variants may be found, from the general issue pattern embroidered in white and light blue cotton to badges partly or wholly embroidered in metal wire; the latter for dress uniforms. The wings worn by the Special Air Service vary from straight, to inclined down or upward.

Glider pilots wore their wings above the left breast pocket. The badge of the 1st glider pilot depicted the royal crest in full colour between two wings; the second qualification depicted a yellow G within a yellow circle and the wings. The former badge is shown, in metal embroidery, for use on full dress.

1, 3. British Army parachute wings 2. Special Air Service 4. 1st Glider Pilot 5. Belgian Army Para/Commando 6. Italian Army Parachutist M.1964, gold

7. French parachute wing M.1937 8. Spanish parachute badge 9. Cambodian wings, basic brevet 10. Ugandan wings, basic brevet 11. US Army glider badge 12. 'Bundeswehr' badge M.1957.

The Belgian para-commando wings were adopted in 1963, in gilt, silver and brass versions according to class of rank. A year later the Italians changed the parachutists' badge from a parachute to wings in gilt or silver and with or without the star.

The basic US Army wings were adopted in 1941, the senior and master (*see* Backing) being introduced in 1950.

There are innumerable types of wings. Most depict the winged parachute, or eagles and the parachute. The *Bundeswehr* made an exception by adopting in 1957 a brevet badge similar to the German wartime clasps; this badge, however, was in use for only one year (Bibl. 30).

WOUND BADGE Although most armies reward war wounds with a medal, the wound badge is still used in Belgium in the form of a stripe of gold or silver lace, 40mm (1½in) long and 4mm (¼in) wide, worn on the left upper sleeve and inclined by 30° towards the front of the wearer.

A similar insignia is worn in Italy, but the stripe measures 50 × 6mm (2 × ⅓in), and it is worn on the right sleeve.

The Red Army adopted two classes of wound stripes, in gold or red braid, in July 1942 to be worn above the left-hand side of the right breast pocket.

The British wound stripes used during both World Wars were worn vertically on the left forearm. A metal stripe, made especially for this purpose, bears the inscription 'The Wounded Stripe' on its back plate.

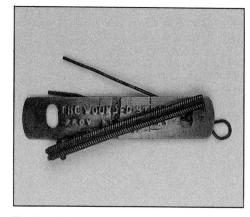

The British 'wounded stripe' shown together with its back plate.

BIBLIOGRAPHY

GENERAL KNOWLEDGE

1. *Handbuch der Uniformkunde* – Knötel-Sieg – H.G.Schulz 1937
2. *Militaria* – F. Wilkinson – Ward Lock & Co. 1969
3. *Battle Dress* – F.Wilkinson – Guinness Signatures 1969
4. *Battledress* I.T.Schick – Weidenfeld & Nicholson 1978
5. *Felduniformen* – F.Wiener – Wehr & Wissen 1975
6. *Military Uniforms in Colour* – P.Kannik – Blandford 1968
7. *Military Uniforms 1689-1918* – R.North and J.Berry – Hamlyn 1970
8. *Soldiers Soldiers* – R.Bowood – Hamlyn 1965
9. *The Armies of Europe Today* – O.von Pivka – Osprey 1974
10. *I Grandi Reggimenti* – V.Melegari – Rizzoli 1968
11. *Armi e Uniformi* (4 volumes) – V.Melegari – C.G.E. 1980
12. *Armies of the World 1854-1914* – D. Woodward – Sidgwick & Jackson 1978
13. *W.W.2 Combat Uniforms & Insignia* – M.Windrow and G.Embleton – PSL 1977
14. *Airborne Warfare 1918-1945* – B.Gregory and J.Batchelor – Phoebus 1979
15. *Army Uniforms of W.W.2* – A.Mollo and M.McGregor – Blandford 1973
16. *Naval, Marine and Air Force Uniforms of W.W.2* – A.Mollo and M.McGregor – Blandford 1975
17. *Army Uniforms of W.W.1* – A.Mollo and B.Turner – Blandford 1977
18. *Military Collectables* – J.Lyndhurst – Salamander 1983
19. *Identification Pamphlet Nos 1, 2 (Britain)* – J.Waring – Waring
20. *Identification Pamphlet Nos 3, 4 (Commonwealth)* – J.Waring – Waring
21. *Identification Pamphlet Nos 5, 6, 7 (U.S.A.)* – J.Waring – Waring
22. *Identification Pamphlet No 8 (Far East)* – J.Waring – Waring
23. *Identification Pamphlet Nos 9, 10 (Europe)* – J.Waring – Waring
24. *Identification* – Military Service Publ. Co. – Harrisburg 1943
25. *Army Badges & Insignia of W.W.1 (1)* – G.Rosignoli – Blandford 1972
26. *Army Badges & Insignia of W.W.2 (2)* – G.Rosignoli – Blandford 1975
27. *Army Badges & Insignia Since 1945* – G.Rosignoli – Blandford 1973
28. *Air Force Badges & Insignia of W.W.2* – G.Rosignoli – Blandford 1976
29. *Naval and Marine Badges and Insignia of W.W.2* – G. Rosignoli – Blandford 1980
30. *Parachute Badges & Insignia of the World* – R.J.Bragg and R. Turner – Blandford 1979
31. *Les Costumes et les Armes des Soldats de tous les Temps* – L.&F. Funcken – Casterman 1967
32. *L'Uniforme et les Armes des Soldats du Premier Empire* – (2 Volumes) – L.&F. Funcken – 1968/69
33. *L'Uniforme et les Armes des Soldats de la Guerre 1914-18* (2 volumes) – L.&F. Funcken – 1972
34. *L'Uniforme et les Armes des Soldats de la Guerre 1939-45* – L.&F. Funcken – 1972
35. *L'Uniforme et les Armes des Soldats de la Guerre en Dentelle* (2 volumes) – L.&F. Funcken – Casterman 1975/76
36. *Navy Uniforms, Insignia and Warships of W.W.II* – W.N.Tantum IV and E.J.Hoffschmidt – WE Inc. 1968

AUSTRIA

37. *Handbuch für Unteroffiziere* – H.Schmid v.B. 1917
38. *Austro-Hungarian Infantry 1914-1918* – J.S.Lucas – Almark 1973
39. *Uniformtafel des Österreichischen Bundesheeres* – Tyrolia 1974 – wall chart
40. *Dienstgrad- und Rangabzeichen, Waffen und Aufschlagfarben des Österreichischen Bundesheeres* – P.Sappl 1980s – wall chart
41. *Truppendienst* – magazine

BELGIUM

42. *Couleurs et Attributs des Armes et Services* – Ministère de la Défense Nationale 1939
43. *Instruction sur les Tenues de l'Armée* – Force de Terre (Plates) c.1950s or early 1960s
44. *Emblemes de Cavalerie* – J.P.Champagne – Everling 1970
45. *L'Aviation Militaire Belge* – Insignes et Traditions – J.P.Champagne – Everling 1972
46. *Infanterie* – Traditions – J.P.Champagne – Everling 1973
47. *Sous Nos Ailes* – J.A.Mangin, J.P.Champagne and M.A.Van Den Rul – Everling 1977
48. *La Cavalerie* – J.P.Champagne – Everling 1978
49. *Artillerie* – J.P.Champagne – Everling 1982

BRITAIN (AND COMMONWEALTH)

50. *Dress Regulations for the Army 1900* – David & Charles Reprints 1970
51. *Regimental Badges worn in the British Army 100 Years Ago* – E.Almack FSA – F.Muller 1970

52. *Regimental Badges* – T.J.Edwards, MBE – Gale & Polden 1951-1957
53. *Regimental Badges* – T.J.Edwards, MBE – Revised by A.L.Kipling – Gale & Polden 1966-1968
54. *Regimental Badges* – T.J.Edwards, MBE – Revised by A.L.Kipling – C.Knight 1974
55. *Military Badge Collecting* J.Gaylor – L.Cooper 1971
56. *Head-dress Badges of the British Army (to 1918)* – A.L.Kipling and H.L.King – F.Muller 1972
57. *Head-dress Badges of the British Army (from 1918)* – A.L.Kipling and H.L.King – F.Muller 1979
58. *Heraldry in War* – H.N.Cole, OBE – Gale & Polden 1946
59. *Badges on Battledress* – H.N.Cole, OBE – Gale & Polden 1953
60. *Badges and Insignia of the British Armed Services* – W.E.May, W.Y.Carman and J.Tanner – 1974
61. *Badges and Emblems of the Services* – N.A.G. 1940
62. *Rank and Badges in the Navy, Army, RAF* – E.C.Talbot-Booth – G.Philip & Son 1940
63. *Regimental Badges and Service Caps* – Philip 1941
64. *Discovering Military Traditions* – A.Taylor – Shire 1969
65. *Discovering English County Regiments* – A.Taylor – Shire 1970
66. *Discovering British Cavalry Regiments* – A.Taylor – Shire 1973
67. *Discovering Military Badges and Buttons* – R.J.Wilkinson-Latham – Shire 1973
68. *Military Metal Shoulder Titles (Infantry)* – R. Westlake – Verner 1977
69. *The Sharpshooters* – B.Mollo – Historical Research Unit 1970
70. *Military Insignia of Cornwall* – D.E.Ivall and C.Thomas – Penwith 1976
71. *Supplement to the above title* – 1976
72. *The Staffords 1881-1978* – G.Rosignoli – Rosignoli 1978
73. *British Airborne Troops* – B.Gregory – Macdonald 1974
74. *British and Commonwealth Armoured Formations (1919-46)* – D.Crow – Profile 1972
75. *Uniforms of the Royal Armoured Corps* – M.Dawson – Almark 1974
76. *British Military Uniforms* – W.Y.Carman – Longacre 1962
77. *Cavalry Uniforms* – R.&C. Wilkinson-Latham and J.Cassin-Scott – Blandford 1969
78. *Infantry Uniforms* – R.&C. Wilkinson-Latham and J. Cassin-Scott – Blandford 1970
79. *A Selection of Badges Designs of the Canadian Forces* – Gutta Percha & Rubber Ltd (Canada)
80. *Croquis d'Insignes Armée Canadienne 1920-50* – D.Mazéas – Mazéas 1970
81. *The Regimental Badges of New Zealand* – D.A.Corbett – R.Richards 1970
82. *Journal of the Society for Army Historical Research*
83. *The Bulletin, of the Military Historical Society*
84. *Dispatch, of the Scottish Military Collectors Society*
85. *Crown Imperial, of the Society for the study of the History, Traditions and Regalia of the Forces of the Crown*
86. *The Formation Sign, of the Military Heraldry Society*
87. *Despatch, Journal of the New South Wales Military Historical Society*

CHINA (Republic of)

88. *Dress Regulations* – Ministry of Defence c.1970

FINLAND

89. *Stusvoimat, Ennen ja Nyt* – K.J.Mikola and V.Tervasmäki – V.S.Salokangas-Porvoo
90. *Miesten Koulu* 1965
91. *Miesten Koulo* 1968
92. *Miesten Koulo* 1969

FRANCE

93. *L'Armée Française 1940* – Editions Militaires Illustrées
94. *Insignes des Troupes Aéroportées Françaises* – C.Malcros – S.P.L. 1975
95. *Les Insignes De Chasseurs* – D.Desjardins – A.S.T. 1981
96. *Uniforms of the French Foreign Legion* – M.Windrow – Blandford 1981
97. *Francais Voici Votre Armée (Service National)*
98. *Uniformes – Les Armées de l'Histoire* – magazine

GERMANY

99. *Uniforms and Organisation of the Imperial German Army 1900-1918* – F.J.Stephens and G.J.Maddocks – Almark 1975
100. *Handbook on German Military Forces* – US War Department 1943
191. *Uniforms, Badges and Intelligence Data, etc. of the German Forces* – Barnards – wartime

102. *Die Waffen SS – Eine Dokumentation* – K.G.Klietmann – Der Freiwillige 1965
103. *German Army Uniforms & Insignia 1933-1945* – B.L.Davis – Arms & Armour 1971
104. *German Military Uniforms & Insignia 1933-1945* – WE Inc 1967
105. *German Combat Uniforms* S.R.Gordon-Douglas – Almark 1970
106. *Waffen SS* – D.S.Fosten and R.J.Marrion – Almark 1971
107. *Waffen SS* – M.Windrow and M.Roffe – Osprey 1971
108. *Uniforms of the SS (Allgemeine 1923–1945)* – A.Mollo – H.R.U. 1969
109. *Uniforms of the SS (Germanishce 1940-1945)* – H.Page Taylor – H.R.U. 1970
110. *Uniforms of the SS (Verfügungstruppe 1933-1939)* – A.Mollo – H.R.U. 1970
111. *Uniforms of the SS (Totenkopfverbände 1933-1945)* – A.Mollo – H.R.U. 1971
112. *Uniforms of the SS (Sicherheitsdienst und Sicherheitspolizei 1931-1945)* – A.Mollo – H.R.U. 1971
113. *Uniforms of the SS (Badges & unit distrinctions 1939-1945)* – A.Mollo – H.R.U. 1976
114. *Orders, Decorations, Medals and Badges of the Third Reich* – D.Littlejohn and C.M.Dodkin – Bender 1968
115. *Waffen SS (vol. 2)* R.J.Bender and H.Page Taylor – Bender 1971
116. *Waffen SS (vol. 3)* – R.J.Bender and H.Page Taylor – Bender 1972
117. *German Uniforms of World War 2* – A. Mollo – MacDonald & Jane's 1976
118. *Uniformen und Abzeichen der deutschen Streitkräfte* – 1956

HOLLAND

119. *De Nederlandse Mariniers* – M.Bosscher and Van Dishoeck – 1966
120. *De Nederlandse Infanterie* – H.Ringoir and Van Dishoeck – 1968
121. *Afstammingen en Voortzettingen der Infanterie* – H.Ringoir – Ministry of Defence – 1977

HUNGARY

122. *Néphadseregünk Jelvényei 1945-1970* – Z.Szórádi and G.Tálas – Éremgyüjtök – 1971
123. *Néphadsereg Jelvényei 1970-1976* – S.Márton and G.Tálas – Éremygyüjyök – 1976
124. *Ungarische Piloten und Fallschirmjäger Abzeichen 1920-1945* – G.Tálas – 1981

IRELAND

125. *An Cosantoir – A Survey of the Uniforms and Insignia of the Defence Forces* – J.M.Hudson and F.G.Thomas – Ministry of Defence – 1975

ITALY

126. *Regolamento sull'Uniforme 1931* – Ministero della Guerra – 1931
127. *Le Uniformi del Partito Nazionale Fascista A.XVII* – S.A.L'Editrice – 1938
128. *Agenda Annuario PNF XX* – Domus – 1941
129. *L'Uniforme Italiana nella Storia e nell'Arte* – A.Gasparinetti – Centro Internazionale di Uniformologia – 1961
130. *Uniformi della Marina* – A. Gasparinetti – Centro Internazionale di Uniformologia – 1964
131. *Uniformi Militari Italiane 1861-1933* – E.&V.Del Giudice -Bramante – 1964
132. *Uniformi Militari Italiane 1934-1968* – E.&V.Del Giudice-Bramante – 1968
133. *Regolamento sulle Uniformi dell'Esercito 1971* – S.M.dell'Esercito – 1971
134. *Caricat!* – R.Puletti – Capitol – 1973
135. *La Marina Militare Italiana* – S.M.della Marina
136. *Fregi, Mostrine, Distintivi della R.S.I.* – H.Küchler-Intergest – 1974
137. *Mostrine, Fregi, Distintivi del Regio Esercito Italiano nella Seconda Guerra Mondiale* – G.Tarlao – Intergest – 1975
138. *Le Uniformi Coloniali Libiche 1912-1942* – P.Crociani and A.Viotti – La Roccia – 1977
139. *Regio Esercito Italiano-Uniformi 1933-1940* – R.Belogi – Belogi – 1978
140. *MVSN 1923-1943* – G.Rosignoli – Rosignoli – 1980
141. *Il Reggimento 'Giovani Fascisti' nella Campagna dell'Africa Settentrionale 1941-1943* – A.Cioci – Ellici – 1980
142. *Le Uniformi dell'A.O.I. (Somalia 1889-1941)* – P.Crociani and A.Viotti – La Roccia – 1980
143. *Italiani Tutti in Divisa* – E.&V.Del Giudice – Albertelli – 1980
144. *Uniformi e Distintivi dell'Esercito Italiano 1933-1945* – P.Marzetti – Albertelli 1981
145. *Le Uniformi Italiane nelle Tavole del Codice Cenni* – Editoriale Nuova 1982
146. *Le Divise del Duce* – U.Pericoli – Rizzoli – 1983
147. *Atlante delle Uniformi Militari Italiane 1934-1984* – E.&V.Del Giudice – Albertelli 1984
148. *L'Uniforme Grigio-Verde (1909-1918)* A. Viotti – S.M.dell'Escercito 1984
149. *Inquadramento della M.V.S.N. e Sue Unità Combattenti* – F.Scandaluzzi 1985

BIBLIOGRAPHY

150. *Disposizioni sulle Uniformi* – Comando 4° C.A.Alpino – 1985
151. *Aquilifer, magazine of the Club Italiano Studi Storico-militari*

JAPAN

152. *Japanese Army Uniforms and Equipment* – R.Dilley and Almark – 1970
153. *Imperial Japanese Army and Navy, Uniforms and Equipment* – 1973
154. *Japanese Army Handbook 1939-1945* – A.J.Barker and Jan Allan – 1979

POLAND

155. *Dziennik Rozkazów Nr 5 (Rek XXIV)* – Naczelny Wódz i Minister Spraw Wojskowych – London 1941
156. *Żolnierz Polski* – K.Linder – H.Wiewióra – T.Woźnicki – Wydawnictwo Ministerstwa Obrony Narodowej – 1965
157. *Polskie Symbole wojskowe 1943-1978* – K.Madej – Wydawnictwo Ministerstwa Obrony Narodowej – 1980
158. *Piechota 1938-1945* – Polish Institute and Sikorski Museum – 1970-74

SPAIN

159. *Uniformes Militares de la Guerra Civil Española* – J. M. Bueno – Editorial San Martin – 1971

SWEDEN

160. *Svenk Soldat* – L.L.Jung and R.Grahn – Överbefälhavaren – 1983

SWITZERLAND

161. *Die Abzeichen der Schweizer Armee* – Herausgeber – 1976

USA

162. *The Officer's Guide* – The Military Service Publ. Co. – 1942, 9th Edition
163. *The Officer's Guide* – Stackpole Books – 1972, 36th Edition
164. *The National Geographic Magazine Vol. LXXXIII, No. 6* – June 1943
165. *Come riconoscere le Forze Armate degli Stati Uniti* – US War Information Office – US 724 IT
166. *Shoulder Sleeve Insignia, Insignia of Rank, Service Ribbons, Decorations and Insignia of the US Armed Forces* – Joel & Aronoff
167. *American Badges and Insignia* – E.E.Kerrigan and L.Cooper – 1967
168. *Field Artillery Battalions of the US Army (1)* – J.A.Sawicki – 1977
169. *Field Artillery Battalions of the US Army (2)* – J.A.Sawicki – 1978
170. *Infantry Regiments of the US Army* – J.A.Sawicki – 1981
171. *Trading Post, of the American Society of Military Insignia Collectors,* and the folowing A.S.M.I.C. catalogs:
172. *Cloth Patch of the U.S. Armed Forces* – Headquarters, Commands, Bases, Theatres, Army Groups, Armies, Divisions 1 to 51
173. *Cloth Patch of the U.S. Armed Forces* – Divisions 51 to 157, Army Corps
174. *Cloth Patch of the U.S. Armed Forces* – Armor and Cavalry
175. *Cloth Patch of the U.S. Armed Forces* – Infantry and Artillery
176. *Infantry Distinctive Insignia*
177. *Armor and Cavalry Distinctive Insignia*
178. *Engineers Distinctive Insignia* – with supplement
179. *Army Aviation Distinctive Insignia*
180. *Transportation Distinctive Insignia*
181. *State Guard Distinctive Insignia*

U.S.S.R.

182. *Uniforms and Insignia of the Soviet Army 1918-1958* – O.V.Haritonov – Leningrad Artillery Historical Museum – 1960
183. *L'Armata Rossa e le sue Uniformi (1917-1945)* E&V.Del Giudice – Edizioni Equestri – 1976

INDEX

Numbers in *italics* refer to illustrations in the Historical Section

ACKNOWLEDGEMENTS

I would like to express my sincerest gratitude to all the friends who helped me with their advice throughout the compilation of this book.

Special thanks to Mr John Lucas, Mr Hugh King and Mr Andrew Mollo for lending me some of the rarest and most valuable badges, and to Mr Christopher Barbarski, Mr H. Diard, Mr Michael Lamb, Mr Ray Westlake, Mr Eddie Dart, Editor of *Military Advertiser*, and to Jeremy Tenniswood, Militaria, of Aldershot.

I am also indebted to the following for their kind help: Lenvay Gesellschaft MBH & CO, KG, Vienna; Mr Markku Melkko, Director, Sotamuseo, Helsinki; Mr Bjørn Nielsen, Curator, Tojhusmuseet, Copenhagen; Major RS Dr Josef Vohralik, Assistant Military and Air Attaché, Embassy of the Czechoslovak Socialist Republic; Colonel Göran De Geer, Military and Air Attaché, Swedish Embassy; Colonel GS W. Hertach, Defence Attaché, Swiss Embassy; Lt. Col. H.L.Zwitzer, Deputy Chief, Military Historical Section, Royal Netherlands Army; Lt.Col. B.J. de Montjamont, Assistant Army Attaché, Embassy of France and Group Captain Onder Aytun, Air Attaché, Turkish Embassy.